The Determinants of Economic Growth

The Determinants of Economic Growth

Edited by

M.S. OOSTERBAAN

THIJS DE RUYTER VAN STEVENINCK

and

N. VAN DER WINDT

Netherlands Economic Institute

KLUWER ACADEMIC PUBLISHERS
Boston / Dordrecht / London

Distributors for North, Central and South America:
Kluwer Academic Publishers
101 Philip Drive
Assinippi Park
Norwell, Massachusetts 02061 USA
Telephone (781) 871-6600
Fax (781) 871-6528
E-Mail <kluwer@wkap.com>

Distributors for all other countries:
Kluwer Academic Publishers Group
Distribution Centre
Post Office Box 322
3300 AH Dordrecht, THE NETHERLANDS
Telephone 31 78 6392 392
Fax 31 78 6546 474
E-Mail <services@wkap.nl>

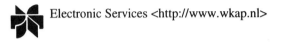 Electronic Services <http://www.wkap.nl>

Library of Congress Cataloging-in-Publication Data

The determinants of economic growth / edited by M.S. Oosterbaan, Thijs de Ruyter
van Steveninck, and N. van der Windt.
    p.cm.
  "Proceedings of the conference on Economic Growth and its Determinants,
which was held on March 23 and 24, 1998, in the "Hague"--Ackn.
  Includes bibliographical references and index.
  ISBN 0-7923-7885-7 (alk. paper)
  1. Economic development. 2. Economic policy. I. Oosterbaan, M.S.
(Maaike S.) II. Ruyter van Steveninck, Thijs de. III. Windt, N. van der (Nico)

HD75 .D482 2000
338.9--dc21   00-044779

Printed on acid-free paper. Printed in the United States of America

Contents

Contributors

Robert Barro	Harvard University
Jean-Claude Berthelémy	Centre d'Etudes Prospectives et d'Information Internationales, Paris
George Borjas	Harvard University
Willem Buiter	University of Cambridge, Bank of England
David Dollar	The World Bank, Washington, DC
William Easterly	The World Bank, Washington, DC
Augustin Fosu	Oakland University
Maxwell Fry	University of Birmingham
Louise Keeley	London School of Economics
Theo van de Klundert	Catholic University of Brabant, Tilburg
Gerard Kuper	University of Groningen
Deepak Lal	University of California, Los Angeles
Robert Lensink	University of Groningen
Ross Levine	University of Virginia
Maaike Oosterbaan	Netherlands Economic Institute
Christopher Pissarides	London School of Economics
Jan Pronk	Minister for Development Cooperation, The Netherlands
Graham Pyatt	Institute of Social Studies, The Hague
Danny Quah	Centre for Economic Performance, London School of Economics
Thijs de Ruyter van Steveninck	Netherlands Economic Institute
Moshe Syrquin	The World Bank, Washington, DC
Aristomene Varoudakis	OECD Development Centre, Paris
Nico van der Windt	Netherlands Economic Institute

Abbreviations and acronyms

BDV   Berthélemy, Dessus, and Varoudakis (1997).
BPV   Berthélemy, Pissarides, and Varoudakis (this book).
CGE   computable general equilibrium model.
CRS   constant returns to scale.
EU   European Union.
FDI   foreign direct investment.
GDP   gross domestic product.
GNP   gross national product
GMM   generalized moments methods
ICOR   incremental capital-output ratio.
LDC   less developed country.
LHS   left hand side (of an equation).
LSDV   least square with dummy variables
MENA   Middle East and North Africa
MRW   Mankiw, Romer, and Weil (1992).
MSV   Murphy, Shleifer, and Vishny (1991).
OECD   Organization for Economic Cooperation and Development.
PPP   purchasing-power parity.
R&D   research and development.
RHS   right hand side (of equation).
TFP   total factor productivity.

Acknowledgements

This book consists of the proceedings of the conference on Economic Growth and its Determinants, which was held on March 23 and 24, 1998, in The Hague. It was organized by the Netherlands Economic Institute (NEI) on behalf of the Netherlands Ministry of Foreign Affairs. Apart from the participants in the conference, we would like to thank Jan Pronk, the then Minister of Development Cooperation for his personal interest and active involvement. The NEI is also grateful to Willem Buiter for his excellent performance as chair and his maintenance of a tight schedule without too many delays, as well as to Sweder van Wijnbergen, at that time Secretary General of the Netherlands Ministry of Economic Affairs, for opening the conference. Support from Frederick Haver Droeze and Freek van den Bosch from the Netherlands Ministry of Foreign Affairs before, during, and after the conference is also gratefully acknowledged. The same goes for Teus van Walderveen, Paulien van Noort, Albert de Groot, and Ulrika Lundgren from the NEI. Finally, Joost van Acht assisted in both the organization of the conference and in a very thorough way with the technical editing of the book.

Introduction

Determinants of economic growth: An overview

Thijs de Ruyter van Steveninck, Nico van der Windt, and Maaike Oosterbaan
Netherlands Economic Institute

What causes economic growth? Why have some countries grown much faster than others? Why do some countries not grow at all, or even experience negative (per capita) growth rates? What can governments do to raise the growth rates of their country? These questions were discussed at a conference on March 23 and 24, 1998, organized by the Netherlands Economic Institute (NEI) on behalf of the Netherlands Ministry of Foreign Affairs. This book contains the proceedings of the conference.

Economic growth is widely considered as a necessary (though not sufficient) condition for poverty alleviation. During the past two decades, scholars and researchers have found a renewed interest in thinking about economic growth, and advances in the understanding of economic growth have taken place. On the one hand, the theoretical understanding of growth has progressed on various fronts, including endogenous technological innovation and increasing returns to scale; the interaction of population, fertility, human capital, and growth; international spill-overs in technology and capital accumulation; and the role of institutions. On the other hand, the increasing availability and use of data sets has given a large incentive to empirical research on cross-country growth, following the path-breaking work of Barro (1991).

In the 1960s and 1970s, economists did not pay much attention to the study of growth. Research focused mainly on short-term fluctuations. The motivation for the renewed interest in the determinants of economic growth in the 1980s was probably the observation that in the long-run economic growth is more important than business cycles or the counter-cyclical effects of monetary and fiscal policies.

Interest in economic growth is not confined to recent times. Adam Smith assumed in 1776 in his classic book *Inquiry into the Nature and Causes of the Wealth of Nations* that the engine of growth was to be found in the division of labor, in the accumulation of capital, and in technological progress. He emphasized the importance of a stable legal framework, in which the invisible hand of the market could function, and he explained how an open trading system would allow poorer countries to catch up with richer ones. In the early nineteenth century David Ricardo formalized the notion of diminishing marginal returns, another concept crucial for the understanding of economic growth. He showed how additional investment in land tended to yield decreasing returns, implying that growth would eventually come to a halt.

The foundations of modern growth theory were laid in the 1950s. Tinbergen (1959) tried to explain the production growth in Germany, Great Britain, France, and the United States with a model that includes, in addition to a Cobb-Douglas production function, rudimentary supply functions of capital and labor. Its model is similar to the models of Robert Solow (1956) and Trevor Swan. Their neoclassical models describe an economy of perfect competition and diminishing marginal returns to each input. They explain economic growth by the growth rate of population (or labor force) and the rate of technological progress. In these models, the technological progress is exogenous—that is, the model itself is not trying to it.

The Solow and Swan models had two crucial implications for the neoclassical growth theory. First, as the stock of capital expands at a faster rate than the labor force, growth slows and eventually returns to the point where, to keep growing, the economy must benefit from continual infusions of technological progress. Second, due to diminishing marginal returns poor countries should grow faster than rich ones. Each slice of new investment gives higher returns in a poorer country.

In practice, however, this neoclassical model does not seem to fit the facts very well. Economic growth has not slowed down over time, if we analyze the developments in the last century; and most poor countries do not seem to catch up with rich ones. Poor countries have even tended to grow more slowly in the last thirty years.

In the 1980s the new growth theory questioned some assumptions of the neoclassical growth model. The research in the mid-1980s began with new theoretical models of the determination of long-run growth, an area that is now called *endogenous growth theory*. Other recent research tried to further bring out the empirical implications of the theory and the relation of these hypotheses to data and evidence. Both disputed the law of diminishing marginal returns. If each extra bit of capital does not yield a lower return than its predecessor, growth can continue indefinitely.

Romer has concentrated on technological progress and showed in his seminal article in 1986 that if the idea of capital is broadened to include human capital (the knowledge and skills embodied in the workforce), the law of diminishing returns may not apply. Romer argued that what is needed is an equilibrium model of endogenous technical change in which long-term growth is primarily driven by the accumulation of knowledge by forward looking, profit maximizing agents. The initial models of Romer imply either constant or increasing returns to capital.

Great efforts have been devoted to huge statistical analyses on economic growth, running millions of regressions (see, for instance, Sala-i-Martin, 1997). Vast sets of data now exist, containing information for more than 100 countries for the last thirty years on growth rates, inflation rates, government spending, and school enrollment. Based on these statistical analyses, it is generally concluded in the literature that high inflation is bad for growth, political stability counts, the results on democracy are mixed (see Barro and Sala-i-Martin, 1995), and so on.

The neoclassical and the new growth theories, both in their purest versions, remain uncommitted about the impact of government policy on economic growth and treat the role of the government only indirectly. Recent empirical work, however, has paid much explicit attention to this issue—for instance, in the context of Barro's finding of conditional convergence. Barro, a pioneer of the new empirical growth studies, has found out that poorer countries indeed tend to grow faster than richer countries, if such factors as a country's fertility rate, its human capital, and its government policies are held constant. In reality, these factors are not constant, and therefore absolute convergence does not take place. Whether these conclusions are frustrating for poor countries depends on what hampers the catch-up process of these countries. Government policies, in principle, can be changed, but the fertility rate, and human capital are more difficult to change.

Most empirical research in this field points to the primacy of government choices. Based on a sample of 111 countries, Sachs and Warner (1995) conclude that "open" economies showed strikingly faster growth than the "closed" ones. Barro, among others, has found that higher government spending tends to be associated with slower growth. As a by-product of financial policy and lack of openness, the lack of financial depth is also discussed (King and Levine, 1993).

Boone (1994) paid attention to the impact of foreign aid on investment and growth and found that no effect could be identified. Burnside and Dollar (1996) found that aid has a positive impact on growth in developing countries with good fiscal, monetary, and trade policies. In the presence of poor policies, aid seems to have been dissipated in unproductive government investment. They have further concluded that inflation, trade openness, and sound fiscal policies have a large effect on growth.

Human capital, education, and skills have also been found to matter. Various statistical analyses have shown that countries with a well-educated workforce (large human capital relative to physical capital) are likely to grow faster than countries with a less educated workforce. One of the major conclusions of the World Bank (1993) on East Asia was that most of the growth in this region has been due to superior accumulation of human capital.

In the theoretical debate between the neoclassical and the new schools, the most important question—What should governments do to promote growth?—was often forgotten. Olson (1996) attempts to deal with this question. He argues that the simplest version of the neoclassical theory as well as new growth theory misses a crucial point. Both theories assume that countries are doing as well as they can and are not wasting resources and that consequently output can be expanded only by an increase in available resources.

Olson argues that if countries are wasting resources, they can achieve a spectacular growth by using their available resources better. Olson presents evidence that labor, capital, and knowledge are being massively squandered in many poor countries. He concludes that the economic potentials of poor countries are enormous, as the Asian tigers have shown. His explanation, together with the work on conditional convergence, offers a rationale for the pattern of growth around the world. As a result, economic policies and institutions are placed at the very center.

The emerging conclusion of most of the recent debate on economic growth is that the poorest countries seem to be able to catch up and that their chances are maximized by the right policies. A number of authors suggest that governments should give a greater role to competition and incentives, but the precise content of these policies still remains under discussion, and empirical findings will always be contested.

In their chapter on "Recent Advances in Economic Growth: A Policy Perspective" (Chapter 7), Robert Lensink and Gerard Kuper give a short and concise overview of the recent history of growth theories. Robert Solow (1956) developed a comprehensive growth theory, which later became known as the *standard neoclassical approach*. This theory states that growth takes place basically by the accumulation of inputs: labor, capital, and (as a residual) technology. An important characteristic is the presence of diminishing marginal returns: the more of a given input is being used, the more marginal (additional) units of it are needed to produce the same marginal unit of output.

As long-term growth rates are determined by variables not explained by the model, the neoclassical models were also called *exogenous growth models*. The main drawbacks of the neoclassical growth theory were that (1) one of the most important explaining factors (technological progress) was in fact determined outside the model and (2) it could not explain some obvious facts.

Recent developments in endogenous growth theory

Robert J. Barro's paper was used as a starting point for the conference, and it is presented as Chapter 1 in this book. It describes recent developments in growth theory and pays special attention to the role of endogenous growth models compared with the traditional neo-classical models. Robert J. Barro (Chapter 1) surveys the empirical effects of a number of government policies on economic growth rates. This study applies to about 100 different countries for three time periods from 1965 to 1990. In a sense, it is an experiment in which many kinds of policies are investigated for their effects on growth performance.

First, government consumption expenditures (excluding education and defense) are considered outlays that do not enhance an economy's productivity and have indeed a negative effect on the growth rate. A rise in the spending ratio by five percentage points lowers economic growth by 0.7 percent per year. Apparently, government consumption exerts a negative effect on both the level and the quality of investment. All these effects are statistically significant.

The second policy variable is the rule of law, which includes, among other elements, secure property rights and a strong legal system. Although there are some measurement problems here, a strong and significantly positive relationship was found between this variable and economic growth and investment. Increased maintenance of the rule of the law therefore applied both to the quantity and quality of investment.

Third, the impact of democracy (such as electoral rights and civil liberties) is theoretically ambiguous. Pressure to redistribute income from rich to poor through high taxes or transfers could be harmful to growth. However, the reduction of political instability (riots or crime) should be expected to result in higher growth, so if democracy *in the margin* contributes to political stability, growth would benefit. Moreover, the incentives for the government to steal the nation's wealth is probably larger under a dictatorship. Again, quantification of this variable is very difficult, but the various definitions that are available show similar results: the overall relation is weak. In practice, there are both democracies and dictatorships with high and low growth rates (like the United States, India, South Korea, and Zaire, respectively). However, an inverted U-curve is found to be statistically significant, both with respect to growth and the propensity to invest. Probably, starting from a 100 percent dictatorship, the main problem is an excess amount of unchecked government power, so an increase in democratic rights will increase growth and investment. However, beyond a certain amount of democracy (the top of the U-curve), factors such as income redistribution start to hamper growth, and the relationship becomes a negative one. Summing up, the data suggest that, after a certain level of democracy has been reached, further democratization goes at the expense of economic performance.

Fourth, it is not surprising that the impact of inflation on growth is negative. However, this effect is statistically significant only with annual inflation rates of larger than 20 percent. This is probably caused by the effects of inflation not on the volume but on the efficiency of investment.

Fifth, school attainment at secondary and higher levels has the strongest impact on economic growth. On average, an additional year of schooling here raises growth by 1.2 percent per year. This effect almost entirely runs through improvements in the quality of human capital and not through the investment ratio.

Sixth, the relationship between levels of public debt stocks and of growth rates and investment ratios are essentially zero. It appears that, at a given budget deficit, the choice between taxes and issuing debt does not matter very much.

Openness to foreign trade

William Easterly (Chapter 2) investigates the relationship between openness and economic growth. His conclusion is that there is a strong connection between growth and openness but that openness is no panacea for economic ills.

There are many dimensions of openness, which can be subdivided into those related to trade and those related to capital flows. Examples in the former case, which could be expressed through the trade share (exports + imports)/GDP, include tariff structures or the degree to which domestic prices are in line with international ones. The latter category mainly includes measures relating to the black market premium for foreign currency.

The data show three kinds of advantages (the "joys") of openness. First, openness promotes the level of domestic investment, as it reduces price distortions of inputs and investment goods. A one standard deviation decrease in the latter variable was found to increase growth by 1.2 percentage points. Moreover, openness was also found to improve the allocation of investment.

Finally, empirical evidence suggests that openness promotes not only growth but also the convergence of rich and poor countries. Among open economies, poorer countries grow faster than rich countries, while there is no such tendency among closed economies. It should be noted, though, that quite often poor countries are in the closed category, so being closed could well be negatively correlated with income level.

On the negative side (the "sorrows") open economies are more vulnerable to terms-of-trade shocks and sudden interruptions of capital flows. The more open a country, the stronger both the negative and positive effects of terms-of-trade shocks. In this sense, there is a risk-return trade-off. Some types of openness make countries more vulnerable than others, such as a large shares of a few commodities in total exports.

Regarding capital flows, the debt crises in Latin America and, more recently, in East Asia show the vulnerabilities to sudden changes in international capital market sentiments. Here also a risk-return trade-off applies: openness to capital imports increases both higher growth (the return) but also vulnerability (the risk).

Poverty clusters occur both on the national and international levels. In the latter case, capital should flow to the poorest countries, where it is theoretically more productive, but it does not. In fact, in the long run there is no evidence of convergence between rich and poor countries. However, the few poor countries that were (became) open actually converged. Apparently, there exists a vicious circle between being closed because you are poor and being poor because you are closed.

Technology

The relationship between technology and growth is reviewed by Louise C. Keeley and Danny Quah in Chapter 3. The impact of technological progress has traditionally been an exogenous variable (the Solow residual) in classical growth theory but has received more attention since the emergence of the new growth school. It is widely agreed that technological progress (caused by R&D) is an important engine for growth and that intellectual property rights play an important role in this. However, the way the latter can be stimulated in an optimal way is still the subject of considerable disagreement.

Patents play an important role in the theoretical literature, as they create rents that allow the creator of the knowledge to have exclusive ownership. Patents are needed to provide the incentives for private firms to conduct R&D, as they enable the users to use the knowledge from R&D to produce output. The information in the patent, however, can be used for additional R&D by other firms, which allows infinite expandability of knowledge. As they have characteristics of non-rival goods, they generate increasing returns for the whole economy. This view is to some extent supported empirically by economic data.

However, it is not just private firms that generate useful knowledge but institutions in the public sector as well, such as universities. Incentive structures here therefore have to be analyzed too. Moreover, patents provide property rights to knowledge, but alternative mechanisms such as research grants or publicly financed contract research may be even more important.

Financial markets and financial flows in LDCs

According to Maxwell J. Fry (Chapter 4), there are four major differences between the financial systems of poor and rich countries (apart from their size, of course). First, financial systems in the former countries are much more than in the latter dominated by commercial banks. Although equity markets are gaining ground in several developing countries, their role in financial intermediation between saving and investment remains insignificant so far. Second, financial systems in LDCs are much more heavily taxed. The inflation tax, in particular, has been used more frequently. Their average inflation rates were only 5.9 percent in 1969, but had risen to 98.6 percent in 1990 (corresponding figures for OECD countries were 4.9 percent and 5 percent respectively). Third, banking systems in developing countries face higher reserve ratios. The ratio of reserves to deposits is about three times higher than in rich countries. This is not reflecting the use of a monetary policy instrument because inflation rates and reserve ratios are positively correlated. Fourth, until recently, financial systems in LDCs were subject to administrative controls over interest rates such as ceilings on loan rates.

Financial markets in market economies perform basically two functions: (1) administering countries' payment systems and (2) intermediating between savers and investors. Almost always high inflation does impair a country's currency not only as a store of value but also as a means of payment. It often makes societies turn to substitute means of payment (barter or foreign currencies—dollarization), thereby passing over the domestic financial system. A credit squeeze might be another consequence, if economic agents may choose to hold smaller money balances, because of the higher costs attached to holding money. Credit squeezes, in turn, may result in larger numbers of bankruptcies and lower levels of output.

Governments can finance their budget deficits in four ways: (1) monetizing by borrowing at zero cost from the central bank (the inflation tax), (2) borrowing at below-market interest rates, by thrusting debt involuntarily down the throat of commercial banks, (3) borrowing abroad in foreign currency, (4) borrowing at market interest rates domestically.

The typical OECD-country government finances about 50 percent of its deficit in voluntary domestic currency markets, the corresponding figure for LDCs is only 8 percent. This means that greater use of sources (1), (2), and (3) results in higher inflation, lower savings, and thus lower growth. Alternatives (1) and (2) constitute taxes on, respectively, money holders and financial institutions, whereas alternative (3) implies that debts have to be repaid in foreign currency.

Fry analyzed the relationship between deficit finance and inflation for seventy LDCs during the 1972 to 1995 period. High growth countries (growth > 8.1 percent annually) exhibited much lower averages of deficits, reserve-money growth, and reserve to deposit ratios than low growth countries (growth < 0.7 percent annually). Given fiscal discipline, removing distortions on financial markets fosters growth, as this will enhance both the quality and quantity of investment. In this case, both domestic and foreign capital will flow toward their most productive use.

It is thus obvious that financial repression reduces economic growth. However, where it does generate significant amounts of public revenues (in LDCs about 2 percent of GDP on average), abandoning it may be harmful nevertheless, as high interest rates are equally damaging. Unless the government is seriously committed to fiscal reform, financial repression may be a second best solution.

Where financial liberalization is introduced, it must therefore be accompanied by fiscal reform to ensure that government debt will not reach excessive levels. Sound prudential supervision of the banking system remains equally important. Finally, in very few areas of the economy, achieving a level playing field is as important as in the financial sector. This is true for the demand of credit, where the government should compete on equal terms with private companies, but also on the supply side, where foreign and domestic financial institutions should receive equal treatment.

Institutional development

The role of institutions (informal constraints like cultural norms) in economic performance has been considered only recently and is the subject of Chapter 5 by Deepak Lal. The Western industrialized countries have promoted their political and economic institutions and values (democracy, the market, human rights, and egalitarianism) as keys to their economic success. However, except for the market, these values have not universally been accepted. For example, Asian values (strong states and extended families) have been held responsible for recent high Asian growth rates.

Two factors are important in any culture: cosmological and material beliefs. The former beliefs are related to how people view their lives—its purpose, meaning, and relationship to others. Material beliefs are about concerns regarding the material world (economy) and how to make a living. Cosmological beliefs most strongly influence the polity. As there is great hysteresis in them, this makes transferring one type of polity (for instance, democracy) into a region with a different cosmology extremely difficult. However, democracy is not essential for development (the Industrial Revolution took place under a system of monarchy), as long as the market is allowed to function, although it is difficult to imagine that in the long run markets can function freely and optimally in an environment of political dictatorship.

In Deepals Lal's view the state should not seek to impose a preferred pattern of objectives (such as general social welfare or human rights) but to facilitate individuals to pursue their own objectives. The state in this way serves as an enterprise association, in which the law is used for, for example, the legislation of morality or nation-building. Egalitarianism is a value unique to Christanity. Implemented in developing countries, it has often resulted in economic failure because it led to dirigisme (for example, in India and China). As a result of this, Eurasian civilizations are turning back to their traditional policies, which were more concerned with civil association and social order than with promoting enterprise. Regarding Africa, where most problems are the result of artificial borders and hence artificial states, the best outcome would be to create states that coincide with tribal homogeneity. This would make it possible for states to be ruled by tribal chiefs, as traditional political forms are more in consonance with people's cosmological beliefs, and imported ones are not.

Institutional development is a form of cultural evolution and is not very well understood. Policies like the welfare state, which impinge on the traditional family, should not be imposed on non-Christian countries. The opposite holds for the market, which is currently spreading throughout the world and is in fact threatened by the West, where the issues like human rights and environmental protection have been used to justify protectionism.

Human capital and rent-seeking activities

In Chapter 6, Jean-Claude Berthélemy, Christopher Pissarides, and Aristomene Varoudakis analyze the importance of human capital for economic growth. At the theoretical level, the impact is unambiguously positive. In classical theory, human capital is a production factor just like capital and (unskilled) labor. In new growth theory, the emphasis is more on the effect of human capital and on R&D that stimulates technological progress. Empirically, the relationship is more controversial, though: often there seems to be no beneficial impact of expenses on education. More generally, the elasticity of economic growth to human capital strongly depends on the national characteristics. A possible explanation for this may be the existence of rent seeking activities.

Rent seeking activities are economic activities that respond to economic policy distortions, such as taxes, price controls, red tape, and trade restrictions. This kind of activities, which are human capital intensive, are privately remunerative but socially wasteful and hence bad for growth. Rent-seeking activities involve much more skilled than unskilled labor. Nevertheless, given the existing distortions rent-seeking activities may enhance the working of free markets and reduce the effect of the distortions on output. However, a world without distortions would be preferable, as the energy of rent seeking could also be used for more productive activities.

Especially in cases when human capital is scarce (such as in Sub-Saharan Africa), the consequences of rent-seeking behavior are serious, as they may pass a threshold that eliminates any growth potential in the country. These countries can easily be trapped in a vicious circle like low equilibrium traps. The elimination of distortions would be the first-best solution, but more investment in education could also help. In this case, however, the government should make sure that the new graduates will not have incentives to work in rent-seeking activities. It should thus not repeat the mistakes that have been made in countries that guarantee university graduates employment in the public sector.

References

Barro R. (1991). "Economic Growth in a Cross Section of Countries." *Quarterly Journal of Economics* 106(2), 407–444.

Barro, R., and X. Sala-i-Martin (1995). *Economic Growth.* New York: McGraw-Hill.

Boone, P. (1994). *The impact of Foreign Aid on Investment and Growth.* London School of Economics, Mimeo.

Burnside, C., and D. Dollar. *Aid, Policies and Growth.* Mimeo, Policy Research Department, World Bank, Washington, DC.

King, R., and R. Levine. (1993). "Finance, Entrepreneurship and Growth, Theory and Evidence." *Journal of Monetary Economics* 32, 513–542.

Olson, M. (1996). "Big Bills Left on the Sidewalk: Why Some Nations Are Rich and Others Poor." *Journal of Economic Perspectives* 10(2), 3–24.

Romer, P. (1986). "Increasing Returns and Long-Run Growth." *Journal of Political Economy* 94(5), 407–444.

Sachs J., and A. Warner. (1995). "Economic Reform and the Process of Global Integration." *Brookings Papers on Economic Activity* 1(1), 1–118.

Sala-i-Martin, X. (1997). "I Just Ran Two Million Regressions." *American Economic Review* 87(2), 178–183.

Solow, R. (1956). "A Contribution to the Theory of Economic Growth." *Quarterly Journal of Economics* 70, 65–94.

Tinbergen, J. (1959). "On the Theory of Trend Movements." In 'Jan Tinbergen. Selected Papers', edited by L.H. Klaassen, L.M. Koyck and H.J. Witteveen. Amsterdam: North-Holland Publishing Company.

World Bank, the (1993). *The East Asian Miracle, Economic Growth and Public Policy.* World Bank Policy Report, Oxford University Press.

Chapter 1

Recent developments in endogenous growth theory

Robert J. Barro*
Robert C. Waggoner Professor of Economics, Harvard University

Since the late 1980s, much of the attention of macroeconomists has focused on long-term issues, specifically, on the effects of government policies on the long-term rate of economic growth. This emphasis reflects partly the recognition that the difference between prosperity and poverty for a country depends on how fast it grows over the long term. Although traditional fiscal and monetary policies matter in this context, other aspects of macroeconomic policy—broadly interpreted to encompass all aspects of government activity that matter for aggregate economic performance—are even more important.

One of these aspects concerns the character of a nation's basic political, legal, and economic institutions. These institutions typically remain stable from year to year and, therefore, have little to do with the latest recession or boom. However, the long-lasting differences in these institutions across countries have proven empirically to be among the most important determinants of differences in rates of economic growth and investment.

The accumulation of human capital is an important part of the development process, and this accumulation is influenced in major ways by public programs for schooling and health. Also important are government policies that promote or discourage free markets, including regulations of labor and capital markets and interventions that affect the degree of international openness. Finally, government policy includes the amount and nature of public investment, especially in areas related to transportation and communication.

The recognition that the determinants of long-term economic growth form the central macroeconomic problem was fortunately accompanied in

* I am grateful to Betsey Stevenson for research assistance, particularly for her compilation of the data on public debt.

the late 1980s by important advances in the theory of economic growth. This period featured the development of endogenous growth models, in which the long-term rate of growth was determined within the model. A key feature of these models is a theory of technological progress, viewed as a process whereby purposeful research and application leads over time to new and better products and methods of production and to the adoption of superior technologies that were developed in other countries or sectors. One of the major contributions in this area is Romer (1990).

Shortly thereafter, in the early 1990s, there was a good deal of empirical estimation of growth models using cross-country and cross-regional data. This empirical work was, in some sense, inspired by the excitement of the endogenous growth theories. However, the framework for the applied work owed more to the older, neoclassical model, which was developed in the 1950s and 1960s (see Solow, 1956; Cass, 1965; Koopmans, 1965; the earlier model of Ramsey, 1928; the exposition in Barro and Sala-i-Martin, 1995). The framework used in recent empirical studies combines basic features of the neoclassical model—especially the convergence force whereby poor economies tend to catch up to rich ones—with extensions that emphasize the role of government policies and institutions. For an overview of this framework and the recent empirical work on growth, see Barro (1997).

The recent endogenous growth models are useful for understanding why advanced economies—and the world as a whole—can continue to grow in the long run despite the workings of diminishing returns in the accumulation of physical and human capital. In contrast, the extended neoclassical framework does well as a vehicle for understanding relative growth rates across countries, for example, for assessing why South Korea grew much faster than the United States or Zaire over the last thirty years. Thus, overall, the new and old theories are more complementary than they are competing.

1.1.   FRAMEWORK FOR THE EMPIRICAL ANALYSIS OF GROWTH

The empirical framework derived from the extended neoclassical growth model can be summarized by a simple equation:

$$Dy = F(y, y^*) \, ,$$

where Dy is the growth rate of per capita output, y is the current level of per capita output, and y^* is the long-run or target level of per capita output. In the neoclassical model, the diminishing returns to the accumulation of capital imply that an economy's growth rate Dy is inversely related to its level of development, as represented by y.[1] In the present framework, this property applies in a conditional sense, for a given value of y^*.

For a given value of y, the growth rate Dy rises with y^*. The value y^* depends, in turn, on government policies and institutions and on the character of the national population. For example, better enforcement of property rights and fewer market distortions tend to raise y^* and, hence, increase Dy for given y. Similarly, if people are willing to work and save more and have fewer children, then y^* increases, and Dy rises accordingly for given y.

In this model, a permanent improvement in some government policy initially raises the growth rate Dy and then raises the level of per capita output y gradually over time. As output rises, the workings of diminishing returns eventually restore the growth rate Dy to a value consistent with the long-run rate of technological progress (which is determined outside of the model in the standard neoclassical framework). Hence, in the very long run, the impact of improved policy is on the level of per capita output, not its growth rate. But since the transitions to the long run tend empirically to be lengthy, the growth effects from shifts in government policies persist for a long time.

1.2.   EMPIRICAL FINDINGS ON GROWTH ACROSS COUNTRIES

The findings on economic growth surveyed in Barro (1997) provide estimates for the effects of a number of government policies. That study applies to roughly 100 countries observed over three time periods—1965 to 1975, 1975 to 1985, and 1985 to 1990. The sample includes countries at vastly different levels of economic development, and places are excluded only because of missing data. The attractive feature of this broad sample is that it encompasses great variation in the government policies that are to be evaluated. In fact, my view is that it is impossible to use the experience of one or a few countries to get an accurate empirical assessment of the long-term growth implications from policies such as legal institutions, size of government, monetary and fiscal policies, and so on.

One drawback of this kind of diverse sample is that it creates difficulties in measuring variables in a consistent and accurate way across countries and

---

[1] The starting level of per capita output y can be viewed more generally as referring to the starting levels of physical and human capital and other durable inputs to the production process. In some theories, the growth rate Dy falls with a higher starting level of overall capital per person but rises with the initial ratio of human to physical capital.

over time. In particular, less developed countries tend to have many measurement errors in national accounts and other data. The hope, of course, is that the strong signal from the diversity of the experience dominates the noise.

The other empirical issue, which is likely to be more important than measurement error, is the sorting out of directions of causation. The objective is to isolate the effects of alternative government policies on long-term growth. But, in practice, much of the government's behavior—including its monetary and fiscal policies and its political stability—is a reaction to economic events. In most cases discussed in the following, the labeling of directions of causation depends on timing evidence, whereby earlier values of government policies are thought to influence subsequent values of economic growth and investment. However, this approach to determining causation is not always valid.

The empirical work focuses on growth over relatively long periods, typically ten years. In one respect, this context is forced by the data because many of the determining variables considered—such as school attainment, fertility, and life expectancy—are measured at best over five-year intervals. Higher frequency observations would be mainly guesswork. The low-frequency context accords, in any event, with the underlying theories of growth, which do not attempt to explain short-run business-cycle fluctuations. In these theories, the exact timing of response—for example, of growth and investment to a change in a public institution—is not as clearly specified as the long-run response. Therefore, the application of the theories to annual or other high-frequency observations would compound the measurement error in the data by emphasizing errors related to the timing of relationships.

The estimation involves the relation between the growth rate of per capita GDP or the ratio of investment to GDP over a period (1965 to 1975, 1975 to 1985, or 1985 to 1990) and prior values of an array of explanatory variables. These variables include an earlier level of per capita GDP, earlier levels of human capital in the forms of education and health, a number of measures of government policies, and some additional variables, such as the fertility rate and the change in a country's terms-of-trade. To illustrate the nature of the effect of each policy variable on growth or investment, it is convenient to use two-dimensional diagrams in which the effects of all the other explanatory variables are held constant.

1.2.1.   Effects of government consumption

As a first example, which typifies the general approach to displaying the results, the left panel of Figure 1.1 relates the rate of economic growth to the

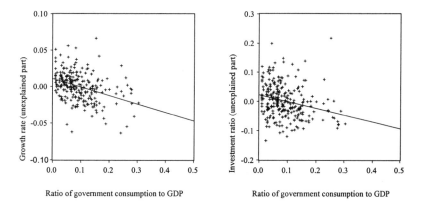

Figure 1.1. Effects of government consumption

ratio of government consumption expenditure (measured exclusive of outlays on defense and education) to GDP.[2] This measure of public spending, plotted on the horizontal axis, is intended to approximate the outlays that do not enhance an economy's productivity. In interpreting the estimated effect on growth, it is important to note that measures of taxation are not being held constant. This omission reflects data problems of constructing accurate representations for various tax rates, such as marginal rates on labor and capital income, and so on. Since the tax side has not been held constant, the effect of a higher government consumption ratio on growth involves partly a direct impact and partly an indirect effect involving the required increase in overall public revenues.

The figure indicates that, for given values of the other explanatory variables, a higher ratio of government consumption to GDP has a negative (and statistically significant) effect on the rate of economic growth. This finding suggests that a greater volume of nonproductive government spending (and the associated taxation) hampers economic performance. Quantitatively, a rise in the spending ratio by five percentage points lowers the growth rate on impact by 0.7 percent per year.

---

[2] The system contains as an explanatory variable the average ratio of government consumption to GDP over the period in which growth is measured. However, the estimation uses a set of instrumental variables that contains prior ratios of government consumption to GDP but not the contemporaneous ratios. The standard international accounts curiously include most public outlays for education and defense as government consumption, but these two categories have been deleted from the measure of government consumption shown in Figure 1.1. If considered separately, the ratio of public spending on education to GDP has a positive, but statistically insignificant, effect on economic growth. The ratio of defense outlays to GDP has roughly a zero relation with economic growth.

The right panel of Figure 1.1 shows the parallel effect of the government consumption ratio on the ratio of investment (private plus public) to GDP. As in the diagram for growth, the effect on investment is shown when all other explanatory variables are held constant. (Note that the investment ratio was not included as an explanatory variable for growth when the upper panel of the figure was constructed.) The estimated effect of government consumption on investment is also significantly negative: an increase in the government consumption ratio by one percentage point is estimated to lower the investment ratio by about one-quarter of a percentage point. This result suggests that one way in which more nonproductive public spending lowers growth is by depressing investment.[3]

1.2.2.   Effects of the rule of law

The next policy variable considered involves the maintenance of the rule of law. Many analysts believe that secure property rights and a strong legal system are central for investment and other aspects of economic activity. The empirical challenge has been to measure these concepts in a reliable way across countries and over time. Probably the best indicators available come from international consulting firms that advise clients on the attractiveness of countries as places for investments. These investors are concerned about institutional matters such as the prevalence of law and order, the capacity of the legal system to enforce contracts, the efficiency of the bureaucracy, the likelihood of government expropriation, and the extent of official corruption. These kinds of factors have been assessed by a number of consulting companies, including Political Risk Services in its publication *International Country Risk Guide.*[4] This source is especially useful because it covers over 100 countries since the early 1980s. Although the data are subjective, they have the virtue of being prepared contemporaneously by local experts. Moreover, the willingness of customers to pay substantial fees for this information is perhaps some testimony to their validity.

Among the various indicators available, the index for overall maintenance of the rule of law (also referred to as *law and order tradition*) turns out to have the most explanatory power for economic growth and investment. This index was initially measured by Political Risk Services in

---

[3]   The significantly negative effect of the government consumption ratio on growth still appears if the investment ratio is held constant. This last property holds also for the other government policy variables that are considered in the following discussion.

[4]   These data were introduced to economists by Knack and Keefer (1995). Two other consulting services that construct these type of data are BERI (Business Environmental Risk Intelligence) and Business International (now a part of the Economist Intelligence Unit).

seven categories on a zero-to-six scale, with six the most favorable. The index has been converted here to a zero-to-one scale, with zero indicating the poorest maintenance of the rule of law and one the best.

To understand the scale, note that the United States and most of the OECD countries (not counting Mexico and Turkey) had values of 1.0 for the rule-of-law index in recent years. However, Belgium, France, Greece, Portugal, and Spain were downgraded from 1.0 in 1996 to 0.83 in 1997. Also rated at 1.0 in 1997 were Hungary, Kuwait, Malta, Morocco, and Singapore. Hong Kong was downgraded on its return to China from 1.0 in 1996 to 0.83 in 1997.

No country had a rating of 0.0 for the rule of law in 1997, but countries rated at 0.0 in some earlier years included Ethiopia, Guyana, Haiti, Sri Lanka, Yugoslavia, and Zaire. Countries rated at 0.5 in 1997 included Algeria, Brazil, Mexico, Peru, Uruguay, South Africa, several countries in Sub Saharan Africa, and much of Central America.

The left panel of Figure 1.2 indicates that, for given values of the other explanatory variables, increased maintenance of the rule of law has a positive (and statistically significant) effect on the rate of economic growth.[5] An improvement by one category among the seven used by Political Risk Services (that is, an increase in the zero-to-one index by 0.17) is estimated to raise the growth rate on impact by 0.5 percent per year.

The right panel of Figure 2 shows that the rule-of-law index also has a significantly positive effect on the ratio of investment to GDP. An improvement by one category in the underlying rule-of-law indicator is estimated to raise the investment ratio by about 1.5 percentage points.

1.2.3.   Effects of democracy

Another strand of research on the role of institutions has focused on democracy, specifically on the strength of electoral rights and civil liberties. In this case, the theoretical effects on investment and growth are ambiguous. One effect, characteristic of systems of one-person one-vote majority voting, involves the pressure to enact redistributions of income from rich to poor.

---

[5] The variable shown on the horizontal axis is the earliest observation available for each country—in most cases 1982 and in a few cases 1985. This variable takes on one of seven possible values. Since the data on the rule-of-law index begin only in 1982 or 1985, later values of this variable are allowed to influence earlier values of economic growth (for 1965 to 1975 and 1975 to 1985). The idea here is that institutions that govern the rule of law tend to persist over time, so that the observations for 1982 or 1985 are likely to be good proxies for the values prevailing earlier. The significantly positive effect of the rule-of-law index on economic growth still emerges if the sample is limited to the growth observations that applied after the early 1980s.

These redistributions may involve land reforms and social-welfare programs. Although the direct effects on income distribution may be

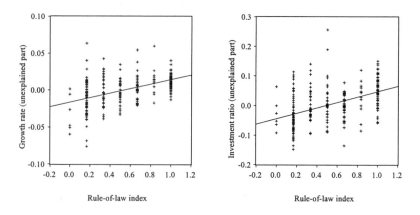

Figure 1.2. Effects of rule-of-law index

desirable (because they are equalizing), these programs tend to compromise property rights and reduce the incentives of people to work and invest. One kind of disincentive involves the transfers given to poor people. Since the amount received typically falls as the person earns more income, the recipient is motivated to remain on welfare or otherwise disengage from productive activity. The other adverse effect involves the income taxes or other levies that are needed to pay for the transfers. An increase in these taxes encourages the non-poor to work and invest less.

One offsetting effect is that an evening of income distribution may reduce the tendency for social unrest. Specifically, transfers to the poor may reduce incentives to engage in criminal activity, including riots and revolutions.[6] Since social unrest reduces everyone's incentives to work and invest, some amount of publicly organized income redistribution would contribute to overall economic activity. However, even a dictator would be willing to engage in transfers to the extent that the decrease in social unrest was worth the cost of the transfers. Thus, the main point is that democracy will tend to generate "excessive" transfers purely from the standpoint of maximizing the economy's total output.

Although democracy has its down side, one cannot conclude that autocracy provides ideal economic incentives. One problem with dictators is that they have the power and, hence, the inclination to steal the nation's

---

[6] Data are available across countries on numbers of revolutions, riots, and so on. However, I find that, once the rule-of-law index is held constant, these measures of social unrest lack significant explanatory power for growth and investment.

wealth. More specifically, an autocrat may find it difficult to convince people that their property will not be confiscated once investments have been made. This convincing can sometimes be accomplished through reputation—that is, from a history of good behavior—but also by relaxing to some degree the hold on power. In this respect, an expansion of democracy—viewed as a mechanism for checking the power of the central authority—may enhance property rights and, thereby, encourage economic activity. From this perspective, democracy would encompass not only electoral rights but also civil liberties that allow for freedom of expression, assembly, and so on.

A number of researchers have provided quantitative measures of democracy, and Alex Inkeles (1991, p. x) finds in an overview study a "high degree of agreement produced by the classification of nations as democratic or not, even when democracy is measured in somewhat different ways by different analysts." One of the most useful measures—because it is available for almost all countries annually on a consistent basis since 1972—is the one provided by Gastil (1982,1983, and other years) and his followers at Freedom House. This source provides separate indexes for electoral rights and civil liberties.

The Freedom House concept of electoral rights uses the following basic definition: "Political rights are rights to participate meaningfully in the political process. In a democracy this means the right of all adults to vote and compete for public office, and for elected representatives to have a decisive vote on public policies" (Gastil, 1986–1987 edition, p. 7). In addition to the basic definition, the classification scheme rates countries (somewhat impressionistically) as less democratic if minority parties have little influence on policy.

Freedom House applies the concept of electoral rights on a subjective basis to classify countries annually into seven categories, where group one is the highest level of rights and group seven is the lowest. This classification was made by Gastil and his associates and followers based on an array of published and unpublished information about each country. The original ranking from one to seven was converted here to a scale from zero to one, where zero corresponds to the fewest rights (Freedom House rank seven) and one to the most rights (Freedom House rank one). The scale from zero to one corresponds to a classification made by Kenneth Bollen (1990) for 1960 and 1965. The Bollen index differs mainly in that its concept of democracy goes beyond electoral rights.

To fix ideas on the meaning of the zero-to-one subjective scale, note first that the United States and most other OECD countries in recent years received the value 1.0, thereby being designated as full representative democracies. Dictatorships that received the value 0.0 in 1995 included Indonesia, Iraq, Syria, Zaire, and several other countries in Africa. Places that were rated in 1995 at 0.5—halfway along between dictatorship and democracy—included Colombia, Dominican Republic, Ghana, Guatemala, Malaysia, Mexico, Nicaragua, Paraguay, Senegal, and Sri Lanka.

The Freedom House index of civil liberties is constructed in a similar way. The definition here is "civil liberties are rights to free expression, to organize or demonstrate, as well as rights to a degree of autonomy such as is provided by freedom of religion, education, travel, and other personal rights" (Gastil, 1986–1987 edition, p. 7). In practice, the indicator for civil liberties is extremely highly correlated with that for electoral rights. Thus, for practical purposes, it makes little difference in the analysis of growth and investment whether one uses the index for electoral rights or the one for civil liberties. The empirical work discussed here uses the index of electoral rights and sometimes refers to this indicator as simply a measure of democracy.

The left panel of Figure 1.3 shows the relation between the growth rate and the electoral-rights index.[7] The overall relation between growth and democracy is weak. In particular, there are examples of dictatorships (values of electoral rights near zero) with high and low rates of growth and similarly for democracies (values of democracy near one). However, there is a suggestion of a nonlinear relation—an inverted U-shape—in which growth rises initially with democracy, reaches a peak at a value for the electoral-rights index of around 0.5, and then declines subsequently with further rises in democracy. This relationship, shown by the curve in the figure, is statistically significant. Moreover, the same kind of nonlinear relation emerges in the right panel of Figure 1.3 when the growth rate is replaced on the vertical axis by the ratio of investment to GDP. That is, democracy also has a nonlinear (inverted-U) effect on a country's propensity to invest.

One way to interpret the results is that, in the worst dictatorships, an increase in electoral rights tends to increase growth and investment because the benefit from the limitations on governmental power is the key matter. But in places that have already attained a moderate amount of democracy, a further increase in electoral rights impairs growth and investment because the dominant effect comes from the intensified concern with social programs and income redistribution.

Specifically, the results suggest that growth would be somewhat reduced by further democratization beyond the levels attained in 1995 in countries such as Malaysia and Mexico (which had index values of 0.5 in 1995). Moreover, political liberalization probably already went by 1995 beyond the point of growth maximization in places such as Chile, South Korea, and

---

[7] The values shown for the electoral-rights index refer to averages over several years. Therefore, these values are not confined to the seven possible values that correspond to the categories used by Freedom House.

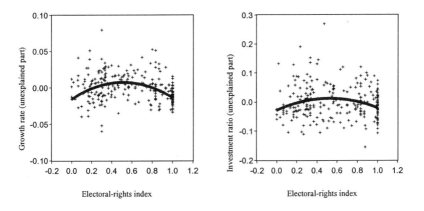

Figure 1.3. Effects of electoral rights index

Taiwan. These countries went from levels of the electoral-rights index of 0.17, 0.33, and 0.33, respectively, in the early 1980s to 0.83, 0.83, and 0.67, respectively, in 1995.

The results should not be taken as saying that dictatorship is desirable from the standpoint of economic performance. There are examples of autocrats—such as Pinochet in Chile, Fujimori in Peru, the Shah in Iran, and Lee and several others in East Asia—that produced good growth outcomes. There are, however, even more examples—including Marcos in the Philippines, Mao in China, Mobutu and numerous other despots in Africa, and many others in South America and Eastern Europe—that delivered poor growth outcomes.

The findings do not support the idea that democracy is necessary for growth—or even that democracy beyond an intermediate range is likely to raise the rate of economic growth. Although it may be unpleasant, the data suggest that, once an intermediate level of democratization has been attained, a further expansion of democracy comes at the expense of economic performance.

1.2.4. Effects of inflation

Figure 1.4 shows the relation between growth and inflation (based on consumer price indices). In the right panel, which includes the full range of inflation, the estimated effect of inflation is significantly negative—quantitatively, a rise by ten percentage points in the inflation rate is associated with a decline by 0.4 percent per year in the growth rate. This kind of effect shows up if growth is related solely to prior values of inflation or if the inflation rate is replaced by measures of money growth (based on M1 or M2 definitions of money). Thus, the timing relationship suggests that higher inflation, related to more expansionary monetary policy, leads to a lower rate of economic growth.[8]

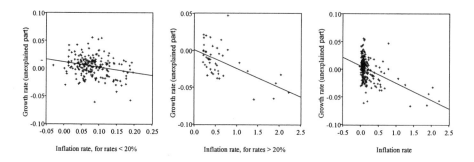

Figure 1.4. Growth versus inflation in three ranges

The left panel of Figure 1.4 shows that the relation between growth and inflation is weakly negative (and not statistically significant) if one considers only moderate inflation, up to rates of 20 percent per year. The middle panel shows that a clear negative relationship applies for higher rates of inflation. However, it turns out that one would accept the hypothesis statistically that the effect of inflation on growth in the low range of inflation (left panel) is the same as that in the high range (middle panel). In any event, there is no indication in the data over any range of a positive effect of inflation on growth. That is, for growth averaged over five or ten years, there is no sign that an economy has to accept more inflation to achieve better real outcomes.

Figure 1.5 shows the estimated effect of inflation on the investment ratio. The overall effect, shown in the right panel, is negative and statistically significant. However, the left and middle panels indicate that the effect is weak within either the moderate or high ranges of inflation. Thus, the more clearly defined negative effects for growth shown in Figure 4 do not involve primarily influences of inflation on investment. Probably the adverse effect of inflation on growth involves an adverse influence on the efficiency with which the economy uses its resources.

[8] Because of the concern about reverse causation—lower growth causing higher inflation—the system that underlies Figure 1.4 does not contain contemporaneous or lagged inflation or money growth in the set of instruments. Rather, the particular results shown use prior colonial history as instruments; these indicators turn out to have substantial predictive content for inflation. (An attempt to use central-bank independence as an instrument failed because this variable turned out to lack predictive content for inflation.) The results shown for inflation in Figure 1.4 turn out to be similar if lagged inflation is included with the instruments.

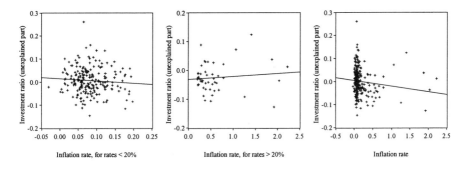

Figure 1.5. Investment versus inflation in three ranges

1.2.5. Effects of education and health

Governments typically have strong direct involvement in the financing and provision of elementary and secondary schooling and in health care services. Hence, public policies in these areas have major effects on a country's accumulation of human capital.

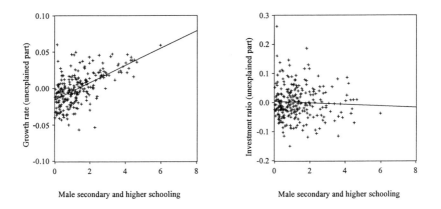

Figure 1.6. Effects of schooling

The left panel of Figure 1.6 shows the estimated effect of one measure of school attainment on economic growth. The variable plotted on the horizontal axis is the average years of attainment of male adults (age twenty-five and over) at the secondary and higher levels. This measure of school years—rather than female attainment or male attainment at the elementary level—turns out to be the one that is most related to subsequent economic growth. The estimated relation implies that an additional average year of schooling of males at the secondary and higher levels raises the growth rate by 1.2 percent per year.[9] Additional results described in Hanushek and Kim (1995) indicate that the quality of schooling, measured by scores on international examinations, matters even more than years of attainment for subsequent economic growth. Barro and Lee (1997) discuss more generally the available cross-country measures of the quality of education.

The right panel of Figure 1.6 indicates that initial schooling has a negligible effect on the investment ratio. Hence, the effect on growth shown in the upper panel likely reflects productivity increases associated directly with human capital. These effects could include a faster rate of absorption of superior foreign technologies when the domestic labor force is endowed with more schooling at the secondary and higher levels.

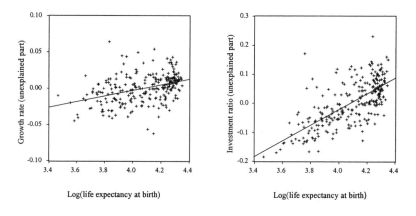

Figure 1.7. Effects of life expectancy

Figure 1.7 shows analogous effects related to another measure of human capital, the population's starting health status as measured by life expectancy at birth. The results indicate that a larger endowment of health capital predicts higher growth and higher investment. However, it may be that life expectancy proxies not only for health status but also in other ways for the quality of the labor force.

1.2.6. Effects of public debt

The results described thus far for traditional fiscal and monetary policy involve government consumption and inflation. The choice of public

[9] However, there is nonlinearity in the estimated relation, which implies that rich countries experience diminishing returns to increased years of schooling.

financing between current and future taxation—or, equivalently, between taxes and public borrowing—is often thought also to matter for economic growth. In a closed economy, the predicted effect is that more public debt would depress national saving and lead thereby to lower growth. This effect would arise for past budget deficits, as reflected in current debt levels, and also for prospective future borrowing. In an open economy, the predicted effects of public debt on domestic investment and growth are mitigated by foreign borrowing but still apply to the extent that international capital markets are imperfect or that the home economy is large enough to matter for world aggregates.

To assess the effects of public debt on economic growth and investment, I use a recently constructed data set on ratios of consolidated central government debt to GDP. The underlying data come from IMF publications and other country sources. The figures refer to five-year averages over the period 1960 to 1994 and are available for a subset of the observations used in Barro (1997).

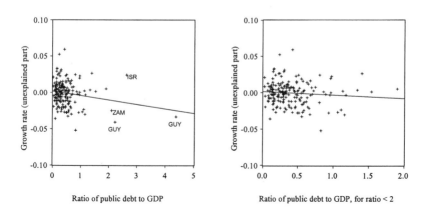

Figure 1.8. Growth rate versus debt-GDP ratio

If the debt-GDP ratio is added to the system used in my prior study, then the results for growth are the ones shown in Figure 1.8. The left panel indicates a negative relationship, which is marginally statistically significant.[10] However, the hint of a negative relation that appears here

[10] The results shown in Figure 1.8 apply when the system includes averages of debt-GDP ratios that are contemporaneous with the measures of growth rates. As with other policy variables, there are important possibilities for reverse causation. The likely effect in the present case is that higher economic growth would reduce the debt-GDP ratio; hence, the negative effect shown in the upper panel of Figure 1.8 could reflect this reverse channel. If the system includes only lagged values of debt-GDP ratios as instruments (which

depends on a few outlier observations, notably the two from Guyana, for which the debt levels are astronomical. If the sample is limited to values for which the debt-GDP ratio is below two, as in the right panel of Figure 1.8, then the estimated relation between growth and this ratio is essentially nil.

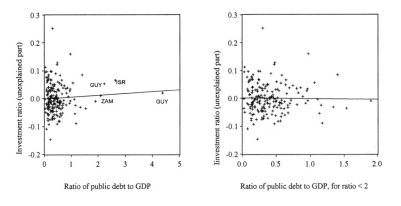

Figure 1.9. Investment versus debt-GDP ratio

Figure 1.9 shows the parallel effects on the investment ratio. In this case, the estimated effects are virtually zero in the whole sample (left panel) and in the truncated sample for which the debt ratios are below two (right panel).

From the standpoint of a supporter of Ricardian equivalence—whereby the choice between taxes and public debt does not matter for much—these cross-country results have to be gratifying. On the other hand, after so much effort was expended in the construction of this new data set on government debt, it would have been nice to obtain stronger findings. At this point, the conclusion seems to be that ratios of public debt to GDP matter little for an economy's subsequent rates of economic growth and investment.

1.2.7.   Effects of labor-market restrictions

Labor-market restrictions imposed by governments are often thought to underlie the sluggish recent performance of many countries in Western Europe. The public interventions include mandated levels of wages and benefits, restrictions on labor turnover, and encouragement of collective bargaining. The assessment of the effects of these kinds of policies for a

---

results in the loss of a substantial number of observations for the 1965 to 1975 period), then the estimated effect of the debt-GDP ratio on growth becomes weaker in magnitude (though it remains negative) and less close to being statistically significant at conventional critical levels.

broad sample of countries has been hindered by lack of good data. To get a rough idea of whether these sorts of restrictions matter much for growth, I used two rough proxies for the extent of these restrictions.

The first approach is based on the labor-standards conventions adopted by the International Labor Organization (ILO).[11] Once ratified by an individual member state (which includes most countries other than Taiwan and Hong Kong), a labor standard is supposed to be binding in terms of international law. Since its inception in 1919, the ILO conference has adopted 174 conventions.[12] Many of these provisions are not very controversial, covering matters such as eliminating forced labor, eliminating discrimination, and guaranteeing freedom of association. Others are more directly related to the kinds of labor-market interventions that would hinder economic performance.

For present purposes, I consider country ratifications of four of the ILO conventions that seem to relate closely to intervention into labor markets: minimum-wage fixing (no. 131, adopted in 1970), restrictions on termination of employment (no. 158, 1982), promotion of collective bargaining (no. 154, 1981), and equal pay for men and women (no. 100, 1951). At one extreme, all four of these provisions had been ratified by 1994 by Spain, Niger, and Zambia, whereas none had been ratified by the United States, Botswana, Mauritius, South Africa, South Korea, Malaysia, Singapore, Thailand, and a few other places.

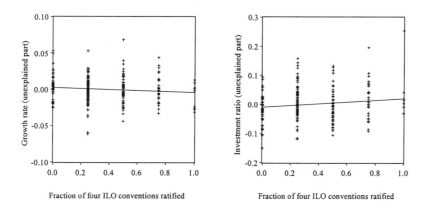

Figure 1.10. Effects of ILO labor-market conventions

---

[11] These measures have been employed previously by Rodrik (1996).

[12] For descriptions of the main conventions, see International Labour Organization (1990). Information on country ratifications is contained in International Labour Organization (1995).

Although the adoption of an ILO convention likely does not matter much directly for a country's labor-market policy, the number of these ratifications may nevertheless proxy for the government's general stance with regard to intervention into labor markets. If the number of ratifications (at any date up to 1994) of the four conventions is added to the system used in Barro (1997), then the relation between growth and this ILO number looks as shown in the left panel of Figure 1.10. The estimated relation is negative, and the implied effect is substantial: the adoption of all four ILO standards would depress the growth rate on impact by 0.7 percent per year.[13] However, since the statistical significance is marginal, this estimate cannot be viewed as highly reliable. In the right panel of Figure 1.10, the relation with investment is also weak statistically (and actually has a positive slope).

Another idea is to use survey information on labor-market regulations compiled in recent years for the World Economic Forum by Jeffrey Sachs and Andrew Warner (available from the authors at the Harvard Institute for International Development, Harvard University). They asked roughly 2000 persons, mostly executives from multinational firms, about labor-market conditions in countries with which they were familiar. Information is updated annually and is available for forty-eight countries. The three questions, all rated initially on a one-to-six subjective scale and applying contemporaneously, concern restrictions on hiring and firing, the nature of labor regulations and collective bargaining agreements, and the ease with which restructuring of labor can be accomplished.

I averaged the three Sachs-Warner indicators for 1994 and transformed them to a zero-to-one scale, with one signifying the most regulation. The most restrictive countries are Germany, India, Belgium, Italy, South Africa, France, and the Netherlands, all measured at 0.7. The least restrictive are Singapore, New Zealand, Hong Kong, the United Kingdom, and Peru, all measured between 0.2 and 0.3. The United States is rated at 0.4 on this scale. The coverage for this indicator is good for the OECD, Asia, and South America but weak otherwise.

The Sachs-Warner indicator was added to the system for economic growth that has already been discussed. One problem here is that the limited data availability on this indicator sharply reduces the sample size. Another difficulty is that the Sachs-Warner variable applies around 1994; that is, after the end of the observation period for economic growth (1965 to 1990). The use of this variable to "explain" prior growth will therefore be satisfactory

---

[13]   Among the four ILO conventions considered, the two that turn out to yield the main negative relation with growth are the one for restrictions on termination of employment and that for equal pay for men and women. The minimum-wage and collective-bargaining conventions are negligibly related to growth.

only if a country's labor-market policies typically remain the same for long periods of time (and do not have an important endogenous component). One example of a problem is Peru, which is rated as having free labor markets in 1994, although its markets were actually highly restricted during the sample period.

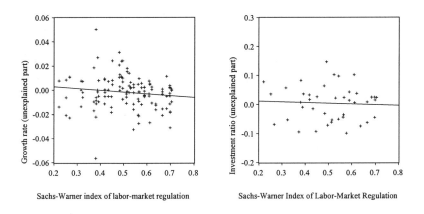

Figure 1.11. Effects of labor-market regulations

In any event, the Sachs-Warner variable has a negative and marginally significant relation with economic growth, as shown in the left panel of Figure 1.11. A shift from the least restrictive labor-market policy (Singapore) to the most restrictive (Germany) is estimated to reduce growth by 0.9 percent per year. This effect is large and similar to that found before with the ILO data. The right panel of Figure 1.11 shows, however, that the relation between investment and the labor-market indicator is basically nil.

The conclusions in this section must necessarily be tentative. Although labor-market restrictions may have quantitatively important effects on long-term growth, the cross-country evidence assembled thus far is not definitive.

1.2.8. Other policy influences on growth and investment

Other researchers have studied additional ways in which government policies affect economic growth. Sachs and Warner (1995) focus on international openness, as reflected in tariff and nontariff barriers, the black-market premium on foreign exchange, and subjective measures of open policies. The overall finding is that increased openness to international trade promotes economic growth. In my own research, I have found, however, that it is difficult to isolate these effects once the variables described earlier are held constant. My view is that this difficulty reflects problems in measuring policies that influence international openness, not the lack of importance of this openness.

King and Levine (1993) analyzed the development of domestic capital markets. They used various proxies for this development, including the extent of intermediation by commercial banks and other domestic financial institutions. The general finding is that the presence of a more advanced domestic financial sector predicts higher economic growth. The main outstanding issue here is to disentangle the effect of financial development on growth from the reverse channel. In particular, it is important for future research to isolate the effects of government policies—for example, on regulation of domestic capital markets—on the state of financial development and, hence, on the rate of economic growth.

Easterly and Rebelo (1993) examined aspects of public investment and also considered the nature of tax systems. One result is that public investment does not exhibit high rates of return overall. The main positive effects on economic growth showed up for investments in the area of transportation. With regard to tax systems, the findings were largely inconclusive because of the difficulties in measuring marginal tax rates on labor and capital incomes in a consistent and accurate way for a large sample of countries. An important priority for future research is better measurement of the nature of tax systems.

1.3.   IMPLICATIONS OF THE CROSS-COUNTRY FINDINGS FOR ADVANCED COUNTRIES

The cross-country evidence provides good and bad news for the growth prospects of the United States and other advanced countries. The basic institutions and policies of these successful places are already favorable in comparison with those of most other countries. In particular, the legal systems and public bureaucracies function reasonably well, markets and price systems are allowed to operate to a considerable extent, and high inflation is unusual. The population is also highly educated, reasonably healthy, and rich. The combination of these factors yields the bad news that it is hard to get the long-run per capita growth rate in the advanced countries much above 1.5 to 2 percent per year. The notion that some tax or other policy change could double the long-term U.S. growth rate therefore looks unrealistic.

The basic problem is that successful countries cannot grow rapidly by filling the vacuum of nonworking public institutions or by absorbing the technologies and ideas that have been developed elsewhere. Moreover, the levels of physical and human capital are already high, and further accumulations are subject to diminishing returns.

Sustained growth in the leading countries depends on innovations that lead to new products and better methods of production, the factors stressed in the endogenous growth theories. This kind of technological progress occurs, and the rate of progress is responsive to policies that shape the economic environment. However, the empirical evidence suggests that feasible policies will not improve technology rapidly enough to raise the long-term per capita growth rate above the range of 1.5 to 2 percent per year. Post World War II U.S. per capita growth exceeded 2 percent in the 1960s but not for other sustained periods (if the Korean War years are excluded).

The numbers should, in any case, be kept in longer term perspective: the average growth rate of U.S. output per person since 1870 was only 1.8 percent per year and has not shown clearly varying trends within this long period. Although this growth rate looks unspectacular, it was high enough to make the United States in 1997 the richest country in the world (in terms of purchasing-power adjusted GDP per capita).

The good news from the cross-country evidence is that some policy actions can be identified that would enhance long-term growth by a few tenths of a percentage point. Moreover, such changes would matter a great deal for standards of living in the long run. For instance, I have made an estimate—based on the cross-country findings for the effects of government consumption expenditure—that a shift in the United States to a flat-rate consumption tax would raise the long-term growth rate by about 0.3 percent per year. Such an improvement means that the level of U.S. real GDP would be higher by around $300 billion after ten years. On the down side, if price stability were abandoned and average annual inflation were to rise by five percentage points, then I estimate that the long-run growth rate would decline by about 0.2 percent per year. In this case, the level of U.S. real GDP would be lower by around $200 billion after ten years.

Aside from basic tax reform and maintenance of price stability, other policies would be important for long-term U.S. growth. Some promising suggestions include improvements in educational quality, notably those that would be stimulated by school-choice programs, privatization of social security along Chilean lines, reduced regulation of labor and other markets, and overhaul of the legal system to limit product-liability awards. Unfortunately, the cross-country growth research is not at a stage to yield reliable estimates for the effects of these reforms on the long-term growth rate.

References

Barro, R.J. (1997). *Determinants of Economic Growth: A Cross-Country Empirical Study.* Cambridge, MA: MIT Press.

Barro, R.J., and J.-W. Lee. (1997). "Determinants of Schooling Quality." Unpublished paper, Harvard University.

Barro, R.J. and X. Sala-i-Martin. (1995). *Economic Growth.* New York: McGraw Hill.

Bollen, K.A. (1990). "Political Democracy: Conceptual and Measurement Traps." *Studies in Comparative International Development* (Spring), 7–24.

Cass, D. (1965). "Optimum Growth in an Aggregative Model of Capital Accumulation." *Review of Economic Studies* 32, 233–240.

Easterly, W.R., and S. Rebelo. (1993). "Fiscal Policy and Economic Growth: An Empirical Investigation." *Journal of Monetary Economics* 32, 417–458.

Gastil, R.D. (1982–1983 and other years). *Freedom in the World.* Westport, CT: Greenwood Press.

Hanushek, E., and D. Kim. (1995). "Schooling, Labor Force Quality, and Economic Growth." Working Paper No. 411, Rochester Center for Economic Research.

Inkeles, A. (1991). *On Measuring Democracy.* New Brunswick, NJ: Transaction.

International Labour Organization. (1990). *Summaries of International Labour Standards.* (2nd ed.). Geneva: International Labour Office.

International Labour Organization. (1995). *Lists of Ratification by Convention and by Country.* Geneva: International Labour Office.

King, R.G., and R. Levine. (1993). "Finance, Entrepreneurship, and Growth: Theory and Evidence." *Journal of Monetary Economics* 32, 513–542.

Knack, S., and P. Keefer. (1995). "Institutions and Economic Performance: Cross-Country Tests Using Alternative Institutional Measures." *Economics and Politics* 7, 207–227.

Koopmans, T.C. (1965). "On the Concept of Optimal Economic Growth." In *The Econometric Approach to Development Planning.* Amsterdam: North Holland.

Ramsey, F. (1928). "A Mathematical Theory of Saving." *Economic Journal* 38, 543–559.

Rodrik, D. (1996). "Labor Standards in International Trade: Do They Matter and What Do We Do about Them?" Unpublished paper, Harvard University.

Romer, P.M. (1990). "Endogenous Technological Change." *Journal of Political Economy* 98, S71–S102.

Sachs, J.D., and A.M. Warner. (1995). "Economic Reform and the Process of Global Integration." *Brookings Papers on Economic Activity* 1, 1–95.

Solow, R.M. (1956). "A Contribution to the Theory of Economic Growth." *Quarterly Journal of Economics* 70, 65–94.

DISCUSSION

David Dollar

Division Chief, Macroeconomics and Growth, Policy Research Department, Development Economics, The World Bank

Robert J. Barro's chapter provides an excellent summary of recent developments in growth theory and empirics. One conclusion from this work is that not much can be done to raise the growth rate of the advanced countries beyond 1.5 to 2 percent per capita. For developing countries, on the other hand, there is a different message — both optimistic and pessimistic.

The optimistic message is that, after controlling for differences in institutions and policies, poor countries tend to grow faster (conditional convergence). Furthermore, some of the relevant policies (for example, maintaining price stability) are not difficult technically. Thus, there is some prospect for the poor countries to catch up with the rich ones. The pessimistic message is that some of the factors that matter for growth are deep-seated institutions, such as the strength of property rights and the rule of law. It is not obvious how a country goes about reforming these. The fact that many poor countries continue to fall further and further behind the developed world indicates that it is not easy to put a growth-enhancing institutional-policy framework in place.

What I would like to do in this brief comment is to examine the results of the empirical growth literature critically. I extract from Barro's chapter four potential messages that developing countries might learn and ask how realistic and counterfactual it is to expect change in these dimensions. And whether we really think that these are causal relationships, in the sense that if a country reforms it will actually move to a higher growth path (permanently or at least for a transitional period of significant length).

Let's start with the easiest lesson: economic policies matter for growth. Two of the most robust associations in the literature are that high inflation (say, above 40 percent) and closed trade regimes are negatively correlated with growth. One of the main criticisms of the empirical growth literature is that it often relies on cross-country associations, raising issues of causality and omitted variables. In the case of economic policies, however, there is robust time-series evidence as well. Countries that stabilize high inflation or liberalize their trade regimes tend to grow more rapidly afterwards (Fischer, 1993; Sachs and Warner, 1995).

Economic policy is clearly an area that developing countries can act on. There are plenty of examples of reform followed by improved growth performance: Taiwan in the 1950s; Indonesia in the 1960s; Bolivia, Peru, Ghana in the 1980s; Vietnam, Uganda, and Ethiopia in the 1990s.

Often several economic reforms are undertaken at once, so that disentangling the independent effect of each reform is difficult. But we can have a fair amount of confidence that the package of macroeconomic and trade reform will produce a better environment for investment and growth. It should also be noted that the time-series and cross-sectional evidence provide consistent quantitative estimates of the impact of reform. A country with high inflation and a closed trade regime can expect to improve its growth rate by about three percentage points through economic reform. That is a large number relative to the average per capita growth of about 1 percent for developing countries in the past thirty years. Nevertheless, the spectacular success of the East Asian countries up until recently may have created exaggerated expectations about the benefits of reform. Good policy alone is not going to achieve the 5 to 6 percent per capita growth rates observed in some East Asian countries.

Thus, the first clear lesson for developing countries is stabilize and join the WTO—and that is a good first step toward a healthy growth environment.

The second potential lesson for developing countries is that there is an important set of institutional issues centering around rule of law, property rights, and efficiency of the public sector (absence of corruption). This is an intuitive result: property rights are at the heart of a good incentive regime for accumulation. Is this something that developing countries can act on?

Unlike economic policy, this is an area where there are not many country examples or time-series evidence to bolster the cross-sectional association. The obvious exception would be the former communist countries, in which there has been a large change in the institutional framework for property rights. It seems likely that in the long run we will find that the shift in favor of private property rights is good for growth, but in my view it is too early to say that these examples provide evidence about the effect of property rights on long-term growth.

In the case of these institutional matters, it is also not clear what a country needs to do to improve. There is some suggestive research into determinants of corruption. Kaufmann and Sachs (1998) find that it is highly associated with regulatory discretion — that is, the perception by firms that rules are vague and leave a lot of scope to bureaucrats. There is not much evidence that the amount of regulation is bad for growth, but vaguely specified regulations appear to create a climate that favors rent-seeking and reduces incentives for productive activities.

A third kind of variable that often shows up in the cross-country regressions is some measure of initial human capital. Thus, a potential (politically correct) lesson for developing countries is that a special effort to build up human capital may be needed to initiate a period of high growth.

However, in this area the time-series evidence is clearly at odds with the cross-sectional findings. In Africa, in particular, there has been a large increase in human capital (measured, for example, by average schooling of the labor force). Countries that achieve this increase do *not* tend to grow faster afterwards.

It is possible that a certain threshold level of human capital is needed before a growth effect is observed. This would fit with certain models in which the human capital creates a good environment for absorbing new technologies from abroad. It is also possible that the cross-sectional result is spurious: there is something unobserved about Taiwan, say, that results in both high levels of human capital at the beginning of a period and rapid growth in the subsequent period. Thus there is association but no causal relationship.

Another problem in the human capital area is that there is not much relationship between public spending and outcomes. Some of the countries with the best results in terms of student achievement on standardized tests spend relatively small amounts of public money on education. Thus, even if it is established that a special effort to build up human capital is warranted, it is not clear what the government can go to bring about this result.

The fourth potential lesson from Barro's chapter is "be democratic, but not too." That is, there is a nonlinear, partial relationship between growth and democracy: the relationship is positive up to a certain level of democracy and then negative beyond. Here, however, it is not clear what the counterfactual is. Democracy is likely to influence the other institutions and policies that are included in the regression (rule of law or openness, for example). In the 1990s there are quite a few examples of democratic revolutions and large policy changes coming together or in close succession.

In summary, the one really robust, actionable finding that comes out of the growth literature is that economic reform (stabilization, trade liberalization) creates a good environment for investment and growth. This does seem to be a lever that individual countries can pull, and there are plenty of successful examples. The lessons concerning institutions and growth are less clear. Democracy has a weak relationship with growth, but it may be that this plays a significant role in establishing economic institutions and policy. And while property rights are obviously important, it is not clear in practice what a country can do to strengthen them. Finally, the evidence on the importance of human capital is mixed. Clearly human capital will be built up endogenously in response to a good incentive regime. The issue for debate is whether a certain level of initial human capital is part of a good incentive regime. The cross-section evidence says yes, whereas the time-series evidence says no.

References

Fischer, S. (1993). "The Role of Macroeconomic Factors in Growth." *Journal of Monetary Economics* 32, 485–512.

Kaufmann, D., and J.D. Sachs. (1998). "Determinants of corruption." Mimeo.

Sachs, J.D., and A. Warner. (1995). "Economic Reform and the Process of Global Integration." *Brookings Papers on Economic Activity* 1, 1–118.

Chapter 2

The joys and sorrows of openness: A review essay

William Easterly[*]
World Bank

Economists have widely celebrated openness as a crucial ingredient in economic success. Yet there are almost as many definitions of openness as there are celebrants. This chapter explores the many dimensions of openness and finds that they are indeed associated with economic growth. But the chapter also notes important limitations to openness as a panacea for economic ills. Open economies are more vulnerable to terms-of-trade and capital market shocks, which suggests that there is a risk-return tradeoff in becoming more open. We also know that openness is no panacea for development because we have considerable evidence of poverty clusters persisting in highly open economies.

2.1. THE MANY DIMENSIONS OF OPENNESS

The most obvious differentiation between types of openness is openness to international trade versus openness to capital flows. The first is the one usually emphasized in the growth literature. However, the wide use of the black-market premium in growth regressions reflects some interest in the second type of openness, since the black-market premium is a direct reflection of the stringency of capital controls. There has also been empirical work on direct measures of capital inflows, like the share of foreign direct investment inflows as a percentage of GDP.

The openness to international trade itself has many dimensions. The trade share (exports + imports)/GDP could be high because the government consciously promotes trade, such as through subsidies to exports. Measures

---

[*] Views expressed here are not necessarily those of the World bank or its member governments.

of openness based on the degree to which domestic prices are aligned with international ones, on the other hand, reflect the degree of neutrality of the government's trade regime. These two kinds of openness could be negatively correlated—a government that gives high subsidies to exports is distorting prices relative to international norms.

A direct measure of government intervention in trade is the average tariff on imports or the share of imports covered by nontariff barriers. These will presumably be reflected in the domestic price distortions mentioned above, but they also can be measured directly.

Other policy measures affect openness in a more indirect way. If the government awards itself a monopoly of a particular commodity export, this may interfere with the comparative advantage the country may have in that commodity. The government may interfere in one of two ways: commodity marketing boards and monopolistic state enterprises.

First, it can create a commodity marketing board with the sole right to buy the product domestically from private producers. For example, Ghana long had a Cocoa Marketing Board, which by law was the sole buyer of cocoa from private cocoa producers. As in many other cases, the Ghanaian government succumbed to the temptation to use the marketing board as a device to heavily tax the commodity exports. Prior to independence, the cocoa producers received 89 percent of the world price of cocoa in 1949. By 1983, sales prices had fallen to 6 percent of the world price. Cocoa exports were 19 percent of GDP in 1955; by 1983 they were only 3 percent of GDP (Easterly and Levine, 1997). Reforms finally began to reverse the punitive taxation in the mid-1980s. It is important to include such phenomena in definitions of openness.

The government can also monopolize exports by having a state enterprise be the sole producer of the export commodity. Many oil companies in the developing world are state enterprises, for example. As with marketing boards, the government finds it hard to risk tinkering with the enterprise for reasons that have nothing to do with maximizing comparative advantage. The government controls prices of domestic gasoline to win the support of urban motorists; it taxes the revenues and controls the investment of the state enterprise to meet fiscal targets. Again, one wants to include the predominance of state enterprises in an openness measure.

Given the diverse dimensions of openness, it is not a complete surprise that the different dimensions are relatively uncorrelated with each other. Pritchett (1996) finds that black-market premia, price-based distortion measures, tariff and quota measures, and shares of trade in GDP are uncorrelated across countries. It is therefore clear that the many dimensions of openness should be investigated individually, which is what I do now.

2.2. THE JOYS OF OPENNESS

The data show three kinds of advantages of the many dimensions of openness. First, most of these dimensions are robustly correlated with economic growth. Second, most of them are still correlated with growth after controlling for investment—suggesting that they raise the efficiency of resource allocation in addition to promoting investment. Third, openness promotes—at least to a limited extent—convergence of poor countries and regions.

2.2.1. Correlations of measures of openness with economic growth

I first review the price-based measures of openness, and then look at trade shares, the black-market premium, and a composite measure of openness. Finally, I look at a direct measure of capital openness: the share of foreign direct investment in GDP.

There are two kinds of price-based measures. The first one measures the overall overvaluation of the currency, which determines whether the country's goods are more expensive in dollars than those of its trade competitors. The second one measures the distortion of relative prices in the economy relative to international relative prices.

Dollar (1992) constructs the first kind of price-based measure. Summers and Heston (1991) have collected information on the dollar prices (converted at the prevailing exchange rate) of 151 commodities in fifty-seven countries. Dollar takes the ratio of the average dollar price of this commodity basket to the dollar price of the same basket in the United States. He corrects for the Balassa-Samuelson effect by which nontradables are cheaper in poor countries with abundant cheap labor, which would mean that his index will show low values in poor countries that have nothing to do with trade policy. He then regresses the index on per capita income and takes the residuals as his measure of openness. Inserting this measure into a growth regression with other plausible controls, he finds a strong association between this indicator of openness and growth: "Reduction of the real exchange rate distortion to the Asian level would add 0.7 percentage points to Latin American growth and 1.8 percentage points to African growth" (Dollar, 1992).

Aitken (1991) proposes another measure of price distortion that captures relative price distortions. For each country, he calculates the dollar price of goods relative to the United States level and corrects it for per capita income. He then takes the variance across all goods of these relative prices. A high variance indicates relative prices are out of whack with international prices:

some goods are artificially cheap by world standards while other goods are artificially expensive. Aitken presumes these price distortions to reflect interventionist trade policy in which tariffs and quotas raise some good prices relative to others.

I applied Aitken's measure as an explanatory variable in a growth regression (Easterly, 1993). Theory predicts that only price distortions of input and investment goods should matter for growth (in an endogenous growth model). Price distortions in input and investment cause the allocation of investment to sectors to diverge from the free-market optimum, and hence these price distortions lower growth. Distortions of consumption-good prices matter for consumer welfare but do not affect growth. Hence, I calculate the variance of prices relative to United States norms only across intermediate inputs and investment goods. This variable had a significant impact on growth: a one standard deviation decrease in the variance of relative input/investment prices raises growth by 1.2 percentage points.[14]

A direct government intervention into openness is the imposition of tariffs and quotas on trade. Harrison (1996) found that an openness index based on tariffs and nontariff barriers was significantly correlated with growth in a cross-country panel of either annual or five year averages. Lee (1993) finds that the average tariff multiplied the trade share had a significant negative effect on growth. Edwards (1997) also finds the average tariff to have a significant negative effect on growth.

The next kind of measure of openness is the share of trade (exports + imports) in GDP. This variable has a troubled history. Levine and Renelt (1992) found that this variable was highly nonrobust across alternative specifications of a growth regression. However, they did find that the trade share was a robust determinant of investment. Harrison (1996) found that the trade share was significant in some regressions but was not robust to changes in methodology (cross-section versus fixed effects in pooled data, annual data versus five-year averages, and so on). However, Easterly, Loayza, and Montiel (1997) found that this variable was strongly significant in an Arrellano and Bond (1991) dynamic panel specification. This econometric method has substantially more power than ordinary least squares and so was able to detect a strong effect of trade share where previous regressions failed.[15] The effect was economically significant: when Latin America increased its trade share by twenty percentage points from 1985 to 1990 to

---

[14] Another related result is in the famous growth regression by Barro (1991), which found that a measure of the absolute deviation of the investment price from the international norm had a negative effect on growth.

[15] Frankel and Romer (1996) found a strong effect of the trade share on income level when they instrumented for the trade share with geographic variables.

1990 to 1993, the effect on growth (controlling for other factors) was plus half a percentage point.

The black-market premium is a measure of openness that has been found to be statistically significant and robust in many studies (Easterly and Levine, 1997; Barro and Sala-i-Martin, 1995; Easterly, 1994; Fischer, 1993; Lee, 1993; Levine and Zervos, 1993). Figure 1 illustrates the results from Easterly and Levine (1997), showing how the deviation from world average growth is correlated with the deviation from the world average black-market premium controlling for other factors. Lee (1993) estimates that for a country with an import share of about 0.2, putting on a tariff of 25 percent and a black-market premium of 50 percent would lower growth at 1.4 percentage points per annum.

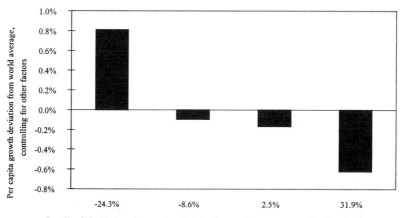

Figure 2.1. The black-market premium and economic growth

The only problem is that we are not sure exactly what the black-market premium is measuring. The premium on foreign exchange in the black-market can exist only if capital controls prevent the free buying and selling of foreign exchange at the official exchange rate. The level of the premium depends on how realistic is the official exchange rate by the purchasing-power-parity criterion. A frequent cause of a high black-market premium is high inflation with a fixed official exchange rate. A high black-market premium will distort prices, since some prices will reflect the official exchange rate (such as producer prices for exporters required to surrender foreign exchange at the official rate) while others reflect the black-market premium. A high black-market premium will cause resources to be diverted to rent seeking, as political interest groups lobby to gain the right to purchase foreign exchange at the official rate. A high black-market premium thus reflects a motley collection of capital controls, official exchange rate overvaluation, inflation, price distortion, and rent seeking. Whichever of these phenomena dominate, the effect is economically and statistically significant: an increase of fifty-six percentage points in the black-market premium (controlling for other factors) is associated with lower growth by one and a half percentage points.

The last openness measure I examine is a composite of several of the above, along with some new measures. Sachs and Warner (1995) classify an economy as "closed" if any of following holds:

1. Black-market premium > 20 percent,
2. Quota coverage of trade > 40 percent,
3. Average import tariff > 40 percent,
4. There is a state monopoly on major exports, or
5. There is a socialist economic system.

If none of the above holds, then the economy is classified as "open." Sachs and Warner have made a valuable contribution by including the state monopoly on export criterion, as well as the socialist economy criterion. Neither of these is contained in any other measure of openness.

Sachs and Warner found dramatic differences between "open" and "closed" economies.

Table 2.1. Growth per capita, 1970 to 1989 (percent)

	Open economies	Closed economies
Developing countries	4.49	0.69
Developed countries	2.29	0.74

Table 2.1 shows their results. Among developing countries, open economies grew 3.8 percentage points faster than closed economies. Over 1970 to 1989, this would imply a doubling of the ratio of income in an open economy to that in a closed economy.

Finally, a direct measure of openness to capital flows is the share of new foreign direct investment in the economy. Borensztein, De Gregorio, and Lee (1994) and Blomstrom, Lipsey and Steiner (1992) have both found strong effects of foreign direct investment (FDI) on growth. Since FDI may be endogenous to growth, both sets of authors instrument for it and still find a strong statistical relationship. The first set of authors found that the effect of foreign direct investment on growth was stronger for countries with more educated populations, which makes sense if FDI is a vehicle for adoption of better technology and thus faster growth.

2.2.2. Openness promotes investment efficiency

All of the studies cited here have found effects of the various measures of openness to be significant even after controlling for the quantity of investment. This suggests that openness improves the allocation of investment and thus raises growth for a given level of investment.

A quick theoretical example (from Easterly, 1993) shows one reason why this might happen. Suppose that output is a function of two capital goods, both tradable internationally:

$$Y = AK_1^{\alpha}K_2^{1-\alpha}$$

Suppose the government imposes an import tariff t on the first capital good but not on the second. Producers will equate the after-tax marginal products of the two capital goods to each other, resulting in a ratio of the two capital goods to be

$$K_1/K_2 = \alpha/[(1 - \alpha)(1 + t)]$$

The optimal ratio of the two capital stocks is just $\alpha/(1-\alpha)$. Hence the imposition of the differential tariff causes there to be too little of the first type of capital and too much of the second type of capital. It is easy to show that this inefficiency in capital accumulation will lower growth for a given amount of capital accumulation. If the above results hold up when controlling for investment, as they do, then this allocation effect must be important empirically.

2.2.3. Open economies converge to each other

Sachs and Warner (1995) not only show that openness promotes growth but also provide a dramatic demonstration that openness promotes convergence of rich and poor countries. Sachs and Warner show that among open economies the poorer countries grow more rapidly (Figure 2.2), while there is no such tendency among closed economies (Figure 2.3). However, note that poor countries are overwhelmingly in the closed category and rich countries are overwhelmingly in the open category, which suggests that being closed is itself correlated with income. I return to this fact later.

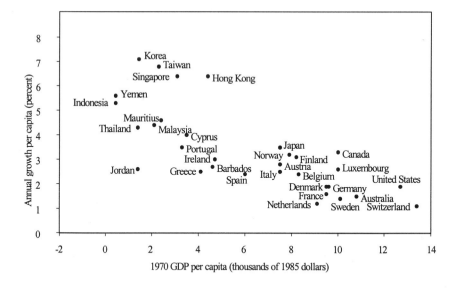

Figure 2.2. Growth and initial income, open economies,1970 to 1989

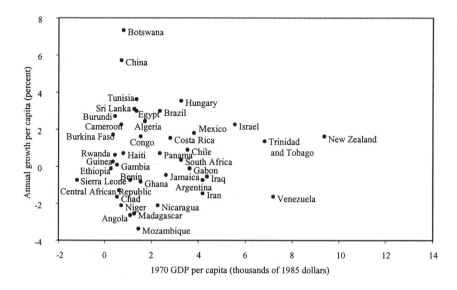

Figure 2.3. Growth and initial income, closed economies, 1970 to 1989

The Sachs and Warner result confirms results by Barro and Sala-i-Martin (1992, 1995) that collections of open economies like the U.S. states, provinces of Europe, and the prefectures of Japan display absolute convergence among themselves. Poorer U.S. states grow faster than richer U.S. states, poorer European provinces grow faster than richer European provinces, and poorer Japanese prefectures grow faster than richer Japanese prefectures. Figure 2.4 shows the impressive Barro and Sala-i-Martin correlation between initial income and growth of US states.

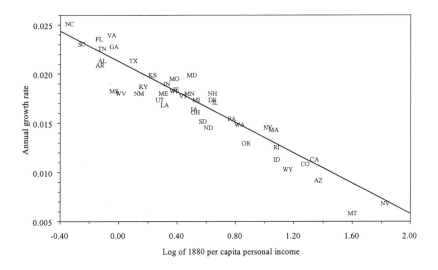

Figure 2.4. Growth and initial income, closed economies, 1970 to 1989

Barro and Sala-i-Martin also note an important qualifier, which again I return to later, that the rate of convergence in all these collections of open economies is fairly slow (about 2 percent a year). At this speed it takes thirty-five years to close half of a gap in per capita incomes. They note that this catchup is much slower than would be expected of economies in the neoclassical model with a capital share of about one-third. A capital share of three quarters would be required to generate this slow speed of convergence (Barro and Sala-i-Martin, 1995), p. 413).

Barro and Sala-i-Martin (1992, 1995) extend their convergence analysis to the international data (including dimensions of openness). In the international data, there is a conditional tendency toward convergence between countries at about the same 2 percent per year.

2.2.4.   Summary of the joys of openness

I should not go further without making the obligatory statement that cross-section regressions show correlation, not necessarily causation. There has been some attempt to deal with causality in many of the works cited here, either by using initial values or instrumental variables. Still the suspicion remains that truly exogenous instruments excludable from the growth regression are hard to find.

I should also mention another justifiable criticism of the recent literature, which is that it fails to acknowledge the contributions of an earlier generation of researchers. These researchers—for example, Bela Balassa, Jagdish Bhagwati, and Anne Krueger—also strongly preached the advantages of openness for development.

To sum up the results surveyed here, caveats aside, open economies do grow more rapidly than closed economies. This is true whether the measure of openness has to do with exchange-rate overvaluation, relative price distortions, tariffs and quotas, share of trade in GDP, the black-market premium, or a composite measure combining some of these with state monopolization of commodity exports and general socialism. Openness promotes efficiency of investment, thus raising growth for a given amount of investment. Open economies converge to each other, albeit if slowly, while closed economies do not converge.

2.3.   THE SORROWS OF OPENNESS

In this section, I review some of the limitations and disadvantages of openness. Open economies are more vulnerable to terms-of-trade shocks. Economies open to capital inflows are more vulnerable to sudden interruption of such flows. Openness only slowly diminishes poverty for backward regions or groups, as poverty traps persist in highly open economies.

2.3.1.   Vulnerability to terms-of-trade shocks

A terms-of-trade shock is defined as the percentage change in export prices times the share of exports in GDP minus the percentage change in import prices times the share of imports in GDP. Easterly, Kremer, Pritchett, and

Summers (1993) found that a one percentage point of GDP terms-of-trade loss lowered growth by 0.85 percentage points. This is a remarkably strong effect, which accounts for significant performance variations among countries. Note that this effect cannot be simply the direct effect on GDP in an accounting sense. First, GDP growth is measured at constant prices and so does not mechanically reflect a terms-of-trade shock. Second, the magnitude of the response is greater than would be predicted by standard neoclassical models.

Figure 2.5 shows the strong simple correlation between terms-of-trade shocks and GDP growth in the 1980s. To look at country examples behind this correlation, Mauritius had among the highest growth rate in the world in the 1980s while Venezuela had among the lowest. Not coincidentally, Mauritius had the most favorable terms-of-trade shock in the world, while Venezuela had the most unfavorable one. Increased openness by the trade share definition means that both positive and negative shocks will be larger in absolute value.

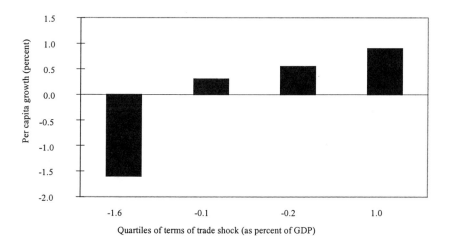

Figure 2.5. Terms-of-trade shocks and economic growth

Sachs and Warner (1995) make a similar point. Their graph of growth of always open economies and always closed economies over time (reproduced here as Figure 2.6) shows that the open economies were hit hard by the great oil price shock of 1973 to 1974, while the closed economies were hardly affected. In general, the volatility of growth is higher in the open economies than in the closed economies, while the mean of the open economies is also

higher than the mean for the closed economies. Taking together the
favorable effect of openness on growth and the unfavorable effect of
openness on the variability of growth, there is a risk-return trade-off in the
degree of openness (although in the case of Figure 6, there is higher growth
in every year for the open economies).

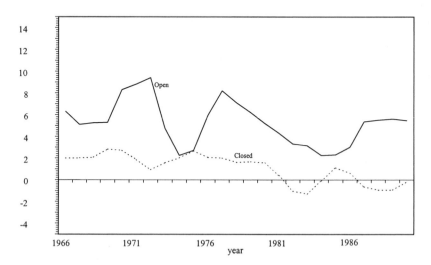

Figure 2.6. Average growth of eight always open and forty always closed economies,
1966 to 1990

Of course, some types of openness are more prone to terms-of-trade
shocks than others. The Interamerican Development Bank (1995) reiterates
the well-known point that countries with a higher concentration of exports in
particular commodities will suffer higher variance of terms-of-trade. Table
2.2 shows their data on the standard deviation of terms-of-trade and the
concentration of the four main commodity exports in total exports:

Table 2.2. Regional export concentration and volatility of terms-of-trade shocks

Region	Share of top four commodities in exports (percent)	Standard deviation of terms-of-trade (percent)
Middle East and North Africa	74	22
Sub-Saharan Africa	73	23
East Asia	60	18
Latin America	50	15
Developing Europe	28	9
South Asia	20	7
Industrialized countries	10	7

Since openness may result in a country being highly concentrated in commodities in which it has a strong comparative advantage, openness in light of this evidence amplifies the risk of terms-of-trade shocks. Poor economies do typically have a heavy weight of primary commodities in exports (Syrquin, 1994). This does not automatically imply such openness is bad; it just reinforces the notion that openness implies a risk-return trade-off: it both increases risk, and increases return.

2.3.2.   Vulnerability to interruption of capital flows

There is no need to present a detailed empirical analysis of the effect of capital market integration on the variability of growth, as nature has provided crystal-clear natural experiments. The debt crisis in Mexico in 1982 (and in the rest of Latin America) was followed by a lost decade of growth. Just when Mexico was starting to find foreign capital inflows and growth again, the debt crisis of 1994 to 1995 struck. It too was followed by recession, although the recovery was quicker than the first time around. The most recent capital-market crisis in East Asia again drives home the point of vulnerability of open economies to sudden changes in capital market sentiments. Given the advantages conferred by foreign direct investment, as discussed above, there is a risk-return trade-off in capital market openness as well.

2.3.3.   Poverty traps in open economies

The conclusion that openness is no panacea comes from the observance of poverty traps in open economies. I do not review here the theoretical increasing returns literature that shows how poverty traps are possible. I just show that poverty clusters exist from both anecdotal and econometric evidence.

In the United States, poverty clusters have both ethnic and geographic dimensions. Borjas (1992) has shown how the immigrant groups that were the poorest in the great migration of 1900 to 1910 continue to be the poorest two generations later. There is some convergence of skill differentials, but it is slow. Thus in 1980 census data, the grandchildren of Portuguese who immigrated sometime in 1900 to 1910 have 21 percent lower wages than the grandchildren of Englishmen who immigrated at the same time. In subsequent work, Borjas (1995) found that both neighborhood and ethnic effects were important in explaining individual wages. In other words, an individual in a poor Portuguese American neighborhood will receive a lower wage than an individual with identical characteristics who lives in a rich English American neighborhood. Obviously, a neighborhood or an ethnic group is open to both trade and capital flows from the outside world, so "closedness" cannot explain the relative poverty of some neighborhoods with respect to others. Borjas postulates "ethnic capital" and "neighborhood capital," in which one learns from the behavior of those around you. If you are in a poor ethnic group or neighborhood, the only available lessons are on how to be poor. A richer neighborhood or ethnic group, by contrast, provides role models for success.

Even completely open economies can endogenously stratify into poor and rich neighborhoods, as shown by Benabou (1996). Locally financed public goods such as schools will be better in the rich neighborhoods. The externalities from role models and good schools will be reflected in high real estate prices. The poor cannot afford to move from the poor to the rich neighborhood because the marginal product of their human capital will be low in light of their history of poor neighborhoods and poor schools.

To see neighborhood poverty traps, it is hardly necessary to examine census data. You can see poverty clusters just driving around any large American city. For example, a drive through the Washington, DC, area from northwest (starting in Potomac, Maryland) to southeast (ending at Andrews Air Force Base, again back in Maryland) takes you on a path that scales the heights of riches and plumbs the valleys of poverty (Figure 2.7). The poorest neighborhood along this drive is the Shaw neighborhood a few blocks to the northeast of the White House, with annual household income less than $20,000. This contrasts with Potomac with annual household incomes above $100,000. Of course, there is a racial dimension to this as Shaw is almost all black and Potomac is almost all white.

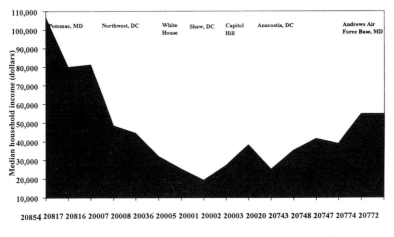

Zipcodes as you move from northwest to southeast Washington, DC, 1989

Figure 2.7. A journey through the Washington, DC area

Even if we abstract from the ethnic dimension, there are clusters of poverty among the white population in the United States. It is well known that the poorest whites in the United States live in the Appalachian Mountains. What is striking is that poverty is not even spread evenly across Appalachia. Instead, the most severe poverty is concentrated in a particular location within Appalachia. Of the twenty poorest white counties in the United States (there are 1484 counties that are 95 percent white or more), eighteen of them are in a small, geographically contiguous area in the mountains of eastern Kentucky. Eastern Kentucky is an open economy with respect to the rest of the United States, but trade and capital inflows have proved to be no panacea for this pocket of poverty. (Of course, individuals can escape the poverty trap by migrating into more promising areas. My grandfather was born in eastern Kentucky and lived his life in the Appalachians, but my parents took the emigration express out of the Appalachians to the promised land of northern Ohio.)

Poverty clusters are ubiquitous throughout the world. Households in the Tangail/Jamalpur district of Bangladesh earn 47 percent less than households with identical characteristics in Dhaka (Ravallion and Wodon, 1998). Households in the poor provinces of southwest China earn less than households with identical skills and other characteristics in Guangdong Province (the latter is next to Hong Kong). The poverty rate in Guangxi Province (right next to Guangdong) is 37 percent, compared to Guangdong's poverty rate of 5 percent (Ravallion and Jalan, 1996; Jalan and Ravallion, 1997).

There is even evidence of poverty traps at national levels. The neoclassical model says that capital should flow to the poorest economies, accelerating their convergence to the rest of the world. This is obviously not happening. The poorest quintile of countries over 1960 to 1995 received $0.06 per capita in portfolio capital inflows; the richest quintile received $189 per capita—over 3000 times more. The poorest economies may have been closed because of national policies, but it is hard to think of policies so punitive that they cause capital flows to poor countries to be 1/3000th of capital flows to rich countries.

More generally, we know there is no tendency toward absolute convergence in the cross-country data. In the very long run, as pointed out by Pritchett (1997), there is clearly strong divergence. Figure 2.8 shows how economies have diverged from 1820 to 1992. Even in the more recent evidence, there is a weak tendency toward divergence of countries. The bottom two quintiles of per capita income have median growth of less than one percent using decade data from 1960 to 1990; the upper three quintiles have median growth of over 2 percent. These differentials are statistically significant. The poorest and richest countries are diverging.

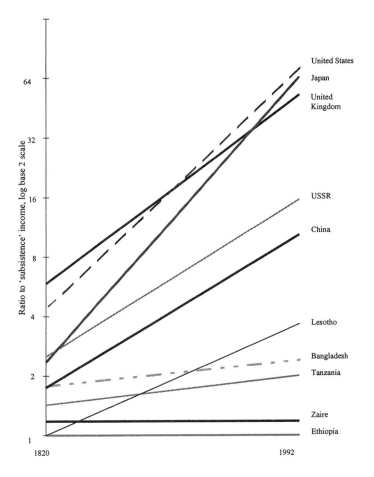

Figure 2.8. Growth rates diverge between rich and poor, 1820 to 1992

Quah (1993) has demonstrated this divergence using the clever device of transition matrices. He asks what is the probability that an economy at below one-quarter of world average income in 1962 will still be below one quarter in 1985. This probability is high — 0.76. When we graph all such probabilities (Figure 2.9), there is a clear tendency for twin peaks of probability. The poorest tend to stay the poorest, and the richest overwhelmingly tend to stay the richest. In between, there is substantial mobility in both directions.

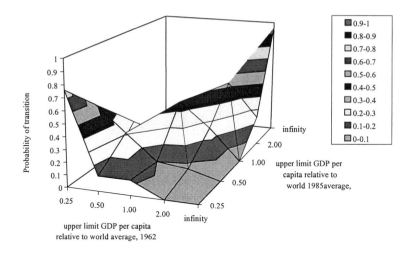

Figure 2.9. Twin peaks: Probabilities of transition from one income bracket to the next,
1962 to 1985, 100 countries

Since we saw from the Sachs and Warner data that poor countries were overwhelmingly closed, we can reconcile the finding of conditional convergence with that of absolute divergence. The few poor countries that were open did converge, while the many that were closed diverged. In the dataset as a whole, the latter dominate the former. There is thus a vicious circle of being closed because you are poor and being poor because you are closed. Why poor countries choose to be closed is an interesting political economy question for future research.

We saw from the eastern Kentucky and Shaw, DC, examples that even perfectly open economies converge only slowly. Recall that Barro and Sala-i-Martin found poor U.S. states to be catching up at only about 2 percent a year. Establishing why these poverty traps exist is beyond the scope of this chapter. I simply speculate that the answer has to do with the vicious circles that can arise in new growth models with spillovers between economic agents. As already noted, the poor are slow to catch up because their opportunities to learn from their neighbors are limited when all of their neighbors are also poor. Openness is fine for the middle-income and the rich among countries, regions, and neighborhoods, but its benefits only slowly trickle down to the poor countries, regions, and neighborhoods.

2.4.　CONCLUSIONS

Openness has many dimensions, virtually all of which prove to be positively correlated with economic growth. But openness brings increased vulnerability to terms-of-trade shocks and external debt crises. There is thus a risk-return trade-off with openness. Perhaps the severity of the trade-off can be ameliorated with insurance mechanisms for trade and financial shocks.

Openness is also no panacea for poor regions and countries, which catch up only slowly with rich regions and countries. The problems of these persistently poor areas deserve more attention from researchers.

References

Aitken, B. (1991). "Measuring Trade Policy Intervention: A Cross-Country Index of Relative Price Distortion." Working Paper 838, World Bank, Washington, DC.

Arellano, M., and S. Bond. (1991). "Some Tests of Specification for Panel Data: Monte Carlo Evidence and an Application to Employment Equations." *Review of Economic Studies* 58, 277–297.

Barro, R. (1991). "Economic Growth in a Cross-Section of Countries." *Quarterly Journal of Economics* 106, 407–443.

Barro, R., and X. Sala-i-Martin. (1992). "Convergence." *Journal of Political Economy* 100, 223–251.

Barro, R., and X. Sala-i-Martin. (1995). *Economic Growth.* New York: McGraw-Hill.

Benabou, R. (1996). "Heterogeneity, Stratification, and Growth: Macroeconomic Implications of Community Structure and School Finance." *American Economic Review* 86, 584–609.

Blomstrom, M., R. Lipsey, and M. Zejan. (1992). "What Explains Developing Country Growth?" Working Paper 4132, NBER.

Borensztein, E., J. de Gregorio, and J.-W. Lee. (1994). "How Does Direct Foreign Investment Affect Economic Growth?" International Monetary Fund.

Borjas, G. (1992). "Ethnic Capital and Intergenerational Mobility." *Quarterly Journal of Economics* 107, 123–150.

Borjas, G. (1995). "Ethnicity, Neighborhoods, and Human-Capital Externalities." *American Economic Review* 85, 365–390.

Dollar, D. (1992). "Outward-Oriented Economies Really Do Grow More Rapidly: Evidence from 95 LDCs, 1976–1985." *Economic Development and Cultural Change* 40, 523–544.

Easterly, W.R. (1993). "How Much Do Distortions Affect Growth?" *Journal of Monetary Economics* 32 , 187–212.

Easterly, W.R. (1994). "Economic Stagnation, Fixed Factors, and Policy Thresholds." *Journal of Monetary Economics* 33, 525–557.

Easterly, W.R., M. Kremer, L. Pritchett, and L. Summers. (1993). "Good Policy or Good Luck? Country Growth Performance and Temporary Shocks." *Journal of Monetary Economics* 32, 459–484.

Easterly, W.R., and R. Levine. (1997). "Africa's Growth Tragedy: Policies and Ethnic Divisions." *Quarterly Journal of Economics* 10, 1203–1250.

Easterly, W.R., N. Loayza, and P. Montiel. (1997). "Has Latin America's Post-Reform Growth Been Disappointing?" *Journal of International Economics* 43, 287–311.

Edwards, S. (1997). "Openness, Productivity, and Growth: What Do We Really Know?" Working Paper 5978, National Bureau of Economic Research.

Fischer, S. (1993). "The Role of Macroeconomic Factors in Growth." *Journal of Monetary Economics* 32, 485–512.

Frankel, J., and D. Romer. (1996). "Trade and Growth: An Empirical Investigation." Working Paper 5476, National Bureau of Economic Research.

Harrison, A. (1996). "Openness and Growth: A Time-Series, Cross-Country Analysis for Developing Countries." *Journal of Development Economics* 48, 419–447.

Interamerican Development Bank. (1995). *Economic and Social Progress in Latin America: Overcoming Volatility.*

Jalan, J., and M. Ravallion. (1997). "Spatial Poverty Traps?" Working Paper 1862, World Bank Policy Research.

Lee, J.-W. (1993). "International Trade, Distortions, and Long-Run Economic Growth." *IMF Staff Papers* 40, 299–328.

Levine, R., and D. Renelt. (1992). "A Sensitivity Analysis of Cross-Country Growth Regressions." *American Economic Review* 82, 942–963.

Levine, R., and S. Zervos. (1993). "What We Have Learned About Policy and Growth from Cross-Country Regressions." *AER Papers and Proceedings* 83, 426–430.

Pritchett, L. (1996). "Measuring Outward Orientation in LDCs: Can It Be Done?" *Journal of Development Economics* 49, 307–335.

Pritchett, L. (1997). "Divergence, Big Time." *Journal of Economic Perspectives* 11, 3–18.

Quah, D. (1993). "Empirical Cross-Section Dynamics in Economic Growth." *European Economic Review* 37, 426–434.

Ravallion, M., and J. Jalan. (1996). "Growth Divergence Due to Spatial Externalities." *Economics Letters* 53, 227–232.

Ravallion, M., and Q. Wodon. (1998). "Poor Areas or Only Poor People?" Mimeo, World Bank.

Sachs, J., and A.M. Warner. (1995). "Economic Reform and the Process of Global Integration." *Brookings Papers on Economic Activity* 1, 1–118.

Summers, R., and A. Heston. (1991). "The Penn World Table (mark 5): An Expanded Set of International Comparisons, 1950–88." *Quarterly Journal of Economics* 106, 327–368.

Syrquin, M. (1994). "Structural Transformation and the New Growth Theory." In L. Pasinetti and R. Solow, eds., *Economic Growth and the Structure of Long-Term Development.* New York: St. Martins Press.

DISCUSSION

Moshe Syrquin*
The World Bank

The mistrust of an open strategy was an important theme in the early development literature. This has mostly been replaced by a strong advocacy of openness buttressed by the, until recently, spectacular performance of several countries in East Asia. Bill Easterly's chapter is a succinct clear

* Comments by Howard Pack are gratefully acknowledged.

summary of what cross-country growth regressions show about the joys of opening balanced by some caveats about its sorrows.

Easterly's arguments are that openness leads to, or is associated with, higher growth rates, higher investment rates, and faster convergence. However, he identifies a potential trade-off: higher growths come at the cost of higher volatility. In addition, he argues that openness is no panacea since pockets of poverty remain even in otherwise successful cases.

In this chapter I will mostly concentrate on the joys and specifically on the effect on growth. I argue that, while there seems to be weighty evidence supporting the thesis that openness has been associated with successful growth, there is an ongoing debate in the literature as to the robustness and applicability of the openness-growth link, its interpretation, and likely mechanisms of transmission. Before proceeding with the discussion of openness and growth, I start with a brief defense of openness from the charges on the sorrows column.

The development literature abounds in arguments about the need to shield the economy from the winds of international commerce, for delinking the internal from the external economy, for regaining the decision centers, and so on. A contemporary version of these themes focuses on the dangers of globalization[16] adding new potential sorrows to the list. The two in Easterly's chapter do not seem to belong here. On poverty, Easterly claims only that openness does not eradicate poverty but not, as some do claim, that it is the cause of that poverty.

On volatility: if openness is measured by trade ratios and a terms-of-trade shock is defined, as in the present case, as the percentage change in export prices times the share of exports in GDP minus the percentage change in import prices times the share of imports in GDP, then trivially the first round measured impact of any shock will be larger in a more open economy. More relevant would seem to be the total effect after taking adjustments into account. Here the bulk of the evidence indicates that open economies have weathered shocks substantially better than their more closed neighbors (Balassa and McCarthy, 1984; Sachs, 1985). Two of the main factors behind the greater sensitivity to shocks in the more closed economies are a high degree of trade concentration in a few primary commodities and lack of flexibility. Both are partly the result of antitrade policies (for Africa, see Collier and Gunning, 1997). The figure from Sachs and Warner (1995) reproduced in the chapter, shows faster growth in the open economies even in the most turbulent periods. This pattern (which Easterly does acknowledge) portrays dominance, not a trade-off.

---

[16] New entries into this version can always count on Krugman to expose their mostly fallacious arguments.

Openness and growth

During the 1950s the strategy of import substitution industrialization (ISI) was widely accepted. The inherent price distortions and the excesses of the ISI strategy led to the beginning of a reevaluation and a gradual shift towards advocacy of an outward or a neutral orientation (see Bruton, 1998; and references there). Additional evidence favoring openness came from more developed countries, where trade liberalization and increased integration were seen as important factors in the prosperity and convergence of the postwar period (Ben-David, 1993).

The emerging view in the last decade, which became part of the Washington consensus, maintains that openness is necessary for sustained growth (sufficiency is discussed below). This view reflects the unprecedented growth of economies in East Asia, as well as the results of various country studies and comparative studies that showed a robust association between measures of openness (or trade reforms) and performance. Among the authors that argued and documented (not just "preached", as Easterly portrays them) the advantages of openness for development are Bela Balassa, Jagdish Bhagwati, and Anne Krueger.

The evidence in Easterly's chapter is limited to results from one particular approach—an extremely useful approach for indicating possible associations but not quite apt to the tasks of providing a solid basis for establishing whether openness has lead to faster growth and of unraveling the mechanisms and highlighting the conditions where this has worked and where it may not necessarily do so.

Mechanisms

Attempts to probe deeper and identify the precise mechanisms of transmission have been less successful. In endogenous growth theory openness influences growth through the exploitation of economies of scale, knowledge spillovers, increased variety of goods, and learning effects. However, it is not unambiguous whether openness leads to faster growth. Whether it does or not may depend on the size of the economy and on other initial conditions including possibly the position of the country in the world economy (Grossman, 1996).

Liberalization, broadly defined but always including a trade component identified as openness, seems to improve performance, though often with a lag and not in every case (Helleiner, 1986; Taylor, 1988). Any increase in growth must take place through higher rates of accumulation or TFP growth. The theoretical literature tends to emphasize the productivity link; the evidence, however, is not very supportive. Careful reviews of micro evidence or of industry studies fail consistently to find it (Pack, 1986; Tybout 1998; Rodrik, 1995).

Definitions, dimensions, and proxies

In cross-country growth regressions, *openness* refers to aspects of an economy's extent of participation in the international economy—primarily to trade flows, sometimes to FDI, and less frequently to other capital flows and migration. An important dimension, not often emphasized, is openness to foreign knowledge. Knowledge from licenses, from consultants, and from the information provided by purchasers has been shown to be no less important than the increase in competition stemming from trade liberalization (Pack, 1992). Furthermore, for long-term growth (really long-term—what the theoretical exercises are presumably studying when they emphasize steady states), a much wider conception of openness would seem to be relevant; such as the one advanced by Landes as the main key for long-term success. This conception of openness, as summarized by De Long (1998) in his review of Landes's book, is "a willingness to borrow whatever is useful from abroad whatever the price in terms of injured elite pride or harm to influential interests. ...A willingness to trust your own eyes and the results of your own experiments rather than relying on old books or the pronouncement of powerful and established authorities."

There is a certain ambiguity in the literature in the use of terms such as *openness, outward orientation, export orientation,* and *trade liberalization.* It is not always clear whether we are dealing with a state (low tariffs) or a process (liberalization). In the case of liberalization, trade usually constitutes only one of many components of a reform package.

Openness is usually measured by variables intended to capture the extent of trade barriers, the resulting wedge between the internal price structure and world prices, or the revealed outcomes of implied policies as in the case of trade shares.[17] Two observations on the measures of openness:

---

[17] The following is Pritchett's (1998, p. 34) list of partial correlates that have been included in growth regressions: "trade barrier measures of various kinds, exchange rate overvaluation, foreign-exchange controls, growth in volume or composition of exports, capital market controls, foreign direct investment, little movement or intellectual interchange, indices of 'economic freedom,' black-market premia, 'outward orientation' measures based on PPP."

- Pritchett (1996) showed that various trade-policy indicators are uncorrelated across countries. Easterly is not surprised by this finding which simply reflects the fact that openness has many dimensions. This multidimensionality, however, is nowhere to be found in the regressions, except in a few cases (Harrison, 1996; Edwards, 1998), where various measures are introduced *one at a time*. This leaves unanswered (actually even unasked) questions about the simultaneous effect of more than one of the dimensions, possible trade-offs, the necessity of each and every one of the effects, or the possibility of substitutability.

- Some of the measures used are at best only tenuous representations of openness or lack of it. Thus, two of the most robust variables used—the black-market premium and the Dollar index (Dollar, 1992) —are better seen as indicators of macroeconomic policy.[18] More worrying, as Collier and Gunning (1997) point out, the parallel premium in the African context is difficult to interpret since it appears to be not monotonic in trade restrictions.

Cross-country regressions

Cross-country comparisons have been an important component of development studies, but, unlike the older tradition that aimed at exploiting the rich variation across countries and over time to uncover uniformities in patterns of development as well as the principal sources of divergence from uniformity, the new strand is more ambitious and less cautious.[19]

Empirical studies that are based on aggregate data of uncertain meaning and questionable validity and that, in addition, pool observations from countries in Western Europe and in Sub-Saharan Africa, can at best yield results that are suggestive, indicative of some associations on average, and give us some rough orders of magnitude. Given the heterogeneity of the observations, the assumption that they are random drawings from a single universe appears too strong. The point is not that a different kind of theory is needed for studying developing countries but rather that there may be significant differences in the validity of some assumptions and in some behavioral and technological relations and parameters.

For understanding development (or lack of development) and for policy, the main criticism can be summarized in an almost trite observation: development is a complex process. While all analysis requires simplification this has gone too far in empirical growth theory. I present now very

---

[18] See, inter alia, Bosworth, Collins, and Chen (1995). For similar views and a critique of the Dollar index, see also Rodrik (1994).

[19] This section draws on Syrquin (1994).

schematically some of the problems in implementation and interpretation of the approach in its application to the issue of openness as summarized in Easterly's chapter.

Omitted variables

Literally hundreds of variables have been tried and found significant in a regression. Levine and Renelt (1992) show most of them to be fragile (one wonders how many policy recommendations have been based on these fragile results). Sala-i-Martin (1997) applies a less stringent test and finds no less than twenty-one variables robustly related to growth. The typical regression in Easterly's summary considers only a small subset of these variables: omitted variables bias is never mentioned.

One example of this problem is the omission of the level of development and its concomitant industrial structure. Most of the arguments of growth theory seem to refer to a modern sector producing manufactures or knowledge-intensive goods and services. How relevant are these for economies where the vast majority of the labor force may be illiterate and is engaged in subsistence agriculture? A similar comment applies to studies that measure openness by the share of exports or exports plus imports. Theoretical arguments about knowledge spillovers arguably do not have oil exports in mind but rather manufacturing or other nontraditional exports. Few studies make this distinction (for one that does, see Pack and Page, 1994).

Causality

It is not uncommon for a growth-regression study to acknowledge that causality has not, or cannot, be established. It is quite common in such cases for the authors to look at this unpleasant fact in the face and then move on to recommend policies that take the causality as established. In the studies cited by Easterly openness enters as an exogenous right-hand-side variable. A strong argument can be made that often trade is the handmaiden of growth rather than the engine of growth (Kravis, 1970). Rapid expansion in trade shares and in various measures of outward orientation may be the result of internally generated productivity growth rather than its cause. The problem of causality is made worse by the heterogeneity of the sample mentioned above. It is quite likely that the direction of causality differs among countries (see, for example, Jung and Marshall, 1985). In such a case what would be the meaning of "instrumenting" even if valid instruments were to be had?

Domain of applicability

Are the results from cross-country regressions supposed to be applicable to a specific period or to a selected group of countries, or, as appears to be implicit in most presentations, are they of (almost) universal applicability? Let us start with time periods. The data for the regressions are mostly five- or ten-year averages, with the range extending from annual to twenty to thirty year periods. Relatively longer periods are supposed to smooth out cycles and to approximate better long-term relations. Pritchett (1998) has recently shown that growth has been relatively smooth in the United States and other OECD countries but that in developing countries there is great instability in growth rates over time. He identifies several distinct growth patterns (hills, plateaus, mountains, and plains), which when thrown together into a uniform regression yield results that are at best hard to interpret. To take just one example from Pritchett's paper: from 1960 to 1992 per capita income in Cote d'Ivoire and Senegal grew at almost the same very low rate (0.22 percent and 0.18 percent respectively). However, while in Senegal the pattern of growth during most of the period was steady resembling a "plain," in Côte d'Ivoire it was more like a "mountain": +3.1 percent for 1960-80 and -4.1 percent afterwards. I join Pritchett (1998, p. 2) in asking, "What is the relevant sense in which the 'growth' experience of Senegal and Côte d'Ivoire explained by growth theory or empirics was the same?"

The majority of the regression studies focus on periods after 1970. How well do the results predict the past? Few researchers ask that question; Vamvakidis (1996, p. 3) does and finds that "the positive correlation between trade openness and growth in the 1970s and 1980s, disappears in the 1950s and 1960s, and becomes negative in the 1920s and 1930s.". In the same vein Fischer (1995, p. 103) in his comment on the Sachs and Warner (1995) paper that found a very strong positive effect of openness on growth argued that by starting in 1970 " the authors stack the deck against the import substituting strategy. Whatever happened later, Latin American and African countries did quite well in the 1950s and 1960s, despite their perverse regimes.".

A cross-country regression runner could argue that universal applicability was never intended; the regressions are designed to study the effects of trade through the mechanisms of endogenous growth theory (knowledge spillovers, economies of scale, and so on), which were less important then. In that case we are back at the problem mentioned above about the relevance of the modern technology arguments for an economy dominated by subsistence agriculture. In one of the earlier studies showing the benefits of an outward orientation, Feder (1983) ran separate regressions for countries with very low incomes and for a group of semi-industrialized countries. The benefits came out clearly only in the latter group.

Interactions and packages

A major shortcoming of the approach is the assumption of additivity. The implication of the way results are usually presented is that the coefficients indicate by how much growth will change if we change a right-hand-side variable by one unit holding all other factors constant.[20] However, as emphasized by Minister Pronk in his closing comments to the Hague conference, policy measures come as a package and the interactions among the various measures are important and cannot be ignored. Each measure in isolation may be ineffective or even counterproductive. Openness or trade liberalization are probably a necessary component of a successful development strategy at millennium's end (some may dispute even this "necessary" part), but even its staunchest advocates have questioned whether it may be sufficient. According to Anne Krueger (1995, p. 23, quoted in Bruton, 1998): "It is widely recognized that an outer-oriented trade strategy cannot succeed unless development of infrastructure (ports, roads, railroads, electric power, communications), increasing educational attainments, and a number of other policies are conducive to growth."[21] And Sachs and Warner (1995, p. 63): "We are strongly aware that trade policy represents just one element—albeit the most important—of an overall economic policy. Among developing countries, open trade has tended to be correlated with other features of a healthy economy, such as macroeconomic balance and reliance on the private sector as the main engine of growth. But to some degree, our measure of trade policy serves as a proxy for an entire array of policy actions."

For Waelbroeck (1998a, p. 26), who thinks the evidence favoring openness is quite conclusive, "why outward orientedness appears to be so effective is a mystery." His solution to the mystery would invoke "able governance", "which produced both the good macroeconomic management and the outward-oriented policies that made the trade balance responsive to currency devaluations" (Waelbroeck 1998b, p. 339).

---

[20] When interactions have been tried results have changed dramatically (see, for example, Burnside and Dollar, 1997). Degrees of freedom and interpretability limit the number of interactions that can be explored simultaneously in cross-country regressions.

[21] Bruton (1998, p. 922) adds: "This statement would mean that as of 1960 very few developing countries could have succeeded with an outer-oriented set of policies."

A summing up

My conclusion from the literature exploring the links of openness and performance (not just the literature mentioned in Easterly) is that inward orientation hampered growth because of the excesses and the inability to shift out of it once its drawbacks were or should have been evident (this inability may in part be a result of the ISI strategy). Trade liberalization is important, but no less so is the recognition that it must come as part of an overall package and that trade liberalization is itself a multidimensional strategy. Notice the debates about the order of liberalization—any guidance from cross-section regressions here? The evidence supporting openness is not uniform, but I believe it is weighty enough to present the case. The evidence from cross-section regressions of growth, ably summarized by Easterly, contributes to this case. If that was all the evidence at hand, I suggest this evidence would be deemed circumstantial and contaminated and would cause the case to be dismissed.

References

Balassa, B., and D. McCarthy. (1984). "Adjustment Policies in Developing Countries." Working Paper 675, World Bank Staff.

Ben-David, D. (1993). "Equalizing Exchange: Trade Liberalization and Income Convergence." *Quarterly Journal of Economics* 108, 653–679.

Bosworth, B., S.M. Collins, and Y.-C. Chen. (1995). "Accounting for Differences in Economic Growth." Brookings Discussion Papers in International Economics 115.

Bruton, H.J. (1998). "A Reconsideration of Import Substitution." *Journal of Economic Literature* 36, 903–936.

Burnside, C., and D. Dollar. (1997). "Aid, Policies, and Growth." Policy Research Working Paper 1777, World Bank.

Collier, P., and J.W. Gunning. (1997). "Explaining African Economic Performance." Working Paper Series No. WPS/97-2, Center for the Study of African Economies.

De Long, J.B. (1998). "Review of David S. Landes, The Wealth and Poverty of Nations: Why Are Some So Rich and Others So Poor?" *Washington Post Book World*, March 15, pp. X05.

Dollar, D. (1992). "Outward-Oriented Economies Really Do Grow More Rapidly: Evidence from 95 LDCs, 1976-1985." *Economic Development and Cultural Change* 40, 523–544.

Edwards, S. (1998). "Openness, Productivity and Growth: What Do We Really Know?" *Economic Journal* 108, 383–398.

Feder, G. (1983). "On Exports and Economic Growth." *Journal of Development Economics* 12, 59–73.

Fischer, S. (1995). "Comment on J. Sachs and A. Warner (1995)." *Brookings Papers on Economic Activity* 1, 100–105.

Grossman, G.M. (1996). Introduction. In G.M. Grossman, ed., *Economic Growth: Theory and Evidence.* The International Library of Critical Writings in Economics: 68.

Harrison, A. (1996). "Openness and Growth: A Time-Series, Cross-Country Analysis for Developing Countries." *Journal of Development Economics* 48, 419–447.

Helleiner, G.K. (1986). "Outward Orientation, Import Instability and African Economic Growth." In S. Lall and F. Stewart, eds., *Theory and Reality in Development: Essays in Honor of Paul Streeten*. London: Macmillan.

Jung, W.S., and P.J. Marshall. (1985). "Exports, Growth and Causality in Developing Countries." *Journal of Development Economics* 18, 1–12.

Kravis, I.B. (1970). "Trade as a Handmaiden of Growth Similarities Between the Nineteenth and Twentieth Centuries." *Economic Journal* 80, 850–872.

Levine, R., and D. Renelt. (1992). "A Sensitivity Analysis of Cross-Country Growth Regressions." *American Economic Review* 82, 942–963.

Pack, H. (1986). "Industrialization and Trade." In H. Chenery and T.N. Srinivasan, eds., *Handbook of Development Economics* vol.1. Amsterdam: North Holland.

Pack, H. (1992). "Technology Gaps Between Industrial and Developing Countries: Are There Dividends for Latecomers?" In *Proceedings of the World Bank Annual Conference on Development Economics*, 283–302.

Pack, H., and J. Page. (1994). "Accumulation, Exports, and Growth in the High Performing Asian Economies." *Carnegie-Rochester Conference Series on Public Policy* 40, 199–250.

Pritchett, L. (1996). "Measuring Outward Orientation in LDCs: Can It Be Done." *Journal of Development Economics* 49, 307–335.

Pritchett, L. (1998). "Patterns of Economic Growth: Hills, Plateaus, Mountains, and Plains." Policy Research Working Paper 1947, World Bank.

Rodrik, D. (1994). "King Kong Meets Godzilla: The World Bank and The East Asian Miracle." In A. Fishlow et al, eds., *Lessons from the East Asian Experience*. Washington, DC: Overseas Development Council.

Rodrik, D. (1995). "Trade and Industrial Policy Reform." In J. Behrman and T.N. Srinivasan, eds., *Handbook of Development Economics* vol.3B. Amsterdam: North Holland.

Sachs, J.D. (1985). "External Debt and Macroeconomic Performance in Latin America and East Asia." *Brookings Papers on Economic Activity* 2, 565–573.

Sachs, J.D., and A. Warner. (1995). "Economic Reform and the Process of Global Integration." *Brookings Papers on Economic Activity* 1, 1–118.

Sala-i-Martin, X. (1997). "I Just Ran Two Million Regressions." *American Economic Review Papers and Proceedings* 87, 178–183.

Syrquin, M. (1994) "Structural Transformation and the New Growth Theory." In L.L. Pasinetti and R.M. Solow, eds., *Economic Growth and the Structure of Long-Term Development*. New York: St.Martin's Press.

Taylor, L. (1988). *Varieties of Stabilization Experience: Towards Sensible Macroeconomics in the Third World*. Oxford: Clarendon Press.

Tybout, J. (1998). "Manufacturing Firms in Developing Countries: How Well Do They Do, and Why?" Policy Research Working Paper 1965, World Bank.

Vamvakidis, A. (1996). "Trade Openness and Economic Growth Reconsidered."

Waelbroeck, J. (1998a). "Half a Century of Development Economics: A Review Based on the Handbook of Development Economics." Policy Research Working Paper 1925, World Bank.

Waelbroeck, J. (1998b). "Half a Century of Development Economics: A review Based on the Handbook of Development Economics." *World Bank Economic Review* 12, 323–352.

DISCUSSION

Augustin Fosu
Oakland University

In his chapter, William Easterly provides a thorough and cogent review of the implications of openness for growth. While much of the chapter recants the usual neoclassical story of the positive economic virtues—joys—of openness, Easterly creditably attempts a balanced account by noting some of its possible deleterious effects as well.

The joys of openness

Although Easterly mentions three, I count two main joys of openness: it promotes growth and may lead to convergence. Openness fosters growth by raising both the level and efficiency of investment. Its various measures can be contradictory, however. For example, export-promoting policies that subsidize exports may contribute to openness and growth but also reduce openness by distorting international prices. Nonetheless, Easterly concludes from the existing evidence, that "open economies do grow more rapidly than closed economies ... whether the measure of openness has to do with exchange-rate overvaluation, relative price distortions, tariffs and quotas, share of trade in GDP, the black-market premium, or a composite measure combining some of these with state monopolization of commodity exports and general socialism" (Easterly, section 2.2.4).

In a gist, the following is the neoclassical story. Openness is likely to facilitate both foreign direct investment (FDI) and domestic investment. Policies that enhance capital inflows and ease impediments for acquiring externally produced capital goods and skills tend to be attractive to both FDI and domestic investment. Such policies would enhance investment productivity as well, as globally competitive forces prompt domestic producers to adopt the most efficient production processes, both technologically and allocatively. As Easterly observes, the evidence in favor of the growth-enhancing properties of openness is substantial.

Openness can also facilitate the catching-up process of less well-off countries. According to the neoclassical thesis, diminishing returns to factors of production would eventually render less well off areas relatively attractive to potential investors. Lower returns to capital in the more developed areas would ensure that capital flows to the lagging regions to promote greater growth. Empirical evidence reviewed by Easterly tends to confirm this convergence hypothesis associated with openness: open economies do converge faster than closed ones.

Thus there is much to celebrate about the joys of openness. The neoclassical dictum is not the entire story, however.

The sorrows of openness

As Easterly additionally argues, there are sorrows of openness as well. Open economies are more likely to be vulnerable to terms-of-trade shocks and capital inflow interruptions. These risks can be substantial as dramatized by the recent Latin American financial and currency crises and even more recently by similar but relatively severe crises in East Asia. Arguably, such risks could have been minimized by countries pursuing the right policies to begin with. Nevertheless, the "contagion" effect can be substantial, and "speculative attacks" may lead to overshooting of the long-run equilibrium exchange rates. Such short-run disequilibria can, nonetheless, be destabilizing and highly deleterious to both economic and political institutions. It is thus conceivable that these "short-run" disturbances would have medium- or even long-term adverse impacts on affected economies.

Easterly discusses one more sorrow of openness: the existence of poverty traps in open economies (poverty pockets have been prevalent even within highly "open" countries like the United States). Casual empiricism suggests that many less developed regions of the world are hardly catching up, if at all. Two explanations may be given for this phenomenon. First, policy and institutional constraints, possibly including the lack of openness, impede the process of convergence. Once these factors are accounted for, however, conditional convergence is usually observed, though at a very slow pace.

Second, under the new endogenous growth theory, openness may not necessarily be accompanied by convergence, for spillovers from human capital investment might result in increasing returns to scale. The marginal product of capital in less developed economies could, therefore, conceivably continue to lag behind that in the more developed advanced countries. Hence, capital need not emigrate from more to less developed economies to result in convergence, contrary to the dictates of neoclassical theory.

Realities

As Easterly's review clearly indicates, the evidence favors the hypothesis that, on average, openness is growth-enhancing. According to this evidence, countries that are more open tend to experience greater growths.

Even laying aside the above sorrows, it is not at all apparent, however, that one can necessarily infer from the existing evidence that openness is desirable for all economies at all times. For example, what degree of openness is optimal for a given economy: complete openness? That is, would a country be best off by charging no tariffs on imports, providing no subsidies for exports, and allowing perfectly free flows of capital no matter the intended uses of such capital? The issues of externalities and fallacy of composition cannot be ignored.

Let us consider first the latter question of the fallacy of composition. The world would be better off as a whole if all tariffs were abolished and if a given country that was relatively open could take advantage of international capital flows. Would it necessarily hold, however, that a completely open country will improve its economic position in the long run vis-à-vis the rest of the world if all countries are similarly open? Even under neoclassical theory, the answer is no, for the theory promises only absolute gains from trade. Its promise of relative gains from trade would be based on the rather static premise of diminishing marginal product of capital, which now seems untenable. Moreover, a given country might, for instance, benefit from an increase in foreign capital if it reduced the tax burden on FDI, but might this be the case if all countries similarly reduced the tax burden?

The distribution of trade is likely to depend in great part on initial conditions. For example, countries with better physical and human capital infrastructure are likely to attract the relatively productive capital and, hence, to garner larger benefits. These countries are, furthermore, likely to be those already economically better off, and such infrastructure might have very little to do with the degree of openness.

In addition, suppose an investor imports hazardous materials with the usual negative externalities. Should the government not intervene to prevent such importation or ensure that resulting externalities are appropriately internalized? Might this not entail less openness? Indeed, drawing the line between desirable and undesirable nontariff barriers is usually a normative nightmare.

What the neoclassical theory lacks is defining an optimal path for openness. For example, the optimal amount of openness is likely to depend on initial conditions. There are simply too many cases where it would be hard to argue that "closedness" at the initial stages did not pay off. The East Asian tigers of Korea, Singapore, and Taiwan, as well as the emerging South East Asian cubs of Thailand, Indonesia, and Malaysia, are excellent examples. There is ample evidence to anchor the view that these economies used, at some points in their initial pushes toward development, interventionist policies that were hardly openness-enhancing.

Nor should one conveniently forget the relatively closed economy of even the United States at its initial stages of development. The most recent success, and perhaps classic story, is likely to be that of China. The evidence is clear that China did not achieve its recent and current economic successes by pursuing open-market policies early on with the rest of the world. Indeed, the historical record is replete with many countries initially adopting relatively restrictive policies to sufficiently develop their industrial structure before subsequently opening up.

The above success-case examples suggest, to the extent there is learning by doing, that it might be desirable for a country to engage in production processes that would provide it with a "dynamic" comparative advantage down the line. Such an advantage may be relatively costly in the short run of course, but it may be a price worth paying. Initially at a comparative disadvantage in industrial production, an industry in a less developed country might require some sort of protection initially in order to be competitive in the world market. In the absence of such protection the industry would likely wither away, and with it the learning-by-doing opportunity required for the future comparative advantage. The importance of this dynamic comparative advantage is bolstered by findings that those countries that diversified their exports away from nonfuel primary toward manufacturing experienced substantially higher growths (e.g., Fosu, 1990, 1996).

Despite the usual short-run costs, "infant industry" protection need not be suboptimal, as long as it is temporary. Harrison (1994), for example, provides recent evidence suggesting that a protected industry experienced greater productivity than its counterpart. Despite Anne Krueger's (1994) subsequent rebuttal, the short-run cost may be justified if expected returns of learning by doing are substantial. Given that such a knowledge-generating process is an important source of innovation, then it is not at all clear that the neoclassical argument against the infant-industry argument has much validity.

What the foregoing discussion suggests is that the optimal openness-growth path may indeed be nonlinear and, more important, non-monotonic. The theory has so far not internalized this possible reality, nor has the econometrics. The evidence abounds, for example, that the Asian tigers and cubs were generally not very open initially but have become increasingly so over time. Unfortunately, the data are simply not good enough to reflect this dynamic phenomenon that less openness was probably required initially to lay the industrial foundation for subsequent sustained growth. The interpretation of the econometric evidence is instead that countries that were more open experienced greater growth and, possibly, that as these countries became more open they improved their growth performance.

What the econometrics does not reflect, unfortunately, is the more realistic scenario that the greater growth probably resulted from countries improving their human capital through learning by doing, which was probably made viable by some degree of protection, that closedness was a constraint to further growth and that openness became a necessary condition for continued growth.

What is lacking in the literature, therefore, is a systematic dynamic treatment of the role of openness, theoretically, to reflect this lifecycle openness-growth relationship. The econometrics must also come to terms with accurately modeling and interpreting this likely nonlinear mapping.

The risk component of the Easterly risk-return trade-off may also actually be worse today than one could have imagined years ago. The greatly improved transactions technology, which can quickly and easily transfer funds across the world with little lag, suggests that market anticipations of the impacts of policies are likely to be accompanied by rapid market sanctioning. This phenomenon is not unlike the distinction between the theories of adaptive and rational expectations associated with the product and labor markets. Current technology is such that international markets are likely to act swiftly in a manner that may not allow national economies room to experiment with policies as many have done in the past—a transition from the regime of adaptive to rational expectations. This suggests that openness with respect to international capital may no longer be as desirable as it once was.

Conclusion

The importance of openness in economic growth, especially in the present highly integrated world, cannot be ignored. Equally, we must be aware of the limitations of openness. History tells us that the role of openness is much more complicated than it is usually acknowledged. Its effect is unlikely to be the linear or monotonic one that is normally portrayed. Indeed, complete openness appears to be neither necessary nor sufficient at every stage of development. While a significant level of it may be desirable at certain points of development, the optimal path of the degree of openness over the development lifecycle need not be horizontal or even linear.

What appears likely is that less openness may actually be required to protect embryonic industries at the initial stages of development, especially in a world where there exists a large variation in the levels of development and abilities toward international competition. Such an infant-industry protection need not be inimical to long-term growth and development, that is, if the learning-by-doing process is an important ingredient in setting the appropriate economic foundations for meeting the fierce external competition from the more advanced economies where knowledge production and acquisition are likely to be relatively high. Uncovering this optimal path probably is the requisite challenge

References

Fosu, A.K. (1990). "Export Composition and the Impact of Exports on Economic Growth of Developing Economies." *Economics Letters* 34(1), 67–71.

Fosu, A.K. (1996). "Primary Exports and Economic Growth in Developing Countries." *World Economy* 19, 465–475.

Harrison, A.F. (1994). "An Empirical Test of the Infant-Industry Argument: Comment." *American Economic Review* 84, 1090–1095.

Krueger, A.C. (1994). "An Empirical Test of the Infant-Industry Argument: A Reply." *American Economic Review* 84, 1096.

Chapter 3

Technology in growth

Louise C. Keely[*] and Danny Quah[**]
*New College, Oxford and Centre for Economic Performance, London School of Economics,
**Professor of Economics, Department of Economics, London School of Economics*

3.1.   INTRODUCTION

This chapter reviews the main insights from the theoretical research and development (R&D) endogenous growth literature and summarizes empirical counterparts to that theoretical work.

A key conclusion can be simply stated in the following set of related statements:

- All analyses recognize that technological progress (or, one concrete manifestation, R&D) is an important engine of growth.

- All analyses acknowledge the significance of economic incentives for determining growth outcomes.

- Knowledge is the accumulation of R&D output, broadly interpreted.

It follows that the economics of knowledge must underlay appropriate policies for growth. In this view the rights accorded intellectual property become central. However, the efficiency, desirability, and precise nature of alternative systems of intellectual property rights comprise issues that are far from settled. Within this broad agenda, the literature has instead emphasized only private-sector R&D and patents, respectively, as the forms of invention and rewards. This focus has arisen for four reasons:

- Tools for modeling private sector behavior are well developed.

- Data on R&D and patents exist to motivate and test hypotheses on growth.

- R&D is a readily identifiable factor input for knowledge production in many technology-driven industries.

- Patents are a readily identifiable, if imperfect, measure of knowledge output.

Economics focuses on the incentives that confront private individuals and firms. The endogenous growth literature follows this tradition in modeling technological progress to result largely from incentives facing profit-maximizing firms. In the theoretical literature firms in the private sector fund and carry out R&D: this, in turn, is the paradigm typically examined in empirical work.

Such a focus might seem excessively narrow. However, this "private R&D with patents" scenario has developed through a series of sensible decisions. Each step along the way applies the traditional tools of economic analysis—optimizing behavior and equilibrium outcomes. Where the reasoning becomes subtle, however, is that R&D output—accumulated knowledge—is infinitely expansible (see below): it can be used by many without itself being drawn down and thus has some of the nature of a public good.

But firms perform R&D only if they can appropriate the rents from it. The mechanism for such appropriation is typically assumed to be patenting, which, in concept, also simultaneously reveals the patent information to all other interested agents. That knowledge, although revealed, is then protected in that only its owner can use it to produce final output. The information in the patent, on the other hand, can be used for additional R&D by rival firms. This allows the infinite expansibility of knowledge to generate increasing-returns effects on the economy overall.

Patent data are plentiful and, at face value, reliable. The empirical literature has therefore been able to exploit the substantial micro- and macro-level data on R&D and patenting. Patents and R&D proxy knowledge production-function outputs and inputs and can therefore be used in empirical production-function analyses. The theoretical literature has, in turn, used those empirical findings to motivate and justify alternative modeling strategies.

As we discuss below, this private-sector R&D-patenting model is highly pertinent for certain industries. In-so-far as this description of knowledge accumulation is adequate, the theoretical and empirical literatures provide credible specific policy recommendations. However, many important forms of knowledge accumulation fall outside this paradigm.

The rest of this chapter is organized as follows. Section 3.2 relates insights from early growth models to those from more recent R&D-driven endogenous growth models. Toward the end of the section we discuss some broader questions on economic growth and knowledge as economic property: research here is thin and, we argue, has thus far failed to deliver concrete conclusions.

Section 3.3 summarizes some of the principal results from empirical work examining the effects of R&D and patents on economic performance of both firms and the aggregate economy. We relate the micro and macro findings to key features of the knowledge-accumulation process in R&D-driven endogenous growth theory. Some of these latter are consistent with empirical findings. Others are not.

Our conclusions from this survey of R&D and economic growth are as follows. We see a continuing need for theoretical and empirical research in this area. While the private-sector R&D and patent framework provides essential groundwork, it has important limitations. Most knowledge accumulation does not occur from private firms' R&D-producing patentable knowledge. Nor is it clear that the institutional mechanisms producing and demanding knowledge more broadly are well understood.

3.2. DEVELOPMENT OF THE LITERATURE

Robert Solow's (1956) analysis of economic growth—with its emphasis on income being driven by transitional dynamics in capital—is so influential and far-reaching that many take physical capital accumulation to be *the* defining feature of neoclassical growth theory. Following quickly from this is the suggestion that neoclassical theory asserts capital accumulation is the principal engine of economic growth.

The observed cross-country variation in savings rates and per capita incomes refutes this suggested importance of physical capital (e.g., Lucas, 1988; Romer, 1986, 1994). If one maintains that physical capital accumulation is the main source of variation in incomes, then—under plausible calibrations of key parameter values—savings rates in the rich developed economies should be orders of magnitude larger than those in the poor developing economies. That predicted range turns out to be greater by far than the observed range in reality. This inconsistency has been used to argue that neoclassical theory provides no credible guide to understanding economic growth. Instead, technological progress and its determinants are deemed central.

3.2.1.   Origins

Early on, however, researchers in the neoclassical tradition were already documenting the importance of technological progress in economic growth.[22]

After noting real U.S. net national product per capita grew fourfold between 1869 to 1978 and 1944 to 1953, Abramowitz (1956) concluded: "The source of the great increase in net product per head was not mainly an increase in labor input per head, not even an increase in capital per head. ...Its source must be sought principally in the complex of little understood forces which caused productivity, that is, output per unit of utilized resources, to rise."

Kendrick (1956) considered U.S. economic performance from 1899 to 1953 and concluded that total factor productivity (TFP) explained 53 percent of the growth in real aggregate output over that half century. Solow's own study (1957) showed technical change accounted for 87.5 percent of the growth in U.S. gross output per work-hour from 1909 to 1949. This sample of findings is, moreover, no artifact of hindsight sample selection.[23] Indeed, its message is how Arrow (1962a) begins a classic article:

"It is by now incontrovertible that increases in per capita income cannot be explained simply by increases in the capital-labor ratio."

By 1969 the economics literature on technology and growth had progressed to where a collection of papers (Stiglitz and Uzawa, 1969) identified the following issues:

---

[22] An important difference between more recent empirical studies and these published in the mid 1950s is that the latter focused almost exclusively on time-series evidence for a single country, while more recent ones, exploiting studies such as Maddison (1989) and Summers and Heston (1991), exploit variation across countries as well (Durlauf and Quah, 1998).

[23] To be clear, our goal is not to claim this is the last word on TFP measurement. Far from it: we intend simply a summary statement on the then-extant state of knowledge in neoclassical growth research. We do not mention, for instance, the large literature following Jorgenson and Griliches (1967) that examines quality adjustments in factor inputs. It seems to us that, conceptually, adjusting for quality cannot show technology to be unimportant. What is quality after all but technology? The tabulation given in Barro and Sala-i-Martin (1995, table 10.8) shows it is the more recent empirical research that has downplayed the importance of technological progress, although admittedly TFP's contribution to growth remains large. It seems that what many now consider the neoclassical preoccupation with physical capital accumulation for growth is the *opposite* of what researchers then actually thought. Instead, that imputed preoccupation follows only more recent empirical analyses. At the same time, however, it is the more recent theoretical work on endogenous growth that emphasizes the importance of technical progress.

- *What determines the rate of technological progress?* Is it purposeful, or is it only incidental to some other deliberate investment—say, physical capital accumulation? What government policies influence it?

- *Does technological progress affect different factors differently?* Are certain kinds of technical change labor-saving? Capital-saving? Biased against labor of different skill levels?. What economic factors determine the differential effects, if any?

- *How does new technology manifest in the economy?* Is technology embodied in physical capital according to different vintages? How does new technology affect the productivity of older capital and earlier investment?

These questions remain the subject of intense and active research in the present.[24]

It is striking how these questions (by 1969) bear phrasings that deny a sharp distinction between "old" and "new" growth theories. Under one (not especially generous) interpretation, recent theories of growth simply carry forward, in different guises, the insight that technical progress is endogenously determined in economically interesting ways. Early growth theorists certainly were aware that technical progress might not be exogenous. As in the old joke about economics examinations, it seems that the fundamental questions have for long remained the same; only the answers have changed.[25]

3.2.2.   The neoclassical mechanism

One can strip away the long-familiar emphasis on physical capital accumulation and reinterpret the formalism of Solow's (1956) neoclassical framework in a way consistent with the time-series empirical observations just described (and, indeed, cross-sectional as well).

Let $y_j(t)$ and $k_j(t)$ denote, respectively, output and capital per worker in economy j at time t:

$$y_j(t) = Y_j(t)/N_j(t) \qquad k_j(t) = K_j(t)/N_j(t),$$

---

[24] The above questions in italics might not be exactly as expressed in the early papers but are issues still being researched that are certainly not out of place relative to the others found here.

[25] For instance, even the most cursory look at the older literature reveals its obsession with the potential instability of the dynamics and with the incipient pathology in defining the production function, neither of which are any longer considered central to economic discussion.

with Y_j and K_j the corresponding aggregate quantities, and N_j the total number of workers. Write $A_j(t)$ for the state of technology in j at t, and suppose that output and capital are related by the production function

$$Y_j = F(K_j, N_j A_j) \Rightarrow y_j = F(k_j, A_j) = A_j f(k_j / A_j), \qquad (3.1)$$

where, by the notation, F is homogenous of degree 1. Assume the worker-intensive production function f satisfies

$$f' > 0, f'' < 0, \quad \text{and} \quad \lim_{k \to \infty} f(k)k^{-1} = 0, \qquad (3.2)$$

and is common across economies.

Let N_j and A_j evolve, respectively, as

$$\dot{N}_j / N_j = v_j > 0, \quad N_j(0) > 0, \qquad (3.3)$$

$$\dot{A}_j / A_j = \xi_j > 0, \quad A_j(0) > 0, \qquad (3.4)$$

and let physical capital decay at a constant exponential rate $\delta \geq 0$ common across economies. Assume savings is a constant fraction τ_j of total income and transforms into physical capital according to

$$\dot{K}_j = \tau_j Y_j - \delta K_j, \quad \tau_j \text{ in } (0,1),$$

so that

$$\dot{k}_j / k_j - \dot{A}_j / A_j = \tau_j \frac{f(k_j / A_j)}{k_j / A_j} - (\delta + v_j + \xi_j). \qquad (3.5)$$

Equation (3.3) says the workforce in economy j grows smoothly at rate v_j. Similarly, (3.4) says the state of technology or TFP grows at rate ξ_j.

No economic model implies that A_j has to be the same across j. Rather, the standard interpretation of the neoclassical model simply *assumes* so. At this level of reasoning, it is unclear why one assumption—equality of A's across economies—is better than any other. Indeed, one might argue that to clarify precisely this point is one of the purposes of a useful economic model of technology and growth.

Standard reasoning, for example, figure 3.1, shows that the model shown in (3.1) to (3.5) displays a *balanced-growth equilibrium* with

$$\dot{y}_j / y_j = \dot{k}_j / k_j = \dot{A}_j / A_j = \xi_j,$$

and thus a steady-state path for output

$$\log y_j^*(t) \qquad = \log f\left(\left[k / A\right]^*\right) + \log A(t)$$

$$= \log f\left(\left[k_j / A_j\right]^*\right) + \log A_j(0) + \xi_j \cdot t \qquad (3.6)$$

$$\overset{def}{=} \Gamma_{j,0} + \xi_j \cdot t .$$

Outside of balanced-growth equilibrium, output per worker follows a convergent trajectory to its steady-state path (3.6) —that is,

$$\log y_j(t) = \log y_j^*(t) + \left[\log y_j(0) - \Gamma_{j,0}\right] e^{\lambda_j t}, \qquad (3.7)$$

where

$$\lambda = \lambda\left(\delta + v_j + \xi_j; f\right) < 0$$

is the *rate of convergence*. In (3.7) output per worker is driven by two factors. The first one is technical progress, described in y_j^*, which simply grows at rate $\dot{A}_j / A_j = \xi_j$. The second one is convergence, which when log $y_j(0) < \Gamma_{j,0}$ produces growth at rate $-\lambda_j$. (Take, for instance, y_2 in Figure 3.2) An important feature of the growth path (3.6) to (3.7) is that given a market for investment that path can be achieved through the competitive mechanism, and, moreover, attains social efficiency.[26]

---

[26] The derivation is so well known that it hardly needs further elaboration, although different expositions in the literature emphasize different details. Our discussion follows Durlauf and Quah (1998).

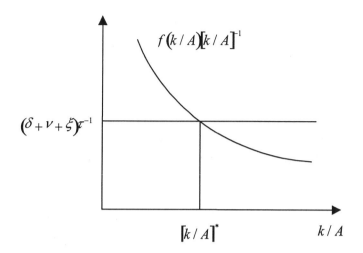

Figure 3.1. Neoclassical growth and convergence[27]

From Figure 3.1 the definition of $[k/A]^*$ as the intersection of the two loci means there is an increasing function g for which

$$\Gamma_{j,0} = g\big((\delta + v_j + \xi_j)^{-1}\tau_j\big) + \log A_j(0).$$

Figure 3.2 graphs some potential timepaths for (3.7): note the wide range of behavior that is possible.

Our immediate goal is to reconcile predictions (3.7) and Figure 3.2 with economic growth observations in reality. First, take the evidence on the relative importance of technological progress versus capital accumulation for explaining growth. In (3.7) the two components $\log y_j^*(t)$ and $\big[\log y_j(0) - \Gamma_0\big]e^{\lambda t}$ evolve due to technological progress and physical capital accumulation, respectively. Saying the first is more important than the second is then simply saying that $\log y_j(0)$ is a particular distance from its

[27] In Figure 3.1 the function $f(\tilde{k})\tilde{k}^{-1}$ is continuous and tends to infinity and zero as $\tilde{k}$ tends to zero and infinity, respectively. Moreover, it is guaranteed to be monotone strictly decreasing. The vertical distance between $f(k/A)[k/A]^{-1}$ and $(\delta + v + \xi)\tau^{-1}$ is $\tau^{-1}[k/A]/[k/A]$. Convergence to steady state $[k/A]^*$ therefore occurs for all initial values k/A.

steady-state counterpart Γ_0, or in words, how far the economy is from steady state. In the model technological progress accounts for all of observed growth when $\log y_j(0)$ happens to be exactly at Γ_0. By contrast, if $\log y_j(0)-\Gamma_0$ is sufficiently large, then capital accumulation explains most of the observed dynamics in y_j.

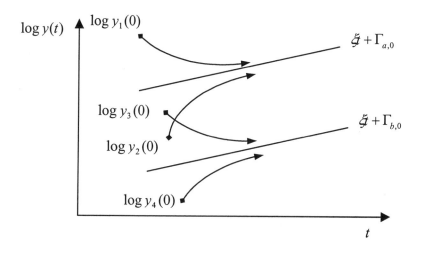

Figure 3.2. Growth and convergence in the neoclassical model[28]

Put differently, using the estimated importance of technological progress—in historical time-series data—to cast doubt on the neoclassical model (3.1)-(3.5) is nothing more than taking a stance on how far an economy is from its steady state. Without independent knowledge of where this steady state is, historical time-series data do not allow us to reject the neoclassical model.

What about the cross-section behavior of incomes? Can the neoclassical model be reconciled with the pattern of incomes and savings rates we observe across economies? Figure 3.2 provides one answer. If A_j is permitted

---

[28] Figure 3.2 shows two different possible steady-state paths corresponding to two possible values for $\Gamma_{j,0} = g((\delta + v_j + \xi_j)^{-1}\tau_j) + \log A_j(0)$. As long as this remains unobserved or unrestricted, *any* pattern of cross-country growth and convergence is consistent with the model. As drawn, the *a* value applies to economies at $y_1(0)$ and $y_2(0)$ while the *b* value to $y_3(0)$ and $y_4(0)$. Economies 1 and 2 converge towards each other, and similarly economies 3 and 4. At the same time, however, economies 2 and 3, although each obeying the neoclassical growth model, are seen to approach one another, criss-cross, and then diverge.

to differ sufficiently across economies, then almost any behavior in cross-sectional income dynamics can be accommodated in the model. Arguments that suggest the opposite invariably assume A_j's are identical across countries.

The issues just described are hardly substantive economic ones: they will not be resolved by application of economic theory. More to the point, many observers (ourselves included) find unconvincing the reconciliation just offered of empirical evidence and the neoclassical model. The model, when it assumes unrestricted A's and Γ_0's, has too many degrees of freedom to shed light on the importance of technology versus capital accumulation in economic growth. But what should replace the unrestricted (A, Γ_0) assumption? Simply taking the other extreme of requiring A's and Γ_0's to be identical across economies cannot be satisfactory either. Nor do we know how far economies are from their steady state, a different question, certainly, from knowing what the rate of convergence λ might be.

To summarize, the problem is not just being able to explain the empirical facts or being able to generate growth in an explicit model. In the model (3.1) to (3.5) we cannot discuss the incentives that form A, the economic mechanisms that explain A's evolution through time, and the economic reasons for A_j's distribution across countries. Without knowledge on these, no policy recommendation can pretend to be well informed. These questions lead us naturally to models of endogenous technological progress.[29]

3.2.3.   Endogenizing technology

Kenneth Arrow's (1962a) model of learning-by-doing is widely viewed as the first rigorous attempt to endogenize technological progress $\dot{A}/A = \xi$.

Interestingly, however, technical change in the model involves no deliberate economic decision. Instead, technical progress is an inadvertent consequence of yet other economic actions, in this case investment. Incentives that affect investment affect, at the same time and in the same way, technological progress.

The model can therefore provide only an incomplete if useful first step. A different but related point: the model also describes an explicit economic

---

[29] A great deal of empirical growth research takes a flexible approach from here. Explaining economic growth is, in that research program, finding explanatory variables—technology or otherwise—that correlate strongly with (proxies for) A_j across countries. In effect the researcher writes ξ on the right of (3.3) as a function of particular observable economic or political variables. This research strategy underscores that while the original neoclassical model refers to A as technology or knowledge, no rigorous economic reasoning precludes A's being something else. In this chapter, though, we concentrate exclusively on its original interpretation as technology.

environment generating from first principles a production function with externalities in capital (as used in, e.g., Romer, 1986).

The model delivers an interesting set of implications:

1. The analogue of the production function (3.1) will show, under one interpretation, increasing returns to scale in K and N.
2. Nevertheless, compensation to the factors of production in decentralized markets will just exhaust total product.
3. Market equilibrium displays underinvestment relative to the socially efficient outcome.
4. Growth in y will, as in the neoclassical model, occur at the same rate as that in k and A. But $\dot{A}/A$ now is endogenous in that it depends on (part of the) economic environment, namely—population growth. Significantly, however, incentives to capital investment do *not* affect the steady-state growth rate.

In the model suppose that technology is embodied entirely in physical capital and that its level varies with the accumulation of all past investment activity. Simplify by assuming no depreciation (that is, $\delta = 0$ in the notation above), so that accumulated investment is the same as the aggregate capital stock K.

From these assumptions technology levels can be indexed by $\kappa \in [0, K]$. Denote by $\widehat{Y}(\kappa)$ and $\widehat{N}(\kappa)$ the output capacity and labor requirements, respectively, of technology level κ, where

$$\widehat{Y}' \geq 0 \quad \text{and} \quad \widehat{N}' \leq 0. \tag{3.8}$$

With advances in technology, output capacities rise (or, more accurately, do not fall) and labor requirements fall. We have simplified by assuming that $\widehat{Y}$ and $\widehat{N}$ depend only on κ; no substitution possibilities are available. However, producers can choose not to operate specific technologies.

From (3.8) it is clear that if a certain technology κ is unused, then so are all technologies with indexes less than κ. Thus, there is a *shutdown threshold* $\underline{K} \in [0,K]$ such that no producer operates any technology with index less than $\underline{K}$. Define the integrals

$$\widetilde{Y}(K) = \int_{\underline{K}}^{K} \widehat{Y}(\kappa)d\kappa \quad \text{and} \quad \widetilde{N}(K) = \int_{\underline{K}}^{K} \widehat{N}(\kappa)d\kappa.$$

Aggregate output and employment are then

$$Y = \int_{\underline{k}}^{K} \hat{Y}(\kappa)d\kappa = \tilde{Y}(K) - \tilde{Y}(\underline{K})$$

$$N = \int_{\underline{k}}^{K} \hat{N}(\kappa)d\kappa = \tilde{N}(K) - \tilde{N}(\underline{K}).$$

Invert the last equation to solve for the shutdown threshold as a function of employment

$$\underline{K} = \tilde{N}^{-1}\left(\tilde{N}(K) - N\right).$$

Using this in the equation for aggregate output gives

$$Y = \tilde{Y}(K) - \left(\tilde{Y} \circ \tilde{N}^{-1}\right)\left(\tilde{N}(K) - N\right) . \tag{3.9}$$

As Arrow (1962a) points out, equation (3.9) is simply an aggregate production function in K and N. The novelty is that it has been derived from a more explicit microeconomic description incorporating, from the beginning, a formulation of technology.

Equation (3.9) can be rewritten in the form (3.1). To see this, it is easiest to work out an explicit example. Assume the functional forms for capacity and labor requirement:

$$\hat{Y}(\kappa) = \alpha \quad \text{and} \quad \hat{N}(\kappa) = \beta\kappa^{-\gamma}, \quad \text{with } \alpha, \beta, \gamma > 0.$$

Using these in (3.9) and dividing through by N we have

$$y = \begin{cases} [1 - (1 - \frac{1-\gamma}{\beta}\frac{1}{k}K^{\gamma})^{\frac{1}{1-\gamma}}]\alpha k & \text{if } \gamma \neq 1 \\ [1 - (e^{\frac{-1}{k}})^{\frac{A}{\beta}}]\alpha k & \text{if } \gamma = 1 \end{cases}$$

Defining $A(K) = K^{\gamma}$, this is simply

$$y = F(k, A) = \begin{cases} [1 - (1 - \frac{1-\gamma}{\beta}\frac{1}{k}A)^{\frac{1}{1-\gamma}}]\alpha k & \text{if } \gamma \neq 1 \\ [1 - (e^{\frac{-1}{k}})^{\frac{A}{\beta}}]\alpha k & \text{if } \gamma = 1 \end{cases} \tag{3.10}$$

Inspection shows that equation (3.10) is homogeneous of degree 1 in k and A and thus is covered by (3.1). When private agents take A in (3.10) as exogenously given, then this is, moreover, exactly the model specification used in Romer (1986). Conversely, taking into account that A depends on K we recognize that the production function (3.9) shows increasing returns in K and N.

Homogeneity of degree 1 in F implies that in balanced growth,

$$\dot{y}/y = \dot{k}/k = \dot{A}/A.$$

But by definition we also have

$$\dot{A}/A = \gamma \dot{K}/K.$$

Combining these relations and provided that $\gamma < 1$, balanced growth occurs with

$$\dot{y}/y = \dot{A}/A = \gamma \dot{K}/K = \frac{\gamma}{1-\gamma} \dot{N}/N. \tag{3.11}$$

Arrow (1962a) shows that (1) compensation to labor and capital can occur sensibly despite increasing returns in (3.9) and (2) competitive equilibrium exists and exhibits underinvestment relative to the social optimum. However, despite (2), steady-state growth rates are identical under both the competitive and socially efficient outcomes, as one would expect from the argument leading up to (3.11).

The model has, of course, endogenized technology A. Since steady-state growth, again, depends on technological progress, it too is similarly endogenous. However, that endogeneity leads only to a dependence on population growth as the determinant of growth. The analysis provides no positive message on the ability to improve economic growth through, say, encouraging capital investment. Indeed, such a policy would have no growth implications, only level ones, which could, of course, be substantial but are of less interest here.

3.2.4. Further endogenizing technology

The work of Aghion and Howitt (1992), Grossman and Helpman (1991), and Romer (1990) are likely the best known for providing explicit theoretical models of endogenous technological progress. Unlike the analysis discussed above, these models produce equilibria where the growth rate of technology is affected by economic incentives on capital accumulation or R&D or both. At the same time, their microeconomic implications are novel and interesting. The models display the tension between policies that allow uncompetitive behavior on the supply side (incurring welfare losses in the process) and policies that foster technical innovations and therefore economic growth.

As described in Jones (1995) and Jones and Williams (1998), these endogenous-technology models share a common structure. They all replace the technical progress equation (3.4) with a version of

$$\dot{A}/A = G(R_A, A), \tag{3.12}$$

where R_A quantifies the resources—skilled labor, R&D spending, research scientists, and engineers—devoted to improving technology, and A describes (the possible absence of) scale effects. In equilibrium, again, balanced growth arises so that $\dot{A}/A$ is then also the growth rate of per capita income or per worker output.

In the simplest versions of these models (3.12) is

$$\dot{A}/A = G(R_A) = R_A, \tag{3.13}$$

where, for instance as in Romer (1990), R_A might be the total quantity of skilled labor working in the aggregate research sector. Here, modulo general equilibrium effects, providing incentives for the skilled to move into research, improves the rate of economic growth.

Jones (1995) argues forcefully against models of endogenous technical progress of the form (3.13). He observes for the advanced economies that while every reasonable measure of R_A has increased dramatically in the last half century, per capita income growth rates have either remained roughly constant or even declined. For example, U.S. scientists and engineers employed in R&D increased fivefold from 1950 and 1990; average U.S. growth rates did nothing anywhere near this.[30]

Function G in (3.13) need not, of course, be linear in R_A. However, almost all models of endogenous technical change (and certainly those of

---

[30] Jones (1995) and Aghion and Howitt (1998), among others, point out that the increase in R&D investment was possibly not as high as the data suggest. After World War II R&D activities became increasingly routine and separately accounted for and their measured resource use increased regardless of any real resource increase. The scale effects predicted in some endogenous growth models might therefore not be as unreasonable as initially thought.

Aghion and Howitt, 1992; Grossman and Helpman, 1991; and Romer, 1990) yield that linearity from explicit microfoundations. Jones (1995) labels this a *scale effect* and argues that it is this feature that empirically invalidates these models.

Jones preferred alternative specification obtains instead from the following reasoning. Identify A as the stock of ideas, and suppose that

$$\dot{A} = \tilde{\rho} R_A^\theta, \qquad \theta \in (0,1]$$

—that is, the flow of new ideas varies with the quantity of resources devoted to research. The factor $\tilde{\rho}$ can be interpreted as the arrival rate of new ideas per effective research unit. When $\theta = 1$, an effective research unit is just the same as an observed research unit. When $\theta < 1$, however, research units can be viewed as congested: there might be, for instance, overlap between projects run by different researchers. (e.g., Dasgupta and Maskin 1987).

The arrival rate $\tilde{\rho}$ depends, in turn, on the stock of ideas already extant:

$$\tilde{\rho} = \rho A^\phi, \qquad \rho > 0, \phi \in (-\infty, \infty).$$

When $\phi < 0$, the stock of ideas outstanding has begun to run out; when $\phi > 0$, ideas build on other ideas already discovered.

Putting these together gives the specification in Jones (1995) and Jones and Williams (1998):

$$\dot{A}/A = G(R_A, A) = \rho R_A^\theta A^{\phi-1}. \tag{3.14}$$

Standard *scale effects* obtain when $\theta = \phi = 1$.

When $\phi < 1$, scale effects are no longer present; since ϕ can be positive, ideas can still build on ideas extant. However, (3.14) then implies growth dynamics that only mimic (3.11) in Arrow's model of learning by doing. In balanced growth, R_A^θ and $A^{1-\phi}$ grow at the same rate so that

$$\dot{A}/A = \frac{\theta}{1-\phi} \dot{R}_A / R_A.$$

When R_A evolves in constant proportion to the population or the labor work force, then this is exactly (3.11), the growth equation in Arrow's model of learning by doing.

3.2.5.   Some outstanding issues

Although not emphasized above, some of (in our view) the most interesting economic issues surrounding technological development relate to the peculiar characteristics of knowledge when viewed as an economic commodity. Emphasizing knowledge as the critical factor input in economic growth while at the same time recognizing the importance of incentives cannot but raise questions regarding property rights on knowledge.

The intriguing properties of knowledge as property were first observed in the formal economics literature in a different 1962 publication of Arrow's (Arrow, 1962b).[31] More recently, Romer (1990) has used them to argue for the necessity of imperfect competition (and transient monopolies) in models of endogenous technology and growth, a Schumpeterian view shared also by the models in Aghion and Howitt (1992) and Grossman and Helpman (1991).

The argument goes as follows. Knowledge and ideas are infinitely expansible (or nonrival); unlike physical-material factor inputs they can be used arbitrarily everywhere without running down their usefulness in any one place or at any one application.[32] Applying the usual replication argument to standard capital and labor factor inputs, the production function therefore displays increasing returns. Perfectly competitive markets and marginal product compensation to factor inputs then would more than exhaust total output. An element of monopoly or other market imperfection circumvents this potential failure, is necessary to allow sensible market equilibrium, and, moreover, generates rents to support research activity.

Equilibrium with these features can be supported by a patents system or some other structure that protects intellectual property rights. Despite the ex post inefficiencies that such systems generate, they provide the ex ante economic incentives to allow ongoing generation of ideas and thus technological progress.

We do not disagree with the motivating observations on knowledge as economic objects given in Arrow (1962b). Indeed, we think those insights assume increasing relevance as modern economies grow and structurally transform (see, for instance Quah, 1997). However, we think there has been an overemphasis here on the supply side of the economy— that is, technology only to push back the frontiers of the production function.

---

[31] Paul David points out to us that a letter of Thomas Jefferson's on the *infinite expansibility* of ideas is an even earlier if nontechnical source of these observations (see Koch and Peden, 1944, pp. 629-630).

[32] We say *infinite expansibility* rather than *nonrivalry*—they have the same meaning —because the positive term seems to us more descriptive and thus more useful than a negation (non-*X* just means everything but *X*).

Instead, the consumption and dissemination aspects of new technology are arguably just as important, and the factors that matter here need not be as strongly tied to the usual systems of intellectual property rights.

Researchers in the economics of science and knowledge have long studied the impact on economic efficiency of alternative definitions of what it means to own and disclose a piece of knowledge. Dasgupta and David (1994), David (1992, 1993), Scotchmer (1991), and Wright (1983) are recent examples. The patent system, a standard formalization of intellectual property rights in endogenous growth theory, is but one of several possibilities.

Likely the best known of these is the system of patents. A patent system grants monopoly rights, for a definite time length, to the original creator or her agents to allow exclusive ownership and thus rent extraction from that idea or discovery. Although legally distinct, copyrights, trade secrets, and design rights (see, e.g., Holyoak and Torremans, 1995) can all be lumped together with patents, and as a group constitute intellectual property proper.

A second system is one of publicly financed prizes or research grants awarded for proposals judged in competition with others. Following a one-time reward the knowledge becomes public property and can be freely used by all agents in the economy.

A third system is one of publicly contracted research. The findings from that research are typically understood to be, again, available to all agents in the economy, although this varies.

Reality contains few pure examples of these three possibilities, but taken together they constitute a useful taxonomy.[33] Patent systems in different countries constitute versions of the first category. The second category includes, say, academic research financed by the National Science Foundation (NSF) in the United States or the Economic and Social Research Council (ESRC) in the United Kingdom An example of the third would be military research. When the research output goes directly into the public good called national defense, benefits do accrue to all in the economy. The findings of military research, however, are not usually available in any detail except perhaps in some mutated form.[34] Both the second and third systems of idea creation would, in general, be financed from general taxation.

Wright (1983) studies the efficiency properties of the three alternative systems. Based on typical structures of individual firms' private information, one would generally expect the patents system to be superior for its

---

[33] David (1992) calls these, respectively, the 3 P's: property, patronage, and procurement.

[34] A different example of the third—of intellectual property in general although not research in the narrow sense—might be royal patronage to support the musical creations of a Bach or Mozart. This example overlaps also with the second category.

emphasis on individual incentives. Wright (1983) shows that this intuition can be misleading and that in many cases patronage and procurement might well dominate patents for producing social efficiency. The principal reason is the social externality costs in researchers working on closely related problems.

Similarly, Scotchmer (1991) shows that even confining attention to the patent system, once one takes into account the cumulative nature of research —that discoveries build on earlier discoveries—the patent system is severely limited in being able to fine-tune appropriate incentives for efficient outcomes. Scotchmer too argues for greater reliance on patronage and procurement.

These subtleties in alternative systems of intellectual property rights have not yet been fully incorporated in analyses of endogenous growth. This area of research seems to us potentially quite fruitful.

Scotchmer's analysis of economic agents who use an initial discovery by a different agent is an example of the *demand side* of the market for ideas. The comparison to draw is with the supply side generating those ideas. In one interpretation, all the endogenous growth models we reviewed above focus only on the latter. Helpman (1993), by contrast, considers a model of innovation and imitation, where advanced and developing economies are explicitly identified. In Helpman's dynamic general equilibrium analysis with endogenous innovation, relaxing control over intellectual property rights can be welfare-improving for all. That economic welfare rises is obvious for the economies doing the imitation. For those economies engaged in innovation, the general equilibrium consequences of having a faster-growing, more productive rest of the world can outweigh the welfare losses from detrimental changes in terms of trade and the shift in patterns of innovation.

Acknowledging R&D as an engine of growth but, at the same time, recognizing the significance of incentives highlights the importance of the economics of knowledge. It is useful then to note that Arrow's observations on knowledge do not end with just infinite expansibility or nonrivalry. Knowledge is also differentially and asymmetrically known, involves setup costs in use, and displays priority significance (the time-series counterpart of the winner-take-all Superstar behavior in the cross section studied in Rosen, 1981). Quah (1998) has used these observations to analyze further the demand side of the market in knowledge. Moreover, since computer software and many other elements of the fast-growing weightless economy (Quah, 1997) share properties in common with knowledge, such analysis takes on increased empirical relevance, for understanding not just R&D and economic growth in particular but economic performance in general.

3.3. EMPIRICAL STUDIES: R&D AND THE IMPACT OF PROPERTY RIGHTS ON GROWTH

Underlying the idea creation in (3.14) is a description of how profit-maximizing firms willingly generate infinitely expansible ideas. Explicit examples of such mechanisms are in Aghion and Howitt (1992), Grossman and Helpman (1991), Jones (1995), and Romer (1990).

The basic insight is that firms agree to devote resources R_A to create new knowledge because their contributions to (part of) $\dot{A}/A$ can be guaranteed by intellectual property rights. As Section 3.2 suggests, we are mindful of the subtleties here. However, following most endogenous growth analyses, we proceed by taking such rights to be described by patents. Viewed thus, equation (3.14) embeds three key features:

- The relation between R_A and $\dot{A}/A$ whereby patented technology is an input into the production function;

- The uni-dimensionality of technology where it is only the aggregate patented stock of knowledge A that matters;

- The public availability of A for research, even if it is protected for owner use in production.

Several strands in the empirical literature on patents, R&D, and growth can help in evaluating these three features. We sacrifice completeness for conciseness in describing the many important pieces of research done in this area. Where empirical findings contradict theoretical assumptions, we suggest ways to address these inconsistencies in future research. We find that empirical work partly confirms the first and the last features. Empirical research suggests that the second is inadequate.

3.3.1. Resources and increases in knowledge

Begin by considering tests of the relation between knowledge inputs proxied by R&D and outputs proxied by patents. A huge empirical literature developed in the 1980s on the relation between patents, R&D, and individual firm performance (Griliches, 1990, and Keely, 1996, provide surveys).

Three main results emerge from this literature. First, private sector patents and R&D are strongly related only contemporaneously (Hall, Griliches and Hausman, 1986; Hausman, Hall and Griliches, 1984). This result contradicts the intuition that there ought to be a dynamic lagged relation between R&D inputs and outputs. However, Jaffe (1986) has provided evidence that patenting occurs very early in the research process, while Pakes (1985) shows that past R&D does have an effect on current patenting.

Second, patents help explain Tobin's q and total factor productivity (TFP) in firms, and R&D effects tend to be much larger and therefore more important for firm performance than for the aggregate economy (Cockburn and Griliches, 1988); Hall, 1998; and Megna and Klock, 1993). The distribution of patent values is highly skewed; most patents are essentially worthless (Schankerman, 1991). When quality weighted with citation data, patent counts have higher explanatory power (compared to unweighted counts) for individual firm performance (Hall, 1998). However, R&D almost always remains the more significant explanatory variable. These results make it doubtful that patents accurately or meaningfully proxy knowledge output.

Third, this research points to the productivity slowdown in advanced economies. In the United States the patent to R&D ratio has markedly declined over the last thirty years. At least three explanations have been given for this: (1) exhaustion of research potential (Evenson, 1984, 1993); (2) expansion of markets leading to increased R&D competition and activity (Kortum, 1993); and (3) decrease in the propensity to patent (Griliches, 1989; Kortum, 1993).[35] Explanation (1) seems to us incomplete because if research opportunities have decreased, so should R&D investment decline. There need be no unambiguous effect on the patent/R&D ratio. Kortum (1993) examined explanation (2), but found insufficient demand growth to explain the increase in R&D activity. Griliches proposed that a decrease in the propensity to patent was due to an increase in bureaucratic costs of patenting. A related explanation for such a decline would be a change in the mix of innovations whereby fewer inventions are patentable (Gittleman and Wolff, 1995; Keely, 1996).

To summarize, the data show correlations between individual firm R&D and patents and between both R&D and patents on the one hand and firm performance measures on the other. The nature of these correlations is, however (acknowledged to be) ill understood. Moreover, the patent to R&D correlation has been recently negative without conclusive corroborating evidence that innovation productivity has fallen. Thus, while final conclusions remain outstanding, a preliminary suggestion—one to which we are sympathetic—is that patents do not at all do a good job of describing the effects of innovation on economic performance.

---

[35] Soete (1996) summarizes discussions of mismeasurement and short-termism in R&D choice.

3.3.2. Significance of aggregate patented knowledge

The knowledge stock that matters for rent appropriation is the aggregate of patented outputs from private-sector R&D. Perhaps the most important information on this subject can be found in the survey summarized in Levin, Klevorick, Nelson, and Winter (1987). The main conclusions of this survey are well known and will only be briefly restated here. Patents were found to be a significant form of rent appropriation in only a few industries: drugs, plastic materials, inorganic chemicals, organic chemicals, and petroleum refining. Overall, however, product and process patents were found to be less effective than any other form of protection or appropriation. Those alternative forms were identified to be secrecy, lead time, moving down the learning curve, and sales or service. Deemed most important were the second and third of these, most usefully viewed, perhaps, as simply learning effects.

The results from this survey cast doubt on the usefulness of the private R&D and patenting paradigm as well as that of endogenous growth models with perfect learning spillovers across firms. Altering these models to be consistent with these survey results seems to us a valuable enterprise, but the implications of doing so have not yet been fully explored.

It is not just profit-maximizing firms that perform R&D. Government and universities do so too. Government-funded R&D constitutes one-third to one-half of total R&D expenditures in the United States and several countries of Europe (Feldman and Lichtenberg, 1997; National Science Foundation, 1996).[36] This type of R&D is sometimes called "basic research" although it is likely not research content that differs so much as the incentives of the scientists involved (Dasgupta and David, 1987, 1994). Academic and government scientists do not work for profit-maximizing firms. Their incentives will not be to patent innovations for appropriating rents but rather to disclose new knowledge in order to receive rewards associated with priority. Adams (1990), Griliches (1986), and Mansfield (1980), among others, have documented the positive correlation between individual firms' "basic research" and their productivity growth. More recent work (e.g., Adams and Griliches, 1996; Cockburn and Henderson, 1997; Henderson, Jaffe, and Trajtenberg, 1995; Pavitt, 1997; Zucker, Darby, and Torero, 1997) find evidence of knowledge spillovers between private and academic science. This work documents the positive effects of these interactions on firm productivity.

The typical explanation for ignoring public R&D in endogenous growth models is that such R&D must be subsidized and is freely available.

---

[36] The 1996 figures are 34 percent United States, 32 percent United Kingdom, 37 percent Germany, and about 45 percent in France and Italy.

Therefore, "the economics of this type of knowledge are relatively straightforward" (D. Romer, 1996). However, empirical work described above as well as theoretical models in industrial organization (e.g., Dasgupta, 1988; and Dasgupta and Maskin, 1987) indicate that the effects of basic scientific research on economic growth could well be important. Nor does the economic theory for understanding basic science seem, to us, at all straightforward.

3.3.3.   Dissemination and spillovers

The knowledge stock is available to all potential inventors for further research. As noted in Section 3.2, when discussing the neoclassical growth mechanism, equations (3.1) and (3.4) in particular, there is no good reason to presume that A or $\dot{A}/A$ are the same across countries or even within countries. In different form, it is this same issue that arises for endogenous growth when one examines this feature.

We consider the empirical evidence in two steps. First, we look at micro- and macroeconomic evidence on whether such spillovers exist across economic agents. Second, we examine evidence on how large such spillovers are, to see how much the same knowledge stock is available to all. We will conclude that spillovers of knowledge do occur across agents and affect their productivity, but the spillovers are not uniform across physical and technological locations.

Microeconomic evidence on physical clustering of innovative activity is remarkably consistent across studies. Ciccone and Hall (1996) conclude that employment density increases labor productivity, supporting therefore the view that knowledge spillovers occur across workers in the same location. Audretsch and Feldman (1996) find that, even after controlling for production density, industries where knowledge is a significant input in production tend physically to cluster innovations more than do other industries. Similarly, Jaffe and Trajtenberg (1996) and Jaffe, Trajtenberg, and Henderson (1993) show that geographical proximity increases patent citations between institutions, again controlling for production density within industries. Finally, apart from physical location, a given firm's R&D productivity increases with the R&D performed by all firms in the same industry, even though the individual firm's profitability might suffer (Jaffe, 1986).

We conclude from this evidence that knowledge spillovers do occur. However, the physical clustering of innovation suggests that spillovers do not happen automatically or completely.

Macroeconomic evidence too supports the hypothesis of knowledge spillovers, although their extent and completeness remain unclear. Much of the empirical research looks for spillovers in international data. In one interpretation, many R&D endogenous growth models are closed-economy ones and thus are silent on the issue of international diffusion. But significant exceptions exist, such as the models in Barro and Sala-i-Martin (1997), Grossman and Helpman (1991), and Helpman (1993).

In an example of seeking knowledge spillovers within a macroeconomy, Caballero and Jaffe (1993) use U.S. patent and citation data to calibrate a model of creative destruction and endogenous technological obsolescence and diffusion. They estimate that diffusion of knowledge from patents occurs with a mean lag of one to two years, but that the decrease over the twentieth century in the patent citation rate indicates a fall in the strength of those spillovers. The result is a decline in growth of the public knowledge stock.

More studies are available on R&D spillovers from advanced to developing countries. Coe, Helpman, and Hoffmeister (1997) document evidence of spillovers via TFP effects in developing countries. They find that TFP in a typical developing country increases with a rise in the country's trade openness, its average rate of secondary school enrollment, its import share from advanced economies, and its import share of GDP. The effect of the foreign R&D stock is strong but significant only when interacted with the import share variable. This finding supports the view that knowledge spillovers occur only via a specific channel of economic interaction such as trade or migration.

Bayoumi, Coe, and Helpman (1998) build on that earlier work in a model of R&D, spillovers, and endogenous growth, where R&D spillovers occur through imports. In both papers, R&D influences growth through TFP and capital accumulation. Simulations support the model as an empirically accurate description of cross-country patterns of growth.

Another way to examine imperfect knowledge spillovers uses cross-country regressions with the dependent variable being either own country R&D (Gittleman and Wolff, 1995) or own-country intellectual property rights protection (Gould and Gruben, 1996). When any one country's R&D stock or flow is small relative to the entire world's, then a significant effect of own R&D in such a cross-country regression indicates that knowledge spillovers are incomplete. Gittleman and Wolff (1995) find that own R&D is insignificant in the regression with all countries included. However, in subsamples chosen by income levels, the regression coefficient is positive for upper, and middle income countries (where almost all R&D occurs). Cross-country spillovers therefore do occur but are incomplete.[37]

---

[37] Gould and Gruben (1996) also report a positive and significant effect of intellectual property right protection on GDP growth. This confirms the hypothesized importance of incentives for accumulating knowledge and promoting growth, a view that this chapter

In a series of papers, Eaton and Kortum (1994, 1995, 1996) develop and calibrate a model of R&D, patenting, knowledge diffusion, and growth to estimate the impact of foreign technology on productivity growth. They examine the hypothesis that foreign technology is difficult to adopt. Productivity levels in the model are affected by the ability to innovate domestically and the readiness to adopt foreign technologies. Therefore, although steady-state income growth rates converge to the same level, productivity level differences persist across countries. Calibrations show consistency with actual growth experiences of different countries. The bulk of technology growth is estimated to originate in the United States, Germany, and Japan.

To summarize, despite the differences in methodologies and emphases in the studies above, the broad conclusion is that spillovers across regions do occur. At the same time, however, these spillovers are generally incomplete.

3.3.4. Extensions

As discussed in Section 3.2, Jones (1995) has forcefully criticized R&D-driven endogenous growth models by documenting their empirical failure on scale effects. The revision, suggested by Jones (1995), posits that research effort duplication could produce decreasing returns in the measured resources devoted to R&D.

The spillover results we have just reviewed suggest another possibility. Although knowledge is in principle infinitely expansible, there might be significant obstacles to its widespread use, even aside from protection in intellectual property rights. Examples that we have in mind given our review of the evidence include the lack of contact between scientists in different physical or technological areas, and the absence of an infrastructure to introduce and utilize new products or processes.

Therefore, a fruitful area of research is to identify the mechanisms by which economic interactions lead to knowledge spillovers. Understanding such mechanisms would aid policy formulation when knowledge spillovers are an important channel for economic growth. In other words, it might be useful to increase research emphasis on the use and dissemination of knowledge on the demand side, not just study legal institutions on the supply side that induce innovation in profit-maximizing firms. Also of interest would be to understand mechanisms whereby researchers in nonmarket environments create and disclose new ideas (e.g., Keely, 1998; Weitzman, 1997). These two—dissemination on the demand side of the market for

---

maintains. The finding does not say, however, that other less obvious forms of knowledge protection and dissemination might not also be important.

knowledge and non-market institutions on the supply side—might well have effects on economic growth that dominate the factors endogenous growth theory traditionally studies.

3.4. CONCLUSIONS

This chapter has reviewed the development of R&D endogenous growth theory, tracing the close relationship between earlier and more recent literatures. The chapter has compared the theoretical paradigm with empirical evidence on the formation and diffusion of new ideas.

A consistent picture emerges. Economic theory emphasizes the importance for growth of incentives in the production of useful knowledge and, more generally, the significance of intellectual property rights. The framework of private-sector R&D as input and intellectual property as output clarifies those incentives for innovation by profit-maximizing firms. This view is one that sees some empirical support in economic data.

However, this framework is an incomplete one for understanding economic growth and the process of idea creation. First, it is not just private sector, profit-maximizing firms that generate the bulk of useful knowledge. Governments and academics do so as well. Incentive structures in this broader nonmarket context are subtle but no less important for economic growth.

Second, it is not just patents that provide property rights to knowledge. Alternative structures that do so are arguably more important in reality, and moreover provide incentive and efficiency implications that differ profoundly from those of a patent system.

These extensions and complications have yet to be incorporated into models of R&D and endogenous growth. The payoffs to doing so are likely high for understanding the effects.

References

Abramowitz, M. (1956). "Resource and Output Trends in the United States Since 1870." *American Economic Association Papers and Proceedings* 46, 5–23.

Adams, J.D. (1990) "Fundamental Stocks of Knowledge and Productivity Growth." *Journal of Political Economy* 98, 673–702.

Adams, J.D., and Z. Griliches. (1996). "Research Productivity in a System of Universities." Working Paper 5833, NBER.

Aghion, P., and P. Howitt. (1998). *Endogenous Growth Theory.* Cambridge, MA: MIT Press.

Aghion, P., and P. Howitt. (1992). "A Model of Growth Through Creative Destruction." *Econometrica* 60, 323–351.

Arrow, K.J. (1962a). "The Economic Implications of Learning By Doing." *Review of Economic Studies* 29, 155–173.

Arrow, K.J. (1962b). "Economic Welfare and the Allocation of Re-sources for Inventions." In R.R. Nelson, ed., *The Rate and Direction of Inventive Activity*. Princeton: Princeton University Press and NBER.

Audretsch, D.B., and M.P. Feldman. (1996). "R&D Spillovers and the Geography of Innovation and Production." *American Economic Review* 86, 630–640.

Barro, R. J., and X. Sala-i-Martin. (1995). *Economic Growth*. New York: McGraw-Hill.

Barro, R.J. and X. Sala-i-Martin. (1997). "Technology Diffusion, Convergence, and Growth." *Journal of Economic Growth* 2, 1–25.

Bayoumi, T., D.T. Coe, and E. Helpman (1999). "R&D Spillovers and Global Growth." *Journal of International Economics*.

Caballero, R.J., and A.B. Jaffe. (1993). "How High Are the Giants' Shoulders: An Empirical Assessment of Knowledge Spillovers and Creative Destruction in a Model of Economic Growth." In O. Blanchard and S. Fischer, eds., *NBER Macroeconomics Annual 1993*. Cambridge, MA: MIT Press.

Ciccone, A., and R.E. Hall. (1996). "Productivity and the Density of Economic Activity." *American Economic Review* 86, 54–70.

Cockburn, I., and Z. Griliches. (1988). "Industry Effects and Appropriability Measures in Stock Market's Valuation of R&D and Patents." *American Economic Review* 78, 419–423.

Cockburn, I., and R. Henderson (1997). "Public-Private Interaction and the Productivity of Pharmaceutical Research." Working Paper 6018, NBER.

Coe, D.T., E. Helpman, and A.W. Hoffmaister. (1997). "North-South R&D Spillovers." *Economic Journal* 107, 134–149.

Dasgupta, P. (1988). "Patents, Priority and Imitation or, the Economics of Races and Waiting Games." *Economic Journal* 98, 66–80.

Dasgupta, P., and P.A. David. (1987). "Information Disclosure and the Economics of Science and Technology." In G.R. Feiwel, ed., *Arrow and the Ascent of Modern Economic Theory* (pp. 519–542), New York: University Press.

Dasgupta, P., and P.A. David. (1994). "Toward a New Economics of Science." *Research Policy* 23, 487–521.

Dasgupta, P., and E. Maskin. (1987). "The Simple Economics of Research Portfolios." *Economic Journal* 97, 581–595.

David, P.A. (1992). "Knowledge, Property, and the System Dynamics of Technological Change." *Proceedings of the World Bank Annual Conference on Development Economics* (pp. 215-248).

David, P.A. (1993). "Intellectual Property Institutions and the Panda's Thumb: Patents, Copyrights, and Trade Secrets in Economic Theory and History." In M.B. Wallerstein, M.E. Mogee, and R.A. Schoen, eds., *Global Dimensions of Intellectual Property Rights in Science and Technology* (ch. 2, pp. 19-61). National Academy Press.

Durlauf, S.N., and D. Quah. (1998). "The New Empirics of Economic Growth." In J.B. Taylor, and M. Woodford, eds., *Handbook of Macroeconomics*, Amsterdam: North Holland.

Eaton, J., and S. Kortum. (1994). "International Patenting and Technology Diffusion." Working Paper 4931, NBER.

Eaton, J., and S. Kortum. (1995). "Engines of Growth: Domestic and Foreign Sources of Innovation." Working Paper 5207, NBER.

Eaton, J., and S. Kortum. (1996). "Trade in Ideas: Patenting and Productivity in the OECD." *Journal of International Economics* 40, 251–278.

Evenson, R. (1984). "International Invention: Implications for Technology Market Analysis." In Z. Griliches, ed., *R&D, Patents, and Productivity.* Chicago: University of Chicago Press.

Evenson, R. (1993). "Patents, R&D and Invention Potential: International Evidence." *American Economic Review* 83.

Feldman, M.P., and F.R. Lichtenberg. (1997). "The Impact and Organization of Publicly-Funded Research and Development in the European Community." Working Paper 6040, NBER.

Gittleman, M., and E.N. Wolff. (1995). "R&D Activity and Cross-Country Growth Comparisons." *Cambridge Journal of Economics* 19, 189–207.

Gould, D.M., and W.C. Gruben. (1996). "The Role of Intellectual Property Rights in Economic Growth." *Journal of Development Economics* 48, 323–350.

Griliches, Z. (1986). "Productivity, R&D, and Basic Research at the Firm Level in the 1970s." *American Economic Review* 76, 141–154.

Griliches, Z. (1989). "Patents: Recent Trends and Puzzles." *Brookings Papers on Economic Activity: Microeconomics 1989.*

Griliches, Z. (1990). "Patent Statistics as Economic Indicators: a Survey." *Journal of Economic Literature* 28, 1661–1707.

Grossman, G.M., and E. Helpman. (1991). "Innovation and Growth in the Global Economy." Cambridge, MA: MIT Press.

Hall, B.H. (1998). "Innovation and Market Value." Working Paper, Oxford University and University of California at Berkeley.

Hall, B.H., Z. Griliches, and J. Hausman. (1986). "Patents and R&D: Is There a Lag?' *International Economic Review* 27, 265–283.

Hausman, J., B.H. Hall, and Z. Griliches. (1984). "Econometric Models for Count Data with an Application to the Patents-R&D Relationship." *Econometrica* 52, 909–936.

Helpman, E. (1993). "Innovation, Imitation, and Intellectual Property Rights." *Econometrica* 61, 1247–1280.

Henderson, R., A.B. Jaffe, and M. Trajtenberg. (1995). "Universities as a Source of Commercial Technology: A Detailed Analysis of University Patenting 1965-1988." Working Paper 5068, NBER.

Holyoak, J., and P. Torremans. (1995). *Intellectual Property Law.* Butterworths.

Jaffe, A.B. (1986). "Technological Opportunity and Spillovers of R&D: Evidence from Firms' Patents, Profits and Market Value." *American Economic Review* 76, 984–1001.

Jaffe, A.B., and M. Trajtenberg. (1996). "Flows of Knowledge from Universities and Federal Labs: Modeling the Flow of Patent Citations over Time and Across Institutional Geographic Boundaries." Working Paper 5712, NBER.

Jaffe, A.B., M. Trajtenberg, and R. Henderson. (1993). "Geographic Localization of Knowledge Spillovers as Evidenced in Patent Citations." *Quarterly Journal of Economics* 108, 577–598.

Jones, C.I. (1995). "R&D-Based Models of Economic Growth." *Journal of Political Economy* 103, 759–784.

Jones, C.I., and J.C. Williams. (1998). "Measuring the Social Return to R&D." *Quarterly Journal of Economics.*

Jorgenson, D.W., and Z. Griliches. (1967). "The Explanation of Productivity Change." *Review of Economic Studies* 34, 249–280.

Keely, L.C. (1996). "Patents: Do They Matter?" Working Paper, London School of Economics.

Keely, L.C. (1998). "Exchanging Good Ideas." Working Paper, London School of Economics.

Kendrick, J.W. (1956). "Productivity Trends: Capital and Labor." *Review of Economics and Statistics* 38, 248–257.

Koch, A., and W. Peden, eds. (1944). *The Life and Selected Writings of Thomas Jefferson.* New York: Random House.

Kortum, S.S. (1993). "Equilibrium R&D and the Patent-R&D Ratio: U.S. Evidence." *American Economic Association Papers and Proceedings* 83, 450–457.

Levin, R.C., A.K. Klevorick, R.R. Nelson, and S.G. Winter. (1987). "Appropriating the Returns from Industrial Research and Development." *Brookings Papers on Economic Activity* 3, 783–820.

Lucas, R.E. Jr. (1988). "On the Mechanics of Economic Development." *Journal of Monetary Economics* 22, 3-42.

Maddison, A. (1989). *The World Economy in the Twentieth Century.* Development Centre of the OECD.

Mansfield, E. (1980). "Basic Research and Productivity Increase in Manufacturing" *The American Economic Review* 70, 863–873.

Megna, P., and M. Klock. (1993). "The Impact of Intangible Capital on Tobin's q in the Semiconductor Industry." *American Economic Association Papers and Proceedings* 83, 265–269.

National Science Foundation. (1996). *National Patterns of R&D Resources: 1996.*

Pakes, A. (1985). "On Patents, R&D and the Stock Market Rate of Return." *Journal of Political Economy* 93, 390–409.

Pavitt, K. (1997). "The Social Shaping of the National Science Base." Working Paper, SPRU, Sussex University.

Quah, D. (1997). "Increasingly Weightless Economies." *Bank of England Quarterly Bulletin* 37, 49–56.

Quah, D. (1998). *"Superstar Knowledge-Products in a Model of Growth."* Working Paper, London School of Economics.

Romer, D. (1996). *Advanced Macroeconomics.* New York: McGraw-Hill.

Romer, P.M. (1986). "Increasing Returns and Long-Run Growth." *Journal of Political Economy* 94, 1002–1037.

Romer, P.M. (1990). "Endogenous Technological Change." *Journal of Political Economy* 98, S71–S102.

Romer, P.M. (1994). "The Origins of Endogenous Growth." *Journal of Economic Perspectives* 8, 3–22.

Rosen, S. (1981). "The Economics of Superstars." *American Economic Review* 71, 845–858.

Schankerman, M. (1991). *"How Valuable Is Patent Protection? Estimates by Technology Field Using Patent Renewal Data."* Working Paper 3780, NBER.

Scotchmer, S. (1991). "Standing on the Shoulders of Giants: Cumulative Research and the Patent Law." *Journal of Economic Perspectives* 5, 29–41.

Soete, L.L.G. (1996). 'Uncertainty and Technological Change: Discussion." In J.C. Fuhrer, and J. Sneddon Little, eds., *Technology and Growth* (pp. 119-125). Boston: Federal Reserve Bank of Boston.

Solow, R.M. (1956). "A Contribution to the Theory of Economic Growth." *Quarterly Journal of Economics* 70, 65–94.

Solow, R.M. (1957). "Technical Change and the Aggregate Production Function." *Review of Economics and Statistics* 39, 312–320.

Stiglitz, J.E., and H. Uzawa, eds. (1969). *Readings in the Modern Theory of Economic Growth*, Cambridge, MA: MIT Press.

Summers, R., and A. Heston. (1991). "The Penn World Table (Mark 5): An Expanded Set of International Comparisons, 1950-1988." *Quarterly Journal of Economics* 106, 327–368.

Weitzman, M.L. (1998). "Recombinant Growth" *Quarterly Journal of Economics* 113(2), 331–360.

Wright, B.D. (1983). "The Economics of Invention Incentives: Patents, Prizes, and Research Contracts." *American Economic Review* 73, 691–707.

Zucker, L.G., M.R. Darby, and M. Torero. (1997). "Labor Mobility from Academe to Commerce." Working Paper 6050, NBER.

DISCUSSION

Graham Pyatt
Institute of Social Studies

The neoclassical parable is a fascinating tale that endogenous growth theory is now refurbishing in its latest attempts to explain the residual factor in economic growth. Earlier, it had been thought that allowing for improvements in human capital (necessitating the remeasurement of the labor input) might do the trick, but empirical efforts to account for the residual on this basis proved to be less than entirely satisfactory. The residual persisted, and some new insight was evidently needed if the edifice of neoclassical growth theory was to be maintained. This has now been provided, as Keely and Quah explain in their elegant paper, by introducing knowledge as a new factor of production that can be produced over time in unlimited quantities through the agency of human capital. And, since knowledge is nonrival, all can benefit from its creation and without apparent cost to others or any diminution of the stock (for reasons other than obsolescence). The production of knowledge can therefore create externalities, which have the potential to offset diminishing returns to other (conventional) factor services. Hence the new growth theories offer the possibility of sustainable growth being generated by explicit production processes that, they imply, can be relied on to invent close substitutes for finite natural resources, if and when it is necessary to do so. Accordingly, the new growth theories promote a technological optimism, which will worry many environmentalists.

There is further cause for pause implicit in the new theories. If knowledge is nonrival then, it can be argued, some way of restricting access to it will be necessary if we are going to rely on private entrepreneurs to articulate the process of knowledge creation. Thus, at the center of the Keely and Quah exposition, we find the notion of a private firm investing in R&D

activity, the objective of which is to create new knowledge that will be sufficiently protected by patents to allow the process as a whole to be profitable. Accordingly, the endogenous growth theories respond to concerns in the United States, in particular, as to how a relatively high living standard can be maintained in an increasingly competitive global environment. They suggest that high-tech is the way forward, but its products need to be protected.

From the perspective of the developing countries, neither of the above messages is especially welcome or encouraging. Nor is the maintained hypothesis that underlies them, whereby the neoclassical growth model is accepted as a useful starting point for addressing the issues. It might be helpful, therefore, to note that this model

- Assumes that growth of real output emanating from the cash economy is the variable that theory needs to explain;

- Assumes that capital is measurable and that labor supply is exogenous to the growth process; and

- Assumes that output per head is a function of the capital-labor ratio, which can be changed instantaneously and without cost.

None of these three assumptions should be allowed to go unchallenged. In relation to the first, it is relatively easy to accept that the real output of the cash economy (gross domestic product per capita) is a useful variable in many contexts, not least because it is strongly correlated with alternative measures of progress, such as life expectation. But so is consumption per capita, which is surely a more relevant growth objective than production. It is not difficult to envisage an economy in which GDP is growing in such a way that an increasing fraction of output must be invested to compensate for environmental losses. It is therefore entirely possible for GDP to grow while consumption stagnates.

A complementary line of criticism notes that conventional measures of GDP leave out of account extensive activity in the non cash economy and are arguably subject, as a result, to a gender bias.[38] They also fail to make any allowance for depreciation and so avoid many of the issues raised by questions of sustainability. This could be seriously misleading, especially if such data are to be used to support a theory of growth and technical change that assumes that population growth is exogenous.

---

[38] This may explain why, in Chapter 1, Robert J. Barro reports having been unable to find evidence that educating girls stimulates economic growth.

The failure to measure output net of depreciation is an aspect of the accepted practice among economists of assuming that capital is measurable as a stock while maintaining that it is not their job to make the necessary measurements. Keely and Quah note that the conceptual problems of measuring capital were the subject of serious debate some forty years ago, but they explicitly dismiss the contemporary relevance of such concerns.[39] I wonder if they are right to do so. For example, as the information economy grows in importance relative to other sectors of the economy, questions about the measurability of its own net output become pressing. The number of patents issued may serve as a useful proxy for the gross output of inventions in some contexts. But its relevance is evidently limited, as Keely and Quah have noted, in an environment in which the protection afforded by the patent system is increasingly seen as being inadequate and may be breaking down in some areas. How, for example, should we measure net output, at constant prices, for the software industry?

The third concern noted above is the presumption in neoclassical theory that capital and labor are substitutes so that the capital-labor ratio can be varied instantaneously and without cost. Surely, no one accepts this part of the neoclassical parable at face value or that full employment can be reached by lowering real wages in all sectors except, perhaps, personal services. The danger here is to miss the central importance of investment as mediator of the transition from invention to innovation and the creation of new jobs.

It is by now many years since Salter provided economics with an alternative formulation of technology that is more in tune with the reality that investment is necessary to create jobs and that older technologies become obsolescent as a result of the invention and subsequent innovation of better ways of doing things (Salter, 1960). In a series of papers written some years ago, I tried to show how, under suitable aggregation, this approach yields an alternative way of accounting for growth to the one that is offered by the surrogate production function (Pyatt, 1964). This alternative obviates the need to measure capital as a stock and shifts the debate about technical change back to the Schumpeterian agenda of explaining invention, with the speed of innovation depending on the rate of investment. From this perspective, the neoclassical parable has apparently seduced its adherents into an unnecessary detour over the years before now returning to the fundamental issues.

None of this is intended to deny that the new growth theories offer new insights and their emphasis on knowledge as a nonrival contribution to the creation of value added is especially important in giving focus and structure to long-standing debates about why some countries are richer than others and

---

[39] See note 25, above.

why some are catching up while others fall behind. Keely and Quah have provided us with a useful review of these developments.

While it is perhaps inevitable that the developed world will remain preoccupied with the creation and maintenance of its technical leadership and that much research will therefore be directed by these concerns for the developing world, the agenda suggested by endogenous growth theories is necessarily somewhat different. For them it is a matter of gaining access to increasingly sophisticated technology and being able to absorb it. This requires the combination of complementary investment activities: in physical capital to acquire the technology and in human capital so that the new technologies can be used effectively. The primary lesson of the new growth theories for developing countries must therefore be to emphasize the importance of balanced development strategies that recognize their need not only to acquire new technologies but also to master their use. A further inference that would then seem to follow is that, to the extent that the developing countries, as a group, can manage the social engineering that is necessary if such strategies are to be successfully implemented, so the protection offered to the developed world by the patents system will be weakened. Direct foreign investment in those developing countries, which are most successful, may then appear to private entrepreneurs from the developed world as offering an attractive alternative. And they are unlikely to be worried by the potential of this scenario to increase the variation of economic growth rates among the developing countries. Some will catch up rapidly as they acquire growing competence in the use of increasingly sophisticated technologies, while others, inevitably, will be left behind.

References

Salter, W.E.G. (1960). *Productivity and Technical Change.* Cambridge: Cambridge University Press.

Pyatt, G. (1964). "A Measure of Capital." *Review of Economic Studies* 30(3).

Chapter 4

Financial markets, financial flows, and economic growth in LDCs

Maxwell J. Fry
Professor of International Finance, International Finance Group, University of Birmingham

4.1.   A FISCAL FOREWORD

All financial systems in market economies, whether they are developed or developing, perform two basic functions: administering the country's payments mechanism and intermediating between savers and investors.[40] On the first function, there is little disagreement that high inflation impairs the domestic currency's attributes not only of a store of value but also of a means of payment. As Tobin (1992) states: "A society's money is necessarily a store of value. Otherwise it could not be an acceptable means of payment." So financial systems are impeded in performing both of their basic functions under high inflation. Society turns to substitute means of payment (foreign currencies or barter trade), thereby bypassing the domestic financial system. This substitution is one manifestation of the law of demand. As the opportunity cost of holding money rises, the demand for money expressed at constant prices or in real terms falls.

In the simplest balance sheet of the banking system, the banks hold loans L and reserves R as their assets and deposits D as their liabilities:

Assets		Liabilities	
Reserves	R	Deposits	D
Loans	L		

---

[40] Gertler and Rose (1994) provide a nontechnical exposition of the theory of financial intermediation. Gertler (1988) offers a more technical analysis.

The balance-sheet identity implies $R + L = D$. Naturally, this balance sheet identity is still preserved if one divides both assets and liabilities by nominal GNP Y:

Assets		Liabilities	
Reserves	R/Y	Deposits	D/Y
Loans	L/Y		

Ceteris paribus, the ratio D/Y falls as inflation accelerates because households and firms choose to hold smaller money balances in relation to their expenditure levels due to the rising cost of holding money. Therefore, the ratio $(R + L)/Y$ must also fall.[41] If the ratio R/L remains roughly constant, then both R/Y and L/Y fall as D/Y falls. Since L/Y is the ratio of bank loans to the nominal value of output, business firms find themselves facing a credit squeeze as inflation rises. Unable to obtain the necessary loans to cover the costs of their working capital, some firms may be unable to stay in business. The aggregate level of output in real terms would then fall. In this case, therefore, the deterioration of money reduces the extents to which the banking system administers the country's payments mechanism and intermediates between savers and investors; performance in both functions is related. Perhaps the former effect reduces income levels while the latter effect reduces income growth.

Fiscal difficulties frequently lie behind many features and problems of financial systems in developing countries. Many developing country governments find it virtually impossible to satisfy their intertemporal budget constraint with conventional tax revenue. Hence, they rely on revenue from the inflation tax, and they reduce their interest costs through financial repression (Agénor and Montiel, 1996; Brock, 1989; Fry, 1997a; Giovannini and de Melo, 1993). Both the theoretical and empirical findings reviewed in this chapter suggest that financial repression is a particularly damaging quasi-tax from the perspective of economic growth.

Governments can finance their deficits in four major ways:[42]

* Monetizing the deficit by borrowing at zero cost from the central bank.

---

[41] Even a competitive banking system cannot raise deposit rates of interest in step with inflation when subject to noninterest-bearing reserve requirements. The reserve tax burden, which increases with inflation, is passed on to depositors or lenders.

[42] Under cash-based budgets, arrears and other deferred-payment arrangements together with unfunded future liabilities such as state pensions constitute additional techniques of disguising the true magnitude of a deficit.

- Borrowing at below-market interest rates by thrusting debt down the throats of captive buyers, primarily commercial banks.

- Borrowing abroad in foreign currency.

- Borrowing at market interest rates from voluntary lenders in domestic currency markets.

The typical OECD country finances about 50 percent of its deficit in voluntary domestic-currency markets, while the typical developing country finances only about 8 percent of its deficit from this source.

Why this matters is that, for any given persistent government deficit, greater use of the first three sources is associated with higher inflation rates, lower saving ratios, and lower rates of economic growth (Fry, 1997a). Government recourse to the central bank inevitably leads to inflation. Indeed, such inflationary finance can be considered a source of tax revenue in that inflation imposes a tax on money holders.

Financial repression, the second way of financing the government deficit, is also taxlike in that it involves forcing captive buyers to hold government debt at interest rates below market yields. By reducing its interest costs, this method reduces the government's recorded deficit. Foreign borrowing, which for all developing countries implies borrowing and repaying foreign rather than domestic currency, constitutes the third method of financing a deficit. Elsewhere, I demonstrate that excessive reliance on these three ways of financing government deficits impedes economic development (Fry, 1997a).

All this conflicts with the views of Barro (1974, 1989) and Buchanan (1976) on Ricardian equivalence. Barro (1989) states that the Ricardian equivalence theorem, proposed only to be dismissed by David Ricardo (1817) himself, holds that

> The substitution of a budget deficit for current taxes (or any other rearrangement of the timing of taxes) has no impact on the aggregate demand for goods. In this sense, budget deficits and taxation have equivalent effects on the economy—hence the term "Ricardian equivalence theorem." To put the equivalence result another way, a decrease in the government's saving (that is, a current budget deficit) leads to an offsetting increase in desired private saving, and hence to no change in desired national saving.

It also follows that Ricardian equivalence implies that the method of financing government deficits has no impact on the macroeconomy.

While Barro (1989) interprets the empirical evidence to provide general support for the Ricardian equivalence theorem, the evidence cited is drawn largely from the United States, where the assumptions of the theorem are perhaps most likely to hold. As Agénor and Montiel (1996) suggest, "In developing countries where financial systems are underdeveloped, capital markets are highly distorted or subject to financial repression, and private agents are subject to considerable uncertainty regarding the incidence of taxes, many of the considerations necessary for debt neutrality to hold are unlikely to be valid." Hence, the assumptions on which Ricardian equivalence rests (Barro, 1989) are almost bound to be violated sufficiently to negate the theorem in these countries. Indeed, Agénor and Montiel (1996) conclude: "the empirical evidence [from developing countries] has indeed failed to provide much support for the Ricardian equivalence proposition." The empirical evidence presented in Fry (1997a) confirms the Agénor–Montiel position.

The negative effect of deficit finance on growth is typically demonstrated by estimating a relationship between inflation and economic growth. Here inflation *INF* is measured by the continuously compounded rate of change in the consumer price index and growth by the continuously compounded rate of change in GDP measured at constant prices *YG*. To confront the problem that inflation have been far more variable (heteroscedastic) in some countries than in others, I estimate the relationship between economic growth and inflation here using iterative three-stage least squares on a system of equations with the same slope parameters but different intercepts for each country. Furthermore, I deal with the problem of simultaneity by treating inflation and money growth as endogenous variables. Initial tests for nonlinearities indicated that the inclusion of both squared and cubed inflation ($INFG^2$ and $INFG^3$) as explanatory variables for economic growth produced better results than the level (*INFG*). The estimate (with *t* values in brackets) for a sample of forty-one developing countries for the period 1971 to 1994 (860 observations, t-statistics in parentheses) is[43]

$$YG = -\underset{(-13.648)}{0.056}\,\hat{INF}^2 + \underset{(10.346)}{0.015}\,\hat{INF}^3 \tag{4.1}$$

$$\bar{R}^2 = 0.154$$

Figure 4.1 illustrates this estimated growth-inflation relationship. The problem I have with this, and similar estimates, is its size. Ceteris paribus, could a rise in inflation from zero to 225 percent, the range covering

---

[43] The instruments are lagged inflation, lagged money and output growth rates, oil inflation, and the OECD growth rate. The estimation procedure, which is asymptotically full-information maximum likelihood, automatically corrects for heteroscedasticity across equations and therefore, in this case, across countries (Johnston, 1984, pp. 486–490).

virtually all the observations, really reduce growth by ten percentage points? Since the magnitude of this estimated effect seems unreasonable to me, I suggest that at least not all of this relationship is causal. Rather, I suggest that economic growth and inflation are both affected in opposite directions by fiscal variables.

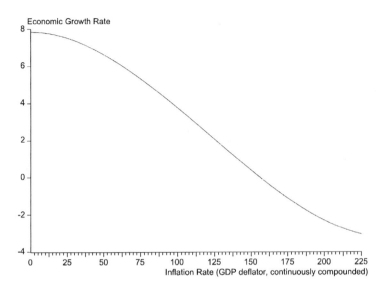

Figure 4.1. Nonlinear relationship between economic growth and inflation

To examine the relationship between deficit finance and economic growth more carefully, I obtained data for seventy developing countries for the period 1972 to 1995. Details of the country sample and the data definitions are presented in Fry (1997a).[44] The sample includes all developing countries with a reasonable number of observations for the relevant fiscal variables. My first examination of the data involved ranking these seventy countries on the basis of various potential discriminating variables. I then selected the ten countries with the highest average values of the discriminating variable and the ten countries with the lowest average values of this discriminating variable during the period 1972 to 1995.

Table 4.1 demonstrates some of the relationships between countries' fiscal attributes and their inflation and growth performance. Table 4.1 compares the mean values of the fiscal variables when countries are selected on growth rates with their mean values when countries are selected on the fiscal variables themselves. The numbers represent means of all annual

---

[44] The instruments are lagged inflation, lagged money and output growth rates, oil inflation, and the OECD growth rate.

values for the country group. In the columns labeled "Low fiscal deficit" and "High fiscal deficit", the countries differ for each fiscal factor. So the ten lowest-deficit countries averaged surpluses of 1.6 percent (deficits of -1.6 percent), compared with average deficits of 12.8 percent in the ten highest-deficit countries. Annual changes in reserve money in the ten countries with lowest reserve-money growth averaged 0.7 percent of GDP compared with 6.6 percent in the ten countries with highest reserve-money growth.[45] Finally, the ratio of bank reserves to bank deposits averaged 6.6 percent in the ten countries with the lowest ratios compared with 46.9 percent in the ten countries with the highest ratios.

Table 4.1. Fiscal attributes in high- and low-growth countries (average annual percentages, 1972 to 1995)

Fiscal attribute	Low growth	High growth	Low fiscal deficit	High fiscal deficit
Government deficit/GNP	9.5	1.4	-1.6	12.8
Δ Reserve money	4.1	1.4	0.7	6.6
Reserve per deposits	29.2	12.5	6.6	46.9
Growth	0.6	8.1	7.0	3.2
Inflation	40.1	8.2	9.4	27.0

In the columns labeled "Low growth" and "High growth", the data related to the same group of countries. So in the ten lowest-growing countries, government deficits averaged 9.5 percent of GDP, reserve money growth averaged 4.1 percent of GDP, and bank reserves averaged 29.2 percent of bank deposits. In the ten highest-growing countries, government deficits averaged 1.4 percent of GDP, reserve money growth averaged 1.4 percent of GDP and bank reserves averaged 12.5 percent of bank deposits. Inflation and growth rates reported in the last two rows are averages for the ten lowest-growth, highest-growth, lowest-deficit and highest-deficit countries.

All the differences between high- and low-growth countries are highly significant. In all cases, high-growth countries exhibit low averages for fiscal variables, that is low deficits, low reserve-money growth, and low reserve to deposit ratios. In other words, countries with good fiscal characteristics perform better economically with higher growth and lower inflation than those with poor fiscal characteristics. I conjecture that these fiscal characteristics explain much of the negative association observed between

---

[45] If reserve money represented 10 percent of GDP, this 6.6 percent would correspond to an annual average rate of growth in reserve money of 66 percent.

inflation and growth.[46] After conducting formal causality tests, Fischer (1993) concludes that "small deficits are good for growth."

A move away from inflationary finance, financial repression, and excessive reliance on foreign currency borrowing toward developing voluntary domestic markets for government debt appears to offer benefits in terms of lower inflation and higher saving and economic growth rates. High growth, in turn, alleviates the deficit. There is, therefore, some hint of a virtuous circle in which less financial repression and greater use of voluntary domestic markets lowers inflation and raises growth, both of which reduce the government's deficit. In general, developing countries make too little use of voluntary lenders in domestic-currency markets.

Given fiscal discipline, removing existing distortions and resisting the imposition of new distortions on financial markets constitute growth-enhancing government policies. Undistorted domestic financial markets promote economic growth by enhancing both the quality and the quantity of investment. Well-functioning domestic financial markets facilitate the allocation of capital inflows from abroad to their most productive uses; they also deter capital flight.

4.2.   DOMESTIC FINANCE

4.2.1.   Financial systems in developing countries

Four specific features of financial systems in developing countries distinguish them from financial systems in industrial countries. First, financial systems in most developing economies are dominated by commercial banks. Assets of insurance and pension companies are minuscule in most developing countries. Development finance institutions such as agricultural and development banks are also small compared with commercial banks. Commercial bond markets are typically thin, and government bond markets are often used only by captive buyers obliged to hold such bonds to satisfy liquidity ratio requirements or to bid for government contracts. Although equity markets are sizable in several developing countries, their role in the process of financial intermediation between household and business sectors remains small. Indeed, the relatively large Taiwanese equity market produces a transfer of resources from the

---

[46]   Elsewhere, I suggest that the effects of poor fiscal policies in developing countries are typically exacerbated by inappropriate monetary policies. Larger deficits and greater reliance by governments on the domestic banking system are associated with less effort exerted toward monetary control (Fry 1998a).

business sector to the household sector in the form of dividends that exceeds the transfer from the household sector to the business sector in the form of new-issue purchases.

Second, financial systems in many developing countries tend to be heavily taxed. Inflation has long been analyzed as a tax and hence as a source of government revenue (Bailey, 1956; Friedman, 1971). The tax collector is the central bank, the tax base is reserve or high-powered money, and the tax rate is the inflation rate. Holders of currency pay the tax through the erosion in the purchasing power of their currency. Banks also pay the tax by holding reserves, invariably in the form of required reserves. For a sample of twenty-six developing countries, I found that the inflation tax yielded revenue for the government equal to 2.8 percent of GNP on average in 1984; this represented over 17 percent of the government's current revenue (Fry 1997b).

In 1969, inflation averaged 5.9 percent in developing countries compared with 4.9 percent in the industrial countries.[47] With the gap widening after 1974, developing country inflation reached 30 percent in 1982 compared with 7.6 percent in the industrial countries. By 1990, the average inflation rate in developing countries had reached 98.6 percent compared with 5 percent in the industrial countries.[48] Evidently, the inflation tax rate has increased rapidly in the developing countries over the past two decades.

Third, banking systems in developing countries face high-required reserve ratios. High inflation tends to be accompanied by high-required reserve ratios. Data from *International Financial Statistics CD-ROM* (September 1993) show that, over the period 1978 to 1987, the ratio of bank reserves (reserve money minus currency in circulation) to bank deposits (including saving and time deposits) averaged 21.2 percent in ninety-one developing countries compared with 7.1 in nineteen industrial countries. In other words, the ratio of reserves to deposits was three times higher in developing countries than in industrial countries. Comparing the ratio of the central government's domestic credit to aggregate domestic credit tells a similar story. The proportion of domestic credit expropriated by central governments averaged 52.6 percent in these ninety-one developing countries compared with 18.1 percent in the nineteen industrial countries.

In contrast to the textbook discussion of higher required reserve ratios as a monetary policy instrument to restrict monetary growth, a cross-country comparison indicates that monetary growth or inflation and the ratio of bank reserves to deposits are positively correlated. There is also a significantly

---

[47] These figures represent geometric means for 113 LDCs and twenty-three industrial countries.

[48] *International Financial Statistics Yearbook* 1992, p.105.

positive relationship between the period-average inflation rate and the reserve ratio in these 111 countries (ninety-one developing and nineteen industrial countries).[49] Evidently countries using the inflation tax tend to combine higher tax rates with a larger tax base in the form of higher required reserve ratios.

Fourth, until recently financial systems in developing countries were subject to administrative controls over interest rates, such as ceilings on deposit and loan rates of interest. Reluctance to rely on market determination of interest rates is still widespread even where administrative controls have been removed. The extraction of the inflation tax from the banking system through high reserve requirements is a form of financial repression. However, the term *financial repression* more commonly refers to interest-rate ceilings. Financial repression can also be analyzed as a tax and hence as another source of government revenue. The tax is imposed directly on depositors when deposit-rate ceilings are set by government fiat. In the absence of deposit-rate ceilings, the financial repression tax may still be borne by depositors to the extent that banks are required to use their own resources to acquire nonreserve assets that yield net returns below the world market interest rate. The tax is also imposed on any other private sector agents that are obliged to hold such assets, for example, as a precondition for bidding on government contracts.

Giovannini and De Melo (1993) estimate the tax revenue from financial repression in the form of private sector holdings of government bonds at yields below the world market rate. They calculate average tax revenue from financial repression equal to 1.8 percent of GDP for twenty-two developing countries over various periods spanning 1972 to 1987. Giovannini and De Melo (1993) state that "the revenue from financial repression is, at least for half of the countries in the sample, of approximately the same size as the revenue from seigniorage."

The term *seigniorage* applied originally to the mint's charges for coinage. Subsequently it meant the difference between the face value and the intrinsic value of a monopoly-supplied money. Under a paper standard, seigniorage virtually equals the face value of the note issue. Seigniorage revenue, therefore, accrues from increasing the note issue or the issue of reserve money. Hence, Giovannini and de Melo measure seigniorage revenue as the change in reserve money divided by GDP.

Revenue from the inflation tax will be lower than revenue from seigniorage in a growing economy because economic growth enables the central bank to issue some more reserve money without causing inflation. The inflation tax starts when the central bank issues so much more reserve

---

[49]   Similar correlations are presented by Brock (1989) and Agénor and Montiel (1996).

money that the general price level starts to rise. For sixteen of the countries in the Giovannini-de Melo sample for which I collected inflation tax data (Fry, 1997b), the average tax revenue from financial repression of 1.9 percent of GDP can be compared with average tax revenue from the inflation tax of 2 percent of GNP.[50]

In broad terms, therefore, it appears that financial repression is as important a source of government revenue in developing countries as the inflation tax. The effect of financial repression on saving, investment, and growth is a major point of disagreement between current theories of the role of financial systems in the process of economic development. The effect of the required reserve ratio on saving, investment and growth is another of the main points of disagreement between these theories (Fry, 1995).

Typically, financial systems in developing countries also differ from those in industrial countries in terms of their small size, lack of competition, absence of debt instruments, and presence of capital controls. Small size, capital controls, and absence of debt instruments all combine to protect banks from competition. To the extent that governments tax banks in one way or another, they are not necessarily keen to promote competition that might kill or seriously reduce the profitability of their golden geese.

4.2.2.   Theoretical models

In their analysis of financially repressed developing economies, Ronald McKinnon (1973) and Edward Shaw (1973) argue that financial repression—indiscriminate "distortions of financial prices including interest rates and foreign exchange rates"—reduces "the real rate of growth and the real size of the financial system relative to nonfinancial magnitudes. In all cases this strategy has stopped or gravely retarded the development process" (Shaw, 1973). The essential common elements of the McKinnon-Shaw model are (1) a saving function that responds positively to both the real rate of interest on deposits and the real rate of growth in output, (2) an investment function that responds negatively to the effective real loan rate of interest and positively to the growth rate, (3) an administratively fixed nominal interest rate that holds the real rate below its equilibrium level (McKinnon, 1973; Shaw, 1973), and (4) inefficient nonprice rationing of loanable funds.

Interest-rate ceilings distort the economy in four ways. First, low interest rates produce a bias in favor of current consumption and against future consumption. Therefore, they may reduce saving below the socially optimum level. Second, potential lenders may engage in relatively low-

---

[50]   Observation periods and denominators differ, so figures are not strictly comparable.

yielding direct investment instead of lending by way of depositing money in a bank. Third, bank borrowers able to obtain all the funds they want at low loan rates will choose relatively capital-intensive projects. Fourth, banks do not allocate credit according to expected productivity of the investment projects in the McKinnon-Shaw model. Their decisions may be influenced by quality of collateral, political pressures, "name" loan size, and covert benefits to loans officers. Even if credit allocation is random, the average efficiency of investment is reduced as the loan rate ceiling is lowered because investments with lower returns now become profitable. Entrepreneurs who were previously deterred from requesting bank loans enter the market. Hence, adverse selection from the perspective of social welfare occurs when interest rates are set too low and so produce *disequilibrium* credit rationing of the type described here.[51]

Figure 4.2 illustrates the inefficiencies created through interest rates that are administratively set below their competitive free-market equilibrium level. Here the demand for credit is equated with investment *I* and the supply of credit is equated with saving *S*. Although saving *S* is depicted as a positive function of the real rate of interest, the interest-elasticity of saving in most countries tends to be small. The line *FF* represents financial repression, taken here to consist of an administratively fixed nominal interest rate that holds the real rate r below its equilibrium level. Actual investment is limited to I_0, the amount of saving forthcoming at the real interest rate r_0.

Suppose that banks' selection process for loan applicants is random. In such case, some investment projects that are financed will have yields below the threshold that would be self-imposed at market-clearing interest rates. The investments that are financed under such conditions are illustrated by the dots in Figure 2. When loan rates in real terms are negative, entrepreneurs who were previously deterred from requesting bank loans now enter the market. Hence, adverse selection in terms of social welfare occurs when interest rates are set too low and so produce disequilibrium credit rationing of the type described here.

Raising the interest rate ceiling from *FF* to *F'F'* (from r_0 to r_1) in Figure 2 increases saving and investment. Changes in the real interest rate trace out the saving function in this disequilibrium situation. Raising the interest rate ceiling also deters entrepreneurs from undertaking all those low-yielding

---

[51] As discussed in Section 2.5 below, adverse selection also occurs when interest rates rise too high because *equilibrium* credit rationing is not working properly. Christophe Chamley and Patrick Honohan (1993) pinpoint another drawback of loan-rate ceilings in that they tend to deter bank spending on loan assessments. Since even in an unrepressed situation banks are likely to underspend on screening, this additional deterrence may be worse for social welfare than another form of repression that affects the financial system at a margin that is initially undistorted.

investments illustrated by the dots below *F'F'*. They are no longer profitable at the higher interest rate r_1. Hence the average return to or efficiency of aggregate investment increases.

In this process, the rate of economic growth rises. Thus the real rate of interest as the return to savers is the key to a higher level of investment and as a rationing device to greater investment efficiency. The increased quantity and quality of investment interact in their positive effects on the rate of economic growth. Growth in the financially repressed economy is constrained by saving; investment opportunities abound here (McKinnon, 1973; Shaw, 1973). The policy prescription for the financially repressed economy examined by McKinnon and Shaw is to raise institutional interest rates or to reduce the rate of inflation. Abolishing interest rate ceilings altogether produces the optimal result of maximizing investment and raising still further investment's average efficiency.

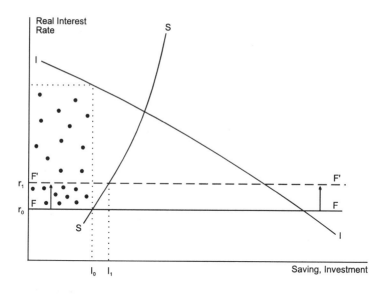

Figure 4.2. Saving and investment under interest rate ceilings

Over the past decade, a second generation of financial growth models incorporating both endogenous growth and endogenous financial institutions has emerged. Typically, financial intermediation is now modeled explicitly rather than taken for granted or treated in simple deterministic terms, as it is in the first-generation financial repression models. Various techniques, such as externalities and quality ladders, are used to model endogenous growth. However, the precise cause of endogenous growth does not affect the role of finance. So it is possible to select alternative financial models for use with alternative endogenous or even non-endogenous growth models.

Finance and financial institutions become relevant in a world of positive information, transaction, and monitoring costs. If monitoring costs are high, a simple debt instrument may dominate a more complicated state-contingent contract that resembles equity. By ignoring all contingencies, however, debt can lead to insolvency, a situation in which the borrower's net worth is no longer positive. The lender may reduce default risk by considering a potential borrower's balance sheet and taking collateral, rationing the borrower by providing less than requested or restricting the maturity of the loan.

One way of showing how financial intermediaries can offer higher expected returns is to construct a model in which individuals can choose between unproductive assets (consumer goods or commodity money) and an investment in a firm (Diamond and Dybvig, 1983). The investment in a firm is illiquid because it takes time to become productive. However, the expected return from a two-period investment in a firm is greater than the return from an inventory of consumer goods or currency. Uncertainty may force some individuals to liquidate or abandon their investments in firms after only one period. In such case, they would be worse off than had they held solely an inventory of consumer goods or currency (Bencivenga and Smith, 1991, 1992; Greenwood and Smith, 1997; Levine, 1993, 1997). Individuals may also be deterred from investing in a firm by productivity risk; some firms do better than others (King and Levine, 1993b).

Without banks, individuals must allocate their portfolios between capital and currency to maximize expected utility. Although they know the probability of the event, which could make a productive investment worthless, their choice will also be affected by their degree of risk aversion. Those with greater risk aversion will choose a higher proportion of currency than those with less risk aversion. Any productive investment bears some risk of becoming worthless.

Bencivenga and Smith (1991, 1992), Greenwood and Smith (1997), and Levine (1993) embed the Diamond-Dybvig financial intermediation model in an overlapping-generations model with production and capital accumulation. With the introduction of banks, individuals can hold deposits that banks then invest in currency and capital. By exploiting the law of large numbers, banks ensure that they never have to liquidate capital prematurely. Banks also rely on the law of large numbers to estimate deposit withdrawals that are unpredictable individually but predictable for the economy as a whole. Hence, banks avoid the uncertainty, which leads to resource misallocation by individuals. By ensuring that capital is never wasted, financial intermediation may produce higher capital per labor ratios and higher rates of economic growth. By engaging in maturity intermediation, financial institutions offer liquidity to savers and, at the same time, longer-term funds to investors. In so doing, they stimulate productive investment by persuading savers to switch from unproductive investment in tangible assets to productive investment in firms.

Those who do not use the Diamond-Dybvig model of financial intermediation posit other ways in which banks can stimulate endogenous growth. For example, Greenwood and Jovanovic (1990) stress the role of financial intermediaries in pooling funds and acquiring information that enables them to allocate capital to its highest valued use, so raising the average return to capital. Specifically, Greenwood and Jovanovic allow capital to be invested in safe, low-yielding investments or risky, high-yielding investments. Risk is created by both aggregate and project-specific shocks. Individuals cannot differentiate between the two types of shock.

With large portfolio holdings, however, financial intermediaries can experiment with a small sample of high-yielding projects to determine the state of the world. With this expenditure on the collection and analysis of information, financial intermediaries determine their investment strategies in the knowledge of the current-period aggregate shock. Were a negative shock to make the high-risk investments less profitable than the low-risk investments, financial intermediaries would invest only in the low-risk projects. Provided the costs of information collection and analysis are sufficiently small, the ability to choose the appropriate set of projects in the knowledge of a given aggregate shock raises the expected return on the intermediaries' portfolios above that of individuals who must choose one or the other technology without any information about the aggregate shock.

King and Levine (1993b) suggest that financial institutions play a key role in evaluating prospective entrepreneurs and financing the most promising ones: "Better financial systems improve the probability of successful innovation and thereby accelerate economic growth" (King and Levine, 1993b). Following Schumpeter (1912), they stress that "financial institutions play an active role in evaluating, managing, and funding the entrepreneurial activity that leads to *productivity growth*. Indeed, we believe that our mechanism is the channel by which finance must have its dominant effect, due to the central role of productivity growth in development'' (King and Levine, 1993b).

The main feature of endogenous growth models is that a broadly defined concept of the economy's capital stock does not suffer from diminishing returns; hence growth is a positive function of the investment ratio. For any endogenous growth model, growth rate comparisons can be made between economies with and without banks. "Relative to the situation in the absence of banks (financial autarky), banks reduce liquid reserve holdings by the economy as a whole, and also reduce the liquidation of productive capital. Then, with an externality in production . . . higher equilibrium growth rates will be observed in economies with an active intermediary sector" (Bencivenga and Smith, 1991, p. 196).

Endogenous growth in all these models magnifies and prolongs the effects of financial conditions. In all cases, financial repression in the form of discriminatory taxes on financial intermediation reduces the growth rate. Financial sector taxes are equivalent to taxes on innovative activity, since they reduce the net returns that financial intermediaries gain from financing successful entrepreneurs. Whereas financial development improves overall productivity, discriminatory taxation of commercial banks, investment banks, mutual funds and stock markets through high reserve requirements, interest and credit ceilings, directed credit programs, and inflation reduces the growth rate by impeding financial development. More generally, "financial repression . . . reduces the services provided by the financial system to savers, entrepreneurs, and producers; it thereby impedes innovative activity and slows economic growth" (King and Levine, 1993b). Indeed, the existence of externalities implies that welfare may be improved through some public subsidy of financial intermediation.

4.2.3. Controversy

Stiglitz (1994) has criticized financial liberalization on the grounds that financial markets are prone to market failures. He suggests that "there exist forms of government intervention that will not only make these markets function better but will also improve the performance of the economy" (Stiglitz, 1994, p. 20). Specifically, he advocates government intervention to keep interest rates below their market-equilibrium levels.

An essential function of financial markets is collecting, processing and conveying information for allocating funds and monitoring their use. Costly information creates market failures. One market failure arising from costly information occurs because monitoring is a public good. If one individual conducts research to determine the solvency of a financial institution and then acts on that information, others can benefit from copying his actions. Because information about the management and solvency of financial institutions is a public good, there is suboptimal expenditure on monitoring them. When financial institutions know that they are not adequately monitored by depositors, they have incentives to take greater risks with their deposits.

Costly information can also produce externalities. For example, when several banks fail, depositors may assume that there is an increased probability that other banks will fail. Their reaction in the form of deposit withdrawal may produce the predicted failures. Externalities can also be transmitted across markets. For example, the provision of a bank loan makes it easier for a firm to raise equity capital. The bank loan provides a signal that the firm is sound, and prospective equity participants can also expect the bank to monitor the firm in which they will be investing. Naturally, financial institutions are rarely concerned about these external effects. Hence, private interest can diverge from public interest.

Given information imperfections, Stiglitz (1994) argues that financial repression can improve the efficiency with which capital is allocated. First, lowering interest rates improves the average quality of the pool of loan applicants. Second, financial repression increases firm equity because it lowers the cost of capital. Third, financial repression could be used in conjunction with an alternative allocative mechanism such as export performance to accelerate economic growth. Fourth, directed credit programs can encourage lending to sectors with high technological spillovers.

The importance of information imperfections and the role of government intervention in the area of prudential regulation and supervision can be accepted without accepting Stiglitz's case for financial repression. First, lowering interest rates does not necessarily increase the average efficiency of investment because lower interest rates can encourage entrepreneurs with lower-yielding projects to bid for funds (Fry, 1995). Second, financial repression may not lower the *marginal* cost of capital if rationing forces borrowers into the curb market. Third, using past performance as a criterion for allocating credit discriminates against new entrants and perpetuates monopoly power. Finally, directed credit programs have invariably raised delinquency and default rates, so increasing the fragility of the financial system by forcing financial institutions to increase their risk exposure with no compensating return.

The overwhelming problem in implementing financial repression as advocated by Stiglitz is that there is such a small range of real interest rates over which financial repression could be appropriate, if it is appropriate at all. Stiglitz claims that it should not reduce real deposit rates below zero. As an upper bound, real loan rates over 10 percent are likely to indicate distress borrowing and pathological behavior by banks. With bank operating-cost ratios in developing countries typically at least twice the level of operating-cost ratios in the OECD countries (Fry, 1995), this implies, if banks are to remain solvent, a maximum real deposit rate of only 4 to 5 percent.

Real deposit rates in eighty-five developing countries for which any data exist ranged from -458 to +234 percent over the period 1971 to 1995.[52] The

[52] For symmetry, I use continuously compounded rates throughout this chapter.

standard deviation of these 1329 annual observations is 32 percent. Hence, discussion over the desirability of manipulating real interest rates by one or two percentage points is akin to the debate over the number of angels that can stand on a pinhead. Establishing and maintaining an environment under which real deposit rates are likely to fall in the 0 to 5 percent range is as much as one can realistically hope to achieve.

Stiglitz has amazing faith in government. The government in his papers is exemplary: disciplined, knowledgeable, long-sighted, objective. It pursues economic objectives without deviating into the many side alleys of patronage and sleaze. My main doubt about actual governments pursuing his policy is that, once they have an intellectual justification for intervention, they will use it for purposes that would horrify him. I agree entirely with Philip Arestis and Panicos Demetriades (1997, p. 796): "Market failure does not necessarily imply government success."

Korea is often cited as an example of a country that has prospered without full-blown financial liberalization. Any economist who has visited Korea and a sizeable sample of other developing countries over the past twenty-five years must concede that economic policy making in Korea approximates Stiglitz's idealized world. Unfortunately, one also has to agree that there are extremely few other developing countries for which the same claim could be upheld. Indeed, the Korean government is particularly noteworthy in both its veracious appetite for economic knowledge and its ability to admit mistakes, such as its encouragement of heavy petro-chemical industries in the late 1970s. Similar flexibility is apparent in the Korean government's reaction to the speculative attack on the Korean won in 1997.

4.2.4.   Qualifications

One concern with the general thrust of the theoretical developments that identify ways in which improved domestic finance may accelerate economic growth lies in the fact that they ignore systemic risk. In the real world, increased financial system fragility seems to accompany the global trend toward market-based financial structures. The convergence hypothesis argues that state-based and bank-based financial systems are becoming increasingly uncompetitive in the global environment (Pérez, 1997; Vitols, 1997). The new financial institution is a lightly regulated financial supermarket offering a range of financial products to a mobile pool of consumers seeking short-term relationships on the basis of price competition.

While the market-based financial structure may dominate international finance at the end of the twentieth century, it tends to substitute efficiency for stability and short-term profit for long-term relationships aimed at

sustained productivity gains. Globalization introduces new problems for
national financial regulators in terms of surges in international capital flows
that can be (and have been in several countries) highly destabilizing. In the
belief that financial structures may well be converging on the market-based
model, I focus here on aspects of the liberalization and globalization process
that are now confronting Pacific Asian countries and may well confront
other developing countries over the next decade as they introduce further
domestic and international financial liberalization.

One caveat concerns reluctant liberalizers and consequent gaps in
financial structure. While macroeconomists may be convinced of the
efficacy of financial liberalization and related economic reforms directed at
producing a more market-based economy, central bankers, ministers of
finance and civil servants may have reservations, which are typically
expressed with vigor at the first signs of trouble. The reluctance to let go and
to rely on market forces is pervasive. But, for example, maintaining the old
system of ratio controls on bank balance sheets as a safeguard or fallback
should things go wrong with the indirect market-based approach to
implementing monetary policy itself retards or thwarts the market-
development process. Hence, one cynical question when confronted with a
liberalization program is: Have these leopards really changed their spots?

Vested interests created under controlled market conditions are bound to
oppose reform. Financial restriction involves protecting the commercial
banks from which government can expropriate significant seigniorage and
discouraging direct markets. Not too surprisingly, when the government
develops direct markets not only for its own debt but for private debt as well,
commercial banks face a competitive threat. Nonbank investors can be
intimidated to some extent from participating in direct markets by fear of
reprisals in some form or another from their banks.

Evidence suggests, however, that financial stability is enhanced by the
existence of a broad variety of financial markets and financial institutions.
As Knight (1998, p. 16) points outs:

> Each financial market—as well as the legal and regulatory framework
> that supports markets—performs a different role that can contribute
> toward achieving a robust financial system. If a key market, law, or
> regulatory practice does not function efficiently, or is missing altogether,
> the robustness of the system is adversely affected . . . most emerging
> market economies have significant "gaps" in the structure of their
> financial systems. . . . the presence or absence of a given non-bank
> financial intermediary or market, the extent to which it offers close
> substitutes for bank liabilities and assets, and the degree to which it
> functions efficiently can affect the soundness of the banking sector. In

this sense, gaps in markets can have a large impact on the robustness of a country's financial system—that is, on the financial system's ability to return to a stable equilibrium following a major shock.

This suggests that financial liberalization could be accompanied to advantage by some explicit efforts to develop financial markets. Again, Knight (1998, p. 16) suggests that

> Just as banks exercise market discipline over borrowing firms by assessing credit risks with a different information set from the firms themselves, so other markets and institutions—if properly regulated and supported by an adequate legal and regulatory framework—can operate to reinforce the soundness of the banking sector.

In many developing countries, establishing voluntary domestic markets for government debt may be particularly efficacious (Fry, 1997a). Markets for government debt provide the central bank with the opportunity to adopt indirect market-based techniques for implementing monetary policy. Abandoning direct controls in favor of indirect market-based techniques can be expected to improve efficiency: all agents face the same market constraint in the form of the market interest rate in their lending and borrowing decisions. According to Knight (1998, p. 16),

> Moreover, by providing a vehicle for collateralizing central bank credit, a government securities market furnishes the means by which the central bank can provide temporary liquidity support without exposing itself to moral hazard problems. Repurchase agreements based on government securities can also be used to develop a collateralized interbank market, yielding additional gains in bank soundness and liquidity.

4.2.5.   Prerequisites

Several interest-rate liberalization experiments have failed to produce the results outlined in the theoretical section above. The basic problem lies in the perverse reaction to higher interest rates by insolvent (or nonprofit-motivated) economic agents—governments, firms, or individuals. By definition, an insolvent agent (one whose liabilities exceed its assets) or "distress borrower" is unable to repay its loans. Hence, it is not deterred from borrowing by a higher cost. It simply continues, if it can, to borrow whatever it needs to finance its losses. These inevitably increase with an increase in the interest rate, which drives up the agent's cost of servicing its loans. Hence such agents exhibit loan-demand functions that respond positively to the interest rate.

Pathologically high positive real interest rates, possibly triggered by fiscal instability, indicate a poorly functioning financial system. Inadequate prudential supervision and regulation enable distress borrowing to crowd out borrowing for investment purposes by solvent firms and so produce an epidemic effect (Fry, 1995; McKinnon, 1993; Rojas-Suárez and Weisbrod, 1995; Stiglitz and Weiss, 1981). Funds continue to be supplied because of explicit or implicit deposit insurance. The end result is financial and economic paralysis.

The international experience over the past twenty years indicates that there are five prerequisites for successful financial liberalization (Fry, 1995):

- Adequate prudential regulation and supervision of commercial banks, implying some minimal levels of accounting and legal infrastructure,

- A reasonable degree of price stability,

- Fiscal discipline taking the form of a sustainable government borrowing requirement that avoids inflationary expansion of reserve money by the central bank either through direct domestic borrowing by the government or through the indirect effect of government borrowing that produces surges of capital inflows requiring large purchases of foreign exchange by the central bank to prevent exchange rate appreciation,

- Profit-maximizing, competitive behavior by the commercial banks,

- A tax system that does not impose discriminatory explicit or implicit taxes on financial intermediation.

Levine (1998) also demonstrates the importance of the legal rights of creditors and contract enforcement.

4.2.6.   Empirical evidence

One way governments finance expenditures in excess of tax revenue is to force private-sector agents to buy government securities at below-market yields. Contractors may be required to hold government bonds as security when bidding for government contracts. Insurance companies and pension funds are often obliged to hold larger proportions of assets in the form of government securities than they would choose voluntarily to hold. But the largest captive buyers of government securities are commercial banks. By setting high liquid asset ratios and ensuring that government securities are the only eligible assets that satisfy this requirement, governments can borrow substantial amounts at below-market rates of interest. A second way of financing government deficits is to set high reserve requirements. In this way, the government can borrow indirectly from the banking system at a zero rate of interest. Finally, governments may set ceilings on institutional interest rates to limit competition from the private sector for loanable funds.

How damaging are these forms of financial repression in terms of higher inflation, lower saving, and lower economic growth? According to economists of almost all persuasions, financial conditions may affect the rate of economic growth in both the short and medium runs. James Tobin's (1965) monetary growth model posits a negative impact of a higher real return on money holdings in the medium run but has nothing to say about the short run. The McKinnon-Shaw school expects financial liberalization (institutional interest rates rising toward their competitive free-market equilibrium levels) to exert a positive effect on the rate of economic growth in both the short and medium runs. The neostructuralists predict a stagflationary (accelerating inflation and lower growth) outcome from financial liberalization in the short run. In the medium run, there is the possibility that the saving ratio will increase by enough to outweigh the negative influence of portfolio adjustments. In practice, neostructuralists, with the possible exception of Buffie (1984), view a dominant saving effect as unlikely.

A simple way of discriminating between the McKinnon-Shaw school and others would be to examine episodes of financial liberalization and see whether these were accompanied by higher or lower rates of economic growth. In practice, however, most clear-cut cases of financial liberalization were accompanied by other economic reforms (such as fiscal, international trade, and foreign exchange reforms). In such cases, it is virtually impossible to isolate the effects of financial components of the reform package. This is unfortunate, since causality can be inferred when financial conditions have been deliberately and substantially changed, as in the case of a discrete financial liberalization. Examining the association between financial conditions and economic growth over time provides in itself no evidence of causality. With this caveat, I now examine the empirical evidence on the association between financial conditions and rates of economic growth.

In one of the earlier studies of the effect of financial repression, Lanyi and Saraco lu (1983) implicitly address the causality issue by dividing twenty-one developing countries into three groups. Lanyi and Saraco lu give a value of 1 to countries with positive real interest rates, 0 to countries with moderately but "not punitively negative" real interest rates, and -1 to countries with severely negative real interest rates. Given the fact that deposit rates were fixed by administrative fiat in all the countries posting negative deposit rates, one can argue that these rates are exogenous to the growth process. The cross-section regression reported by Lanyi and

Saraco lu (1983) indicates a positive and significant relationship between the average rates of growth in real gross domestic product (GDP) and the interest rate dummy variable for the period 1971 to 1980.

The World Bank (1989) uses the same methodology as Lanyi and Saraco lu for a sample of thirty-four developing countries. Table 4.2 shows that economic growth in countries with strongly negative real deposit rates (lower than -10 percent on average over the period 1974 to 1985) was substantially lower than growth in countries with positive real interest rates. Although the investment ratio was only 17 percent higher in the countries with positive real interest rates, the average productivity of investment, as measured by the incremental output per capital ratio, was almost four times higher. As confirmed by others, financial repression exerts its main impact on the quality rather than the quantity of investment. It has very little, if any, *direct* effect on saving. Second, the World Bank also reports a regression showing a positive and significant cross-section relationship between average growth and average real interest rates over the period 1965 to 1985.[53]

Table 4.2. Growth and interest rate policies in 34 developing countries, 1974 to 1985

	Positive real interest rates	Moderately negative real interest rates	Strongly negative real interest rates
Real interest rate	3.0	-2.4	-13.0
GDP growth rate	5.6	3.8	1.9
Investment per GDP	26.9	23.2	23.0
Change in GDP per investment	22.7	17.3	6.2

Source: World Bank (1989, p. 31)

Several other studies present pooled time-series regression estimates showing positive and significant relationships between the rate of economic growth and the real deposit rate of interest. The empirical results reported in Fry (1978, 1979, 1980, 1981) suggest that on average a one percentage point increase in the real deposit rate of interest toward its competitive free-market equilibrium level is associated with a rise in the rate of economic growth of about half of a percentage point in Asia, that is, the coefficient of the real deposit rate of interest averages 0.5. The World Bank (1989) estimates a coefficient of 0.2, Alan Gelb (1989) estimates coefficients of 0.2 to 0.26 for his sample of thirty-four countries, while Jacques Polak (1989) estimates coefficients of 0.18 to 0.27 when regressing the average annual rate of growth in real GDP on the median real interest rate for forty developing

---

[53]   In this regression, two observations, one for 1965 to 1973 and the other for 1974 to 1985, are included for each country, as well as a dummy variable for the 1974 to 1985 period.

countries. For fifty-three countries over the period 1960 to 1985, Roubini and Sala-i-Martin (1992) also find that countries with real interest rates less than -5 percent in the 1970s experienced growth rates that averaged 1.4 percentage points less than growth rates in countries with positive real interest rates. If the difference is approximately 10 percentage points, the implied interest-rate coefficient is 0.14.[54] The global evidence suggests that Asian developing countries may be more sensitive to real interest-rate changes than other groups of developing countries.

Recent empirical work has tended to resort to far larger data sets than were used in studies before 1990. For example, Ghani (1992) estimates growth equations for a sample of fifty developing countries following an approach used by Barro (1991). The initial levels of human capital (as measured by years of schooling) and financial development (as measured by the ratio of total assets of the financial system to GDP or the ratio of private sector credit to GDP) in 1965 yield significantly positive coefficients, while the initial level of per capita real GDP produces a negative coefficient in an equation explaining average growth rates over the period 1965 to 1989 (Ghani, 1992). De Gregorio and Guidotti (1995) produce similar results for middle- and low-income countries using Barro's data set.

King and Levine (1993a, 1993b, 1993c) examine links between finance and growth in a cross-section of seventy-seven developing countries over the period 1960 to 1989. They construct four financial indicators: (1) liquid liabilities divided by GDP (usually *M2* divided by GDP),[55] (2) domestic assets in deposit money banks divided by domestic assets of both deposit money banks and the central bank, (3) domestic credit to the private sector divided by aggregate domestic credit, and (4) domestic credit to the private sector divided by GDP. King and Levine also construct four growth indicators: (1) average rate of growth in per capita real GDP, (2) average rate of growth in the capital stock, (3) the residual between (1) and 0.3 of (2) as a proxy for productivity improvements, and (4) gross domestic investment divided by GDP.

King and Levine (1993a, 1993b) show that each financial indicator is positively and significantly correlated with each growth indicator at the 99 percent confidence level. The same positive relationship is illustrated by dividing the seventy-seven countries into four groups with respect to the growth indicators; countries are divided into those with average per capita income growth above 3 percent, greater than 2 but less than 3, greater than 0.5 but less than 2, and less than 0.5 percent. There are about twenty

---

[54] See also Asian Development Bank (1985), Easterly (1993), and Fry (1991).
[55] To obtain mid-year estimates, beginning-of-year and end-of-year values of all financial variables are averaged.

countries in each group. In each case, the average value of the financial indicator declines with a move from a higher to a lower growth group. Multivariate analysis produces much the same picture (King and Levine, 1993c, Levine, 1997). Extending this work, Levine and Zervos (1998) find that stock market liquidity as well as banking development predict, positively and significantly, capital accumulation, productivity improvements, and accelerated economic growth.

De Gregorio and Guidotti (1995) claim that real interest rates are not a good indicator of financial repression or distortion. They suggest that the relationship between real interest rates and economic growth might resemble an inverted U-curve: "Very low (and negative) real interest rates tend to cause financial disintermediation and hence tend to reduce growth, as implied by the McKinnon-Shaw hypothesis . . . On the other hand, very high real interest rates that do not reflect improved efficiency of investment, but rather a lack of credibility of economic policy or various forms of country risk, are likely to result in a lower level of investment as well as a concentration in excessively risky projects."[56]

In fact, the point made by De Gregorio and Guidotti holds up well with data from eighty-five developing countries for the period 1971 to 1995.[57] First I estimated the relationship between the annual rate of economic growth YG and the real rate of interest RR in equations of the basic form $YG = \beta_0 + \beta_1(RR + \beta_2)\cdot(RR + \beta_2)$. Since the parameter β_2 was not significantly different from zero, although its negative value implies that growth is maximized at some positive real interest rate, I dropped it from the estimate reported here. A pooled time-series fixed-effect estimate including both the squared real interest rate and the absolute value of the cubed real interest rate gave the following result (1.296 observations):

$$YG = \underset{(-3.949)}{-0.033}\,RR^2 + \underset{(-3.598)}{0.008}\left|RR\right|^3 \tag{4.2}$$

$$\overline{R}^2 = 0.163$$

No intercept is reported because the fixed-effect model estimates separate constants for each country; this equation estimates eighty-five intercepts. The effect of a rising real interest rate on growth produced by equation (4.1) is illustrated in Figure 4.3. Evidently, growth is maximized when the real

---

[56]   This criticism is based on work by Calvo and Coricelli (1992).

[57]   Not all countries report data for the entire period. For the interest rate series, I use the geometric average of commercial bank deposit and loan rates, since these are the most prevalent interest rate data reported in the March *1996 International Financial Statistics CD-ROM*. The continuously compounded inflation rate is then subtracted from the continuously compounded nominal interest rate.

interest rate lies within the normal or nonpathological range of, say, -5 percent to +15 percent.

As noted earlier, government expropriation of domestic credit through the imposition of liquid asset ratios and reserve requirements represent two forms of financial repression. Elsewhere, I report significant negative relationships between economic growth, on the one hand, and both the proportion of domestic credit expropriated by government and the reserve/deposit, ratio on the other hand, for a sample of eighty-five developing countries over the period 1970 to 1995 (Fry, 1997a). My interpretation of these negative relationships is that the more the government takes from the financial system at below-market rates, the lower will be the return to depositors and so the less willing will the public be to hold deposits.[58] This produces a doubly destructive effect on the ability of the banking system to lend for productive investment. First, its resource base in the form of deposits is reduced. Second, the government takes a larger share of the smaller pie. Most important, the average quality of investment is impaired; this lowers growth, which, in turn, reduces saving.

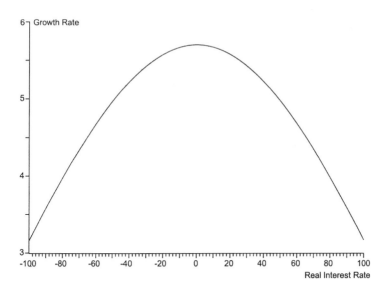

Figure 4.3. Annual growth and real interest rates, 1971 to 1995

In fact, financial repression is usually even more damaging than this. Captive buyers receive below-market returns on their forced holdings of government debt. Typically, such a method of financing the government

---

[58] Saving is then channeled into other repositories, such foreign bank accounts and traditional small-scale investments, that may yield relatively low returns.

deficit is accompanied by a range of financially repressive measures that include interest-rate ceilings on bank deposits, bank loans, and various other financial claims. When interest rates are fixed under conditions of high inflation, the concomitant negative real interest rates produce growth-inhibiting effects that have been described earlier in this chapter and are examined in detail elsewhere (Fry, 1995).

Finally in this section, I extend the empirical work on financial repression by estimating a simultaneous-equation system in which saving and investment ratios as well as export and output growth rates are affected by financial conditions. I also examine the effects of the excessively high real interest rates that have been experienced after several financial liberalization experiments. These distorted financial conditions appear to be just as debilitating as financial repression. Following Shaw (1973), I use both the real deposit rate of interest *RR* and the black-market exchange-rate premium *BLACK* as proxies for financial distortions. Negative real interest rates generally reflect some government-imposed distortion in domestic financial markets (Fry, 1995; Giovannini and De Melo, 1993). Since governments using financial repression as a source of revenue attempt to prevent capital outflows that would erode their tax base, black-market exchange-rate premia also provide an indicator of financial repression.

The De Gregorio-Guidotti effect discussed earlier could also apply to saving behavior. Increased risk and uncertainty leading to very high real interest rates can reduce measured national saving, particularly if the increased domestic risk encourages savers to remove their savings abroad through under- and overinvoicing. Again, I resolve the problem that both very low and very high real interest rates could deter saving not by abandoning real interest rates but rather by using the square of the real deposit rate. This ensures that large positive and negative values exert the same, presumably negative, effect on the saving ratio.[59]

For the empirical work reported here, I use data from a sample of sixteen developing countries—Argentina, Brazil, Chile, Egypt, India, Indonesia, Korea, Malaysia, Mexico, Nigeria, Pakistan, Philippines, Sri Lanka, Thailand, Turkey, and Venezuela—for the period 1970 to 1988.[60] I use iterative three-stage least squares which is, asymptotically, full-information maximum likelihood (Johnston, 1984, pp. 486-492). The estimation technique corrects for heteroscedasticity across country equations and

---

[59] I tested various alternative functional forms for the real interest rate in all the estimates reported here. None produced noticeably better or different results.

[60] The ending date was determined by the availability of black-market exchange rates taken from the World Bank's *World Development Report 1991: Supplementary Data* diskette. All other data come from *International Financial Statistics CD-ROM* and the World Bank's *Socio-economic Time-series Access and Retrieval System: World Tables* diskette.

exploits contemporaneously correlated disturbances. I estimate the sixteen individual country equations for saving, investment, export growth, and output growth as systems of equations with cross-equation equality restrictions on all coefficients except the intercept. Hence, the estimates apply to a representative member of this sample of developing countries.

The equations presented in Table 4.3 are derived from Fry (1998b). The estimates indicate that financial distortions, as measured by the real interest rate squared and the black-market exchange-rate premium, reduce investment ratios, and export growth. In turn, lower investment ratios and export growth reduce output growth rates. Output growth is also reduced directly by financial distortions, possibly through an impact on investment efficiency. Because a major determinant of saving ratios is the output growth rate, saving ratios are influenced substantially, albeit *indirectly*, by financial distortions through their effects on investment ratios, export growth, and output growth.

I now use the four equations in Table 4.3 to examine both the direct short-run and overall long-run effects of financial distortions on saving and output growth by comparing the estimated variations in the saving ratio and output growth rate caused by changes in the financial distortion variables in equations (4.2) and (4.5) with the estimated variations caused by changes in the financial distortion variables in the system of equations consisting of equations (4.3), (4.4), (4.5) and (4.6). The simulated changes in the financial distortion variables are confined to the observed range recorded in this sample.

Table 4.3. A simultaneous-equation system of financial distortions

$$SNY = 0.289\,\hat{Y}G - 0.038BLACK - 0.006RR^2 \tag{4.3}$$
$$(123.359) \qquad (-39.816) \qquad (-3.981)$$

$$-0.198(\hat{Y}G\cdot BLACK) - 0.205(\hat{Y}\,G\cdot RR^2) + 0.812SNY_{t-1}$$
$$(-12.487) \qquad\qquad (-5.696) \qquad\qquad (748.272)$$

$$R^2 = 0.861$$

$$IY = 0.251\hat{Y}G - 1.628RR^2 + 0.692IY_{t-1} \tag{4.4}$$
$$(32.671) \quad (11.661)(43.998)$$

$$R^2 = 0.794$$

$$XKG = 0.364\,\hat{Y}G + 0.179\,\hat{I}Y + 0.496\,SIY - 0.224\hat{BLACK}^2 \tag{4.5}$$
$$(5.797) \qquad (3.756) \qquad (11.941) \qquad (-2.846)$$

$$R^2 = 0.153$$

$$YG = 0.226\,\hat{IKY} - 0.999(\hat{IKY}\cdot BLACK) - 0.354(\hat{IKY}\cdot RR^2) + 0.098\,\hat{XKG} \qquad (4.6)$$
$$\quad\;\;(16.850)\qquad\;\;(-9.786)\qquad\qquad\quad(-11.389)\qquad\quad(19.691)$$

$$R^2 = 0.202$$

Endogenous variables:
SNY   National saving/GNP (current prices)
IY   Domestic investment/GNP (current prices)
SIY   SNY – IY
YG   Rate of growth in GNP (constant prices, continuously compounded)
IKY   Domestic investment/GNP (constant prices)
XKG   Rate of growth in exports (constant prices, continuously compounded)

Exogenous variables:
RR   Real deposit rate of interest (interest minus inflation rate, continuously compounded)
BLACK   Black-market foreign exchange rate premium

Figure 4.4 illustrates both the direct effect from equation (4.3) and the overall effect from the joint simulation of equations (4.3), (4.4), (4.5) and (4.6) of a rising real interest rate on the national saving ratio. The simultaneous-equation model used to estimate the overall effect also contains identities defining the saving-investment gap and the equivalence of the nominal and real investment ratio. Figure 4 is produced using the mean values of all the explanatory variables with the exception of the real deposit rate of interest. The mean value of the real deposit rate for the entire country sample is zero with a standard deviation of 23 percent. Its minimum value is -83 percent and its maximum value 221 percent. Figure 4.4 shows that the relationship between the real interest rate and the national saving ratio resembles an inverted U. Both very low and very high real interest rates reduce national saving mainly through the effects of these interest rates on output growth.

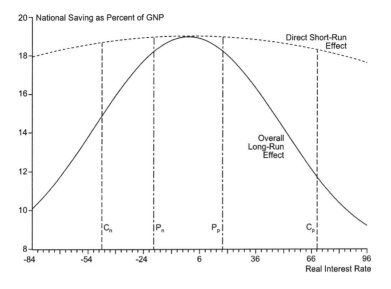

Figure 4.4. Effects of real interest rates on national saving ratios

The line P_n denotes two standard deviations below the mean of all negative interest rates in the five Pacific Asian economies (Indonesia, Korea, Malaysia, the Philippines, and Thailand), C_n denotes two standard deviations below the mean of all negative interest rates in the remaining eleven countries (the control group), P_p denotes two standard deviations above the mean of all zero or positive interest rates in the Pacific Asian economies, while C_p denotes two standard deviations above the mean of all zero or positive interest rates in the control group countries. Evidently, real interest rates deviated from their saving-maximizing level far more in the control group countries than they did in the Pacific Asian economies.

Figure 4.5 illustrates both the direct effect from equation (4.6) and the overall effect from the joint simulation of equations (4.3), (4.4), (4.5) and (4.6) of a rising real interest rate on output growth. This figure captures the multiplicative effects of the lower quantity and quality of investment produced by both very low and very high real interest rates on economic growth. Again, real interest rates deviated from their growth-maximizing level far more in the control group countries than they did in the Pacific Asian economies. In contrast to the considerable differences between direct and overall effects of real interest rates on national saving ratios, Figure 4.5 indicates that the direct effects of real interest rates on growth rates are very similar to their overall effects. The direct and overall simulated effects of black-market exchange rate premia on saving and growth rates are similar.

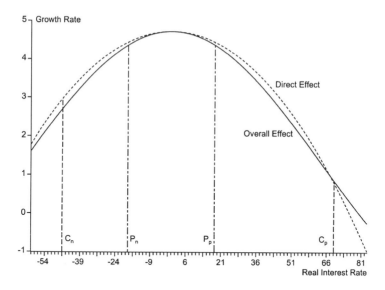

Figure 4.5. Effects of real interest rates on output growth rates

Over the period 1970 to 1988, the national saving ratio in the five Pacific Asian countries averaged 23.8 percent compared with 16.0 percent in the eleven countries of the control group, while the continuously compounded output growth rate in the Pacific Asian countries averaged 6.2 percent compared with 3.9 percent in the control group. Over the same period, the black-market exchange rate premium averaged 6.2 percent in the Pacific Asian countries compared with 42.6 percent in the control group, while the square of the real interest rate was ten times greater in the control group than it was in Pacific Asia.

The overall effects of both financial distortion variables are estimated by simulating the model consisting of equations (4.3), (4.4), (4.5) and (4.6), together with identities defining the saving-investment gap and the equivalence of the nominal and real investment ratio. These simulations indicate that differences in the average values of the financial distortion variables in each country group account for 3.7 of the 7.8 percentage point difference in the national saving ratios between the Pacific Asian and control group countries and for 1.7 of the 2.3 percentage point difference in their output growth rates. In other words, these two financial distortions explain approximately 50 percent of the difference in saving ratios and 75 percent of the difference in output growth rates between these two country groups.

Much of the above-average economic performance of the Pacific Asian developing market economies can be explained by their economic policies that ensured negligible levels of financial distortions, as measured both by the real rate of interest and the black-market exchange rate premium. The macroeconomic policies that prevented seriously distorted financial and foreign exchange markets stimulated investment and export growth. High investment and rapid export growth accelerated output growth. Higher output growth rates and undistorted financial and foreign exchange markets raised both saving and investment ratios. The evidence suggests that conducive financial conditions fostered by government policies played an important role in producing the virtuous circles of high saving, investment, output growth, and export growth found in Pacific Asia.

4.2.7. Summary

The available empirical evidence reviewed here does indicate a positive link between financial and economic development. Financial systems that are stunted and repressed are typically found in stagnant economies with low per capita incomes. Financial repression reduces economic growth. But abandoning financial repression that has been used as a revenue-generating device to finance the government deficit may result in extraordinarily high real interest rates that can be just as damaging. Experience indicates that, to be successful, financial liberalization must be accompanied by fiscal reform aimed at ensuring that government debt will not explode in the aftermath of the liberalization, as well as sound prudential supervision and regulation of the banking system.

In practice, financial repression appears to have yielded government revenue in the order of 2 percent of GDP on average in samples of developing countries (Fry, Goodhart, and Almeida, 1996; Giovannini and De Melo, 1993). If government finances are stable with this revenue from financial repression, the loss of such revenue requires higher revenue from alternative sources or expenditure cuts of a similar magnitude. Unless the government is committed to fiscal reform in conjunction with financial liberalization, financial repression may be lesser of two evils. "Good-bye financial repression, hello financial crash" is the verdict of Díaz-Alejandro (1985) on the Latin American experiments with financial liberalization since the mid-1970s. If government expenditure cannot be reduced or traditional tax revenue increased, abandoning financial repression may lead to an explosion in government debt, economic instability, and lower economic growth.

4.3.   FOREIGN DEBT ACCUMULATION

4.3.1.   Some balance-of-payments accounting

The balance-of-payments accounts show that current account deficits are financed by capital inflows or decreases in official reserves. One way of presenting this identity is (ignoring errors and omissions)

$$CAY + KAY \equiv \Delta RY ,\qquad\qquad\qquad (4.7)$$

where CAY is the current account as a proportion of GNP, KAY is the capital account ratio, and ΔRY is the change in official reserves also expressed as a ratio of GNP. If the change in official reserves is unaffected, an increased capital inflow is matched by a smaller current account surplus or a larger current account deficit.

Capital inflows allow domestic investment to exceed national saving when they finance a current account deficit. Domestic investment equals national saving plus the current account deficit, which is identical to foreign saving, as shown by the national income definition of the balance of payments on current account:

$$IY \equiv SNY + SFY\qquad\qquad\qquad\qquad (4.8)$$

or

$$CAY \equiv SNY - IY\qquad\qquad\qquad\qquad (4.9)$$

where SFY is foreign saving, which equals the current account deficit and so is equal but of opposite sign to CAY the balance of payments on current account, SNY is national saving, and IY is domestic investment, all divided by GNP.[61] Hence, capital inflows that finance the current account deficit can increase investment and the rate of economic growth.

The current account ratio can also be defined as the export ratio XY plus the ratio of net factor income from abroad to GNP $NFIY$ minus the import ratio IMY:

$$CAY \equiv XY + NFIY - IMY .\qquad\qquad (4.10)$$

---

[61]   This definition of the current account ratio is derived from the national income rather than the balance-of-payments accounts. It differs from the balance-of-payments definition by excluding unrequited transfers.

If capital inflows increase capital formation in the host country, the increased investment could involve increased imports of raw materials or capital equipment. Alternatively, it could reduce exports by diverting them into the additional investment. In either case, the current account must deteriorate in equation (4.10) by exactly the same amount as it does in equations (4.7) and (4.9).

4.3.2.   Stabilizing financial effects

The extent and financing of a current account deficit depend both on a country's desire to spend more than its income and on the willingness of the rest of the world to finance the deficit from its saving. In other words, a current account deficit is determined simultaneously by both the demand for and the supply of foreign saving. My saving-investment model of a semi-open developing economy attempts to capture the essential determinants of this interactive process (Fry, 1989, 1993a, 1995).

Based on the assumption that foreign saving takes the form of foreign loans to or guaranteed by the government, my model also permits the ratio of foreign debt to GNP to converge to a constant and hence sustainable steady state. A steady state exists if a higher level of foreign indebtedness improves the current account. If foreign indebtedness reduces investment by more than it reduces saving or raises investment by less than it raises saving, rising foreign indebtedness improves the current account and so slows down the buildup of foreign debt. Hence, the model contains an informal error-correction process. The model also specifies a monetary policy reaction function, since domestic credit expansion usually worsens a current account.

The key components of this open-economy model are represented in Figure 4.6. This figure echoes Metzler (1968) in viewing the current account deficit as the difference between domestic investment and national saving. It shows the planned levels of national saving, foreign saving, and domestic investment at different levels of real interest rates r. The domestic investment function I slopes downwards, indicating that there is more investment at lower interest rates. The national saving function Sn is nearly vertical indicating that changes in the domestic real interest rate have little *direct* effect on national saving.

Most developing countries face an upward-sloping supply curve of foreign saving Sf_0. However, the effective cost at which foreign saving begins to be supplied in any particular year depends on the country's foreign debt position inherited from past borrowing. In this model, the effective cost of foreign borrowing is also the effective domestic real interest rate. At an effective interest rate of r_0, domestic investment I_0 exceeds national saving

*Sn*₀. Hence, the inflow of foreign saving is positive, and the country runs a current account deficit on its balance of payments equal to $I_0 - Sn_0$.

The accumulation of foreign debt resulting from the current account deficit in year 0 raises the foreign saving curve to Sf_1 in the next year. This change produces an effective cost of foreign borrowing of r_1 in year 1. In this case, foreign debt accumulation reduces domestic investment and raises national saving through a higher domestic real interest rate. As this process continues in subsequent years, the current account deficit declines until it

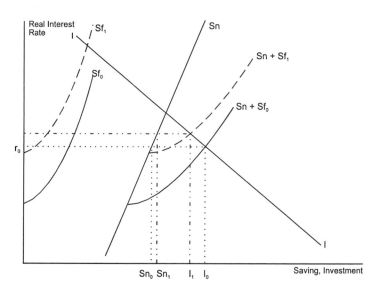

Figure 4.6. Stabilizing financial effect of foreign debt accumulation on saving, investment and the current account deficit

reaches a steady-state equilibrium in which the foreign debt to GNP ratio is constant. This is the stabilizing financial effect of foreign debt accumulation.

4.3.3.   Destabilizing fiscal effects

Much foreign debt in developing countries takes the form of government and government-guaranteed foreign debt. The level of this type of foreign debt accumulated from past current account deficits may itself affect the position of the saving and investment functions in Figure 4.6. Presumably the modern Ricardian equivalence view would hold that if households expect the existence of government-guaranteed foreign loans to necessitate government expenditure and hence higher taxation in the future, private saving would rise as more guarantees were extended. Hence, the Ricardian equivalence hypothesis suggests that more foreign debt could actually raise the national saving ratio, since this *future* contingent government liability does not reduce the *current* level of government saving.

While rising government and government-guaranteed foreign debts could well lead households to anticipate higher future tax burdens for debt service and repayment, they may respond in the alternative way suggested by Ricardo (1817, p. 338).

> A country which has accumulated a large debt is placed in a most artificial situation; and although the amount of taxes, and the increased price of labor, may not, and I believe does not, place it under any other disadvantage with respect to foreign countries, except the unavoidable one of paying those taxes, yet it becomes the interest of every contributor to withdraw his shoulder from the burden, and to shift this payment from himself to another; and the temptation to remove himself and his capital to another country, where he will be exempted from such burdens, becomes at last irresistible, and overcomes the natural reluctance which every man feels to quit the place of his birth, and the scene of his early associations. A country which has involved itself in the difficulties attending this artificial system, would act wisely by ransoming itself from them, at the sacrifice of any portion of its property which might be necessary to redeem its debt.

Here Ricardo is clearly refuting the Ricardian equivalence proposition that the way governments finance their expenditures is immaterial.

Savers could also perceive that a high and rising foreign debt ratio may goad the government into stimulating exports, which would involve a devaluation in the real exchange rate. Indeed, a steady-state equilibrium necessitates a depreciation in the real exchange rate at some stage. In this case, the real returns on assets held abroad could be higher than the real returns on domestic assets.

Most developing countries prohibit capital outflows. Hence, the removal of capital abroad takes place through over-invoicing imports and under-invoicing exports. Typically, an exporter submits an invoice for a smaller sum than that actually received for the exports when surrendering foreign exchange to the central bank; the difference can then be deposited in the exporter's bank account abroad. Conversely, an importer submits an invoice for an amount exceeding the true cost of the imports in order to siphon the difference into his or her foreign bank account.

This method of removing capital from a country reduces measured national saving, even in the unlikely event that the true level of saving remains constant. Hence, one might expect a higher value of government plus government-guaranteed foreign debt to reduce measured national saving, implying a leftward shift in the saving function in Figure 4.6 as illustrated in Figure 4.7. Here, therefore, is an explanation of a *negative* effect of foreign debt on the current account; an increase in foreign debt can worsen the current account. By raising the effective costs of foreign borrowing and shadow domestic real interest rates, higher foreign debt also reduces investment and growth. Lower growth reduces saving, implying another leftward shift in the saving function in Figure 4.7. This is the destabilizing fiscal effect of foreign debt accumulation, which may or may not outweigh the stabilizing financial effect of foreign debt accumulation discussed in the previous section.

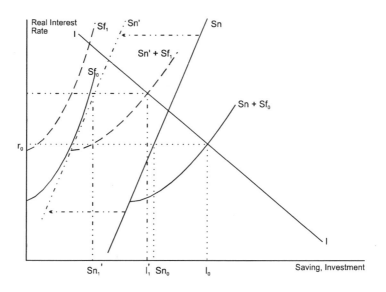

Figure 4.7. Destabilizing fiscal effect of foreign debt accumulation on saving, investment, and the current account deficit

The magnitude of capital flight caused by a buildup of foreign debt can be, and in several developing countries has been, destabilizing. Instead of an increase in foreign debt *reducing* domestic investment and *increasing* national saving, the foreign debt buildup shifts the national saving function to the left; hence the current account deficit *increases*. Real interest rates can reach, and in several developing countries have reached, astronomical levels without reducing the current account deficit.

The variable representing this foreign debt factor *DTGY* is the stock of government plus government-guaranteed foreign debt converted from dollars to local currency divided by GNP. In addition to its effect on the position of the national saving function, *DTGY* also affects the supply of foreign saving. By reducing foreign saving from Sf_0 to Sf_1, a higher debt ratio produces a higher domestic real interest rate and hence a movement up the saving function in Figure 4.6. This financial or interest rate effect on saving (a movement up the saving function) can be of opposite sign to the fiscal effect of *DTGY* (the leftward shift in the saving function shown in Figure 4.7). To allow for these conflicting and possibly nonlinear influences of debt on saving, the debt to GNP ratio is used in quadratic, cubic, and level forms.

An increase in government and government-guaranteed foreign debt may also deter domestic investment because it raises the probability of higher taxes on domestic assets in the future (Ize and Ortiz, 1987). This would shift the investment function in Figures 6 and 7 to the left. Krueger (1987, p. 136) concludes: "When debt-service obligations are high, increasing public resources to service debt will be likely to reduce incentives and resources available to the private sector sufficiently to preclude the necessary investment response." Sachs (1986, 1989, 1990) documents the deleterious effects of the foreign debt buildup on investment in Latin America.

In its early stages, however, foreign debt buildup could actually stimulate investment. Entrepreneurs may perceive that there would be profitable investment opportunities in export activities as debt service mounts and the government is forced to intensify its drive to raise foreign exchange earnings. Again, therefore, the impact of foreign debt accumulation on investment and hence on growth need not be linear.

4.3.4.   Empirical evidence

The estimates of saving, investment, and growth functions for twenty-eight heavily indebted developing countries (Fry, 1995) show that the national saving ratio is increased by higher growth *YG* and by terms-of-trade improvements. Income growth attributable to terms-of-trade improvements raises the saving ratio by more than income growth attributable to output growth. In a permanent income framework, this is consistent with the perception that terms-of-trade changes are more temporary than output changes. A higher world real interest rate and a higher ratio of net government credit to total domestic credit reduces the national saving ratio, as does higher foreign debt after foreign debt *DTGY* exceeds 30 percent of GNP. The Ricardian equivalence hypothesis with respect to foreign debt is rejected; higher government plus government-guaranteed foreign debt reduces rather than raises national saving ratios in these countries.

The domestic investment ratio is raised by faster real growth *YG*, lagged improvements in the terms-of-trade, and a higher real exchange rate that makes imported capital goods cheaper. Capital inflows allow domestic investment to exceed national saving, a movement down the investment curve from its intersection with national saving in Figures 4.6 and 4.7. They also stimulate domestic investment by appreciating the real exchange rate and so moving the investment curve itself to the right. Higher investment accelerates the rate of economic growth. However, a higher ratio of net government credit to total domestic credit reduces the investment ratio, as does a higher foreign debt ratio after foreign debt exceeds 50 percent of GNP.

Estimates of a five-equation model, which includes these saving and investment functions together with export, import, and growth functions, indicate that capital inflows raise economic growth by allowing investment to exceed saving and by stimulating investment indirectly through a real exchange rate effect (Fry, 1989). However, a rising ratio of foreign debt to GNP eventually has three negative impacts on growth: it reduces the saving ratio, it deters domestic investment, and it lowers the efficiency of investment (Fry, 1989). The lower quantity and quality of investment exert a multiplicative negative effect on economic growth. Lower saving stimulates these direct effects on growth by accelerating the debt buildup. The negative effects of debt *stock* start to outweigh the positive effects of debt *flow* when the debt to GNP ratio reaches about 0.5; this corresponds to a debt to export ratio of about 2.4 for this sample of countries. In fact, debt to GNP ratios ranged from 0.02 to 1.28 in this sample of countries. The problem arises from the lack of any automatic deterrent to continued debt accumulation after its effects turn malign and economic growth starts to decline.

Figure 4.8 shows the direct and indirect effects of increasing foreign debt on the national saving and domestic investment ratios (Fry, 1989). These are short-run equilibrium effects, since the values of all lagged endogenous variables are held constant while *DTGY* is increased from 0 to 200 percent.The gap between the saving ratio and the investment ratio increases monotonically as the debt ratio rises. The same result occurs whether the foreign debt ratio is entered linearly or to the third or fourth power with beginning- or end-of-year values in both the saving and investment ratio equations. Whether entered linearly or in quadratic form, the debt to export ratio also produces the same result but has a somewhat lower explanatory power than the debt to GNP ratio in both the saving and investment functions. In all cases, higher debt ratios eventually reduce economic growth.

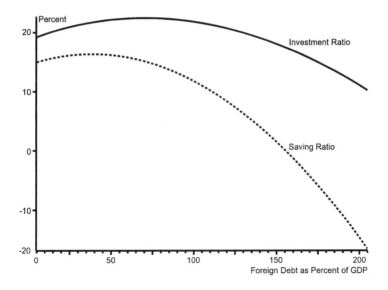

Figure 4.8. Effects of a rising foreign debt ratio and saving and investment ratios

4.3.5. New estimates of economic growth and foreign debt accumulation

Using annual data for sixty-nine developing countries with a minimum set of ten observations for debt and economic growth, the most satisfactory functional form for this bivariate relationship gives the following result (1495 observations, *t* statistics in parentheses):[62]

$$YG = \underset{(-2.587)}{-\,0.015\,DTGY^{2}} + \underset{(2.753)}{0.004\,DTGY^{3}}$$

$$\overline{R}^{2} = 0.113$$

(4.11)

Figure 4.9 shows the effect of foreign debt ratio on growth. Consistent with the results reported earlier, the negative impact of foreign debt accumulation is not pronounced at small levels but increases as the debt ratio itself rises.

---

[62] The data are taken from *International Financial Statistics*, CD-ROM, March 1996, and World Bank, *World Data 1995*, CD-ROM, September 1995.

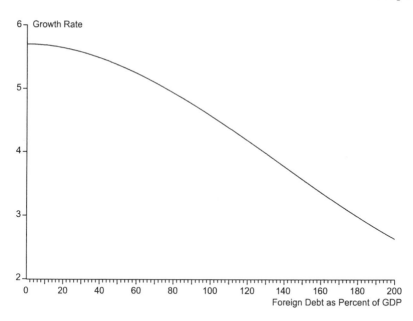

Figure 4.9. Growth and foreign debt ratios, 1970-1995

4.3.6.   Summary

That some developing countries have overborrowed (and some lenders have overlent) is certainly not a new finding. Among others, Bruno (1985), Cooper and Sachs (1985), Díaz-Alejandro (1985), Harberger (1986), McKinnon (1991), and McKinnon and Pill (1996) provide explanations for why private sectors will borrow more abroad than is socially optimal unless restrained from so doing.

Bruno (1985) and Harberger (1986) show that the optimum tariff theory can be applied to the taxation of foreign capital inflows when a country faces a rising supply schedule of foreign loans. In such a case, the country's general welfare can be increased by reducing the incentives to borrow abroad through a tax on foreign indebtedness. Bruno (1985) also argues that differential speeds of adjustment justify restrictions on capital inflows during a liberalization program. Cooper and Sachs (1985) show that a laissez-faire policy toward foreign borrowing is justified only under very restrictive conditions. Specifically, the private sector must have rational expectations regarding the possibility of a liquidity crisis, the probability of such a crisis must not be a function of the overall level of foreign debt, the private sector must believe that the government will not bail it out, and the liquidity crisis must not cause a wave of disruptive bankruptcies.

McKinnon and Pill (1996) examine the "overborrowing syndrome" that has plagued capital-account liberalization, particularly in Latin America. The basic problem is that a credible domestic reform leads to overoptimistic forecasts of future economic growth and "excessive" capital inflows to finance consumption smoothing in the light of anticipated higher future incomes. McKinnon and Pill use an extended Fisherian two-period model of production, consumption, borrowing, and lending to illustrate three cases: the financially repressed economy in which all agents are borrowing-constrained so that they can invest only in traditional technology, the domestically liberalized economy in which some agents can now borrow from the banking system at high real interest rates to invest in high-return modern technology, and the internationally liberalized economy in which all agents can now borrow through the domestic banking system at the world real interest rate to invest in the new technology.

In most countries, the main constraint to higher growth lies in their modest saving ratio. However, if the government convinces the population that the growth rate will accelerate in the near future to double digits, the rational individual may well react by consuming more now anticipating that he or she will also be able to consume more in the future as well. This is simply consumption smoothing. The result is a reduction in the present saving ratio, exactly the opposite of what is needed for the higher growth rate to be achieved.

Saving ratios in the Tiger economies of Pacific Asia lie in the 40 percent range. Elsewhere, saving ratios are typically under 20 percent. One can detect a virtuous circle in which high growth causes high saving so financing higher investment that in turn causes higher growth in output and exports. Export growth itself stimulates growth in other parts of the economy. Before anticipating a sustainable acceleration in economic growth outside Pacific Asia, therefore, signs of substantial increases in both the quantity and quality of investment are generally required.

Market failure arises as a result of overoptimistic, albeit rational, beliefs about returns to the new technology combined with implicit or explicit deposit insurance. Under these conditions, capital inflows into insured deposits with the domestic banks will prove to have been excessive when lower than anticipated returns to investments are realized. If the first-best solution of removing deposit insurance is not feasible, McKinnon and Pill (1996) recommend the imposition of reserve requirements on foreign as well as domestic deposits combined with some discouragement of consumer credit as the best practical solution. Whether or not this is a second-best solution or simply adds a further distortion to a market failure can probably be evaluated only on a case-by-case basis.

If the predicted growth acceleration fails to materialize, in part because of lower saving induced by triumphalistic pronouncements on the economic front by government, the country may well find that it has overborrowed in international capital markets. If the triumphalism has convinced both residents and nonresidents, it may have produced capital inflows that are unsustainable and reversible as soon as the euphoria ends. Such large capital inflows appreciate the real exchange rate, so deterring exports, which are invariably a strong engine of growth. When reality strikes, large capital outflows then cause a balance-of-payments crisis and currency depreciation.

One measure that appears to have had the opposite result to that intended is relaxing capital outflow controls. Experience suggests that liberalizing outflows induces greater capital inflows. While Folkerts-Landau and Ito (1995, p. 101) interpret this phenomenon in terms of sending "a positive signal that increases the confidence of foreign investors," another interpretation is that a substantial proportion of foreign capital inflows to developing countries takes the form of recycled domestic capital that was previously removed in the form of flight capital. When outflow restrictions are relaxed, confidence of *residents*, who now have an increased incentive to repatriate their savings, increases.

Díaz-Alejandro (1985) and McKinnon (1991) pursue the bailout condition. They argue that government guarantees and deposit insurance in the lending countries combined with inadequate regulation have produced a strong incentive for the multinational banks to overlend to developing countries. In sum, government involvement in both borrowing and lending countries has contributed to foreign debt instability that has afflicted developing countries since the mid-1970s.

4.4.   FOREIGN DIRECT INVESTMENT

Foreign capital inflows to developing countries constitute part of the world's saving. Over the past two decades, world saving as a proportion of world income has fallen. As world saving has shrunk, so the world real interest rate has risen from 0.8 percent during the period 1971 to 1978 to 5.7 percent in the period 1979 to 1986 (*International Financial Statistics*, CD-ROM, September 1994; *World Economic Outlook*, October 1997, p. 221).[63]

---

[63] The world real interest rate is the London interbank offered rate on U.S. dollar deposits adjusted for the percentage change in the U.S. GDP deflator. The world real interest rate averaged 3.1 percent during the period 1987 to 1994 and 3.6 percent during the period 1995 to 1998 (*World Economic Outlook*, October 1997, p. 221).

It is against this background that foreign direct investment (FDI) has appeared increasingly attractive to developing countries facing declining domestic investment and higher costs of foreign borrowing. Foreign direct investment seems an attractive form of capital inflow because it involves a risk-sharing relationship with the suppliers of this type of foreign capital. This kind of risk sharing does not exist in the formal contractual arrangements for foreign loans. Furthermore, as the World Bank (1993, p. 3) claims, there may be dynamic benefits: "Foreign direct investment is a large and growing source of finance that may help developing countries close the technology gap with high-income countries, upgrade managerial skills, and develop their export markets."

This section is concerned not with the determinants of FDI inflows to developing countries but rather with their effects. If FDI finances additional capital formation of the same value as the FDI, equation (4.7) demonstrates that the current account deteriorates to the same extent that FDI increases capital inflows, provided saving remains unchanged. In such case, FDI cannot provide additional foreign exchange to finance a pre-existing current account deficit. The extra foreign exchange is entirely absorbed in financing a larger current account deficit.

However, an increase in FDI could provide additional finance for the balance of payments if it failed to result in additional capital formation in the host country. In undertaking any analysis of FDI, one must recognize that FDI data record financial flows, which may or may not correspond to changes in capital formation. Whether or not they do depends on the extents of crowding out of domestically financed investment and substitutability of this type of financial flow for other types of financial flows.

Suppose that FDI capital inflows were used for new capital formation. If this capital formation would have taken place in any event or if this capital formation deters an equal amount of domestically financed investment in other projects, then total domestic investment I remains unchanged. In such case, FDI does not affect the current account unless it changes the level of national saving. If the current account and the change in official reserves remain the same, this FDI becomes one of the sources of finance for the pre-existing current account deficit.

An inflow of FDI also provides balance-of-payments financing if it is not used for new capital formation. For example, privatization programs in a number of countries have produced capital inflows in the form of FDI. The privatization has resulted in foreign ownership of an existing company and its capital assets, but not necessarily in any new capital formation. Typically, a capital inflow used to acquire ownership of an existing firm is recorded as FDI if it achieves ownership of 10 percent or more in the company. Again, this FDI is not accompanied by additional capital formation and so does not increase the current account deficit. It does, therefore, provide additional or alternative balance-of-payments financing.

Some of the literature on FDI suggests that FDI can serve two purposes—namely, increase investment and relieve foreign exchange shortages. For example, Cockcroft and Riddell (1991, p. 3) note: "Two of the principal factors inhibiting higher levels of economic growth in Sub-Saharan Africa in the 1990s are low levels of investment and foreign exchange shortages. The first attraction of foreign investment lies in its potential to address both these constraints."

Unless it affects national saving, however, FDI can increase domestic investment or provide additional financing for a pre-existing current account deficit or achieve some combination of the two, but these two effects must always sum to one. In other words, if U.S. $100 FDI increases capital formation by U.S. $75, it would provide U.S. $25 for additional current-account financing.

In summary, there are three alternative polar cases:

- Foreign direct investment increases capital formation and so worsens the current account by exactly the same amount as the FDI inflow.

- Foreign direct investment is embodied in capital formation but crowds out locally financed investment that otherwise would have occurred. In this case, FDI deteriorates the current account by increasing foreign-financed investment but improves the current account by deterring locally financed investment. The net effect is that the reduction in locally financed investment effectively frees the FDI capital inflow to finance the unchanged pre-existing current account deficit.

- Foreign direct investment acquires ownership of existing capital in the host country and so has no effect on capital formation. In this case, it substitutes for other capital inflows in providing an alternative source of financing for the unchanged pre-existing current account deficit.

Which of these three cases, or combinations of them actually occurs in any particularly country is entirely an empirical question, to which I now turn.

By analyzing FDI to developing economies within a macroeconomic framework, I identify five channels through which FDI influences the macroeconomy and hence the balance of payments on current account (Fry, 1995). Specifically, I examine the effects of FDI on saving, investment, exports, imports, and economic growth. As well as estimating the effects of FDI flows, I have attempted to estimate the effects of FDI stocks on the same five variables. As a proxy, I use the average ratio of FDI to GNP over the previous five years.

Whether or not substitutability and fungibility are so high that FDI flows provide no relevant economic information at all is an empirical question. Indeed, some recent estimates of current account financing requirement equations suggest that FDI is either a close substitute for at least one other type of capital flow or is autonomous in a sample of sixteen developing countries (Fry, 1993a). In an attempt to discriminate between these two possibilities, I investigate whether or not FDI affects the ratio of gross domestic investment to GNP. To do this, I use FDI as an explanatory variable rather than as the dependent variable in a five-equation macroeconomic model. Since causation could run both ways and could well be determined simultaneously with saving and investment, I treat it as an endogenous variable.

I estimated behavioral equations for five Pacific Asian developing market economies (Indonesia, Korea, Malaysia, Philippines, and Thailand) and a control group of eleven other developing economies (Argentina, Brazil, Chile, Egypt, India, Mexico, Nigeria, Pakistan, Sri Lanka, Turkey, and Venezuela). The estimates of domestic investment as a ratio of GNP indicate that, in the Pacific Asian economies, FDI corresponds to capital formation on a one-to-one basis since the coefficient of the ratio of FDI to GNP is not significantly different from 1. This implies that FDI may not be a close substitute for other forms of capital inflow in these economies. Furthermore, it suggests that FDI does not crowd out or substitute for domestically financed investment. Ceteris paribus, it increases the current account deficit by the magnitude of the capital inflow. This conclusion that FDI is not a close substitute for other capital inflows in these Pacific Asian developing economies corroborates the same conclusion reached by Rana and Dowling (1990) for a similar sample of Pacific Asian developing economies.

For the control group, the estimated coefficient of the FDI ratio in the investment function is significantly negative. The Pacific Asian economies may differ from the control group because a number of Latin American countries have combined debt-equity swaps with programs of privatization; this has not happened in Pacific Asia. In these cases, the deliberate aim of attracting FDI was not to increase capital formation but rather to substitute one form of capital inflow for another. The recorded net FDI inflow cancelled part of the country's foreign debt and was used to acquire holdings in the newly privatized industries. While this process of privatization continues, private investors may take a wait-and-see stance before undertaking new investment projects. Hence, the net inflow of FDI may be associated with a degree of uncertainty that clouds the investment outlook and so reduces capital formation.

Use of FDI in debt-equity swap programs may also have been a last resort measure taken under crisis conditions. Hence, the significantly negative coefficient for the control group may reflect the fact that FDI increased when the investment climate deteriorated in the wake of debt crises. In such case, the foreign debt crises may well have simultaneously reduced domestic investment and increased FDI. If so, higher FDI did not cause the decline in domestic investment but was associated with it since both were caused by some other factor.

In an attempt to pin down the key factors causing such disparate effects of FDI on domestic investment ratios across these two country groups, I interacted the black-market exchange rate premium, the domestic real interest rate, the degree of openness (the average ratio of exports plus imports to GNP over the preceding five years), the investment climate (the average investment ratio over the preceding five years) and the lagged foreign debt ratio with the FDI ratio. Except for the real interest rate and the proxy for the investment climate, these variables produce significant interactive terms for the complete sample (356 observations). The results show that high black-market exchange rate premia and foreign debt ratios produce the negative association between FDI and the domestic investment ratio (Fry, 1995).

If FDI constitutes a last-resort source of external financing during debt and balance-of-payments crises, it may well be associated with a reduction in investment productivity. In a direct test, I find that investment productivity does deteriorate as a country accumulates foreign debt (Fry, 1989) In any event, an open economy with a low black-market exchange rate premium (perhaps signifying open capital as well as current accounts) and a low foreign debt ratio experiences a positive association between FDI and the domestic investment ratio and, through this capital formation, higher economic growth.

While the coefficient of the FDI ratio in the estimate of national saving as a proportion of GNP is not significant for the Pacific Asian economies, it is significantly negative for the control group. As with the investment function, I interacted the black-market exchange rate premium, the degree of openness, the investment climate and the lagged foreign debt ratio with the FDI ratio in an attempt to detect any systematic influence of these variables on the relationship between FDI and saving behavior. In this case, the degree of openness and the investment climate produce significant interactive terms for the complete sample. The estimated coefficients suggest that a more open economy can anticipate a less negative effect of FDI on its national saving ratio. Therefore, greater openness induces greater positive effects of FDI on both domestic investment and national saving ratios. An improved investment climate also reduces the negative effect of FDI on national saving ratios (Fry, 1995).

The contemporaneous effect of FDI on exports is significantly negative in the control group but insignificant in Pacific Asia. However, FDI over the previous five years exerts a significantly positive, albeit small, effect on the export ratios in both country groups. An increase in FDI is associated with a one-for-one increase in imports in both country groups. The immediate effect of FDI, therefore, is to finance a larger import bill. However, FDI inflows over the preceding five years are associated with a significant decline in the import ratio outside Pacific Asia. In these control countries, FDI seems to have been directed not only into export industries but also into import-substitution activities. In both country groups, higher lagged FDI inflows improve the current account. In the control group, FDI inflows over the preceding five years raise exports and reduce imports.

Finally, I show that FDI raises the rate of economic growth in the absence of financial repression and trade distortions in the sixteen sample developing countries taken together. However, financial repression as measured by the real deposit rate of interest and trade distortions as measured by the black-market exchange rate premium can both cause FDI to be immiserizing. When the domestic economy is distorted, FDI inflows are associated with a low or negative growth rate. When real interest rates are positive, however, FDI can accelerate the rate of economic growth more when restrictions on the sectoral location of this investment are relaxed.

In the absence of domestic distortions and counterproductive triumphalism, foreign capital inflows can augment domestic resources available for capital formation and hence can accelerate economic growth In another empirical study of FDI inflows to six Pacific Asian economies (Indonesia, Korea, Malaysia, the Philippines, Singapore, and Thailand), I find that FDI increases capital formation in this sample of Pacific Asian countries on a one-to-one basis, since the coefficient of the FDI variable is again not significantly different from 1 (Fry, 1996). However, this investment effect on the current account is offset by the fact that both current and lagged FDI ratios increase national saving ratios in this sample of Pacific Asian countries.

In these Pacific Asian economies, FDI also increases imports on a one-to-one basis, since the coefficient of the FDI variable is again not significantly different from 1. In contrast, FDI has no immediate effect on export supply, although it does increase exports significantly in the medium run (over the subsequent five years). This suggests that FDI in Pacific Asia has been concentrated in the export sectors of these economies.

The growth rate estimate shows that FDI does not have a significantly different effect from domestically financed investment on growth in this sample of Pacific Asian countries. Hence, its impact on growth is exerted indirectly through its effects on the investment ratio and the export growth rate.

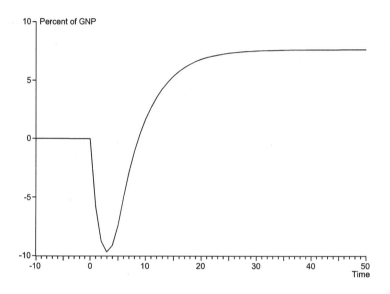

Figure 4.10. Current account effect of a ten percentage point increase in foreign direct investment

Table 4.4 presents the estimated equations that form the simulation. Figure 4.10 illustrates the simulation of the effects of an increase in FDI from zero to 10 percent GNP in year 1 and in all subsequent years through investment, saving, imports, exports and growth on the current account. While the current account deteriorates from zero to -9.7 percent of GNP by year 3, thereafter the current account improves until it reaches +7.6 percent of GNP in the long run. Figure 4.11 shows their simulated effects on economic growth.

Table 4.4. A simulation model of foreign direct investment

$$IY = 0.745\,F\hat{D}IY - 0.148\,FD\hat{I}YL + 0.400\,D\hat{D}CY + 0.063\,R\hat{E}XL + 0.354\,\hat{Y}G + 0.718IY_{t-1}\,(4.12)$$
$$\quad\ (3.675)\qquad\quad (-0.484)\qquad (5.555)\qquad\quad (3.796)\qquad (4.934)\qquad (13.253)$$

$$R^2 = 0.857$$

$$SNY = 0.162\,F\hat{D}IY + 0.330\,FDIYL + 0.438\,\hat{Y}G + 0.812SNY_{t-1} \qquad\qquad (4.13)$$
$$\qquad\ (2.680)\qquad\qquad (2.575)\qquad\ (10.051)(24.182)$$
$$R^2 = 0.904$$

$$IMKY = 1.169\,\hat{FDIY} + 0.461FDIYL + 0.197\,\hat{OKY} + 0.121\,\hat{REXL} + 0.322\,\hat{IKY} \qquad (4.14)$$

$$\ \underset{(5.737)}{} \qquad \underset{(1.101)}{} \qquad \underset{(4.960)}{} \qquad \underset{(12.491)}{} \qquad \underset{(11.073)}{}$$

$$+\, 0.323\,\hat{XY} + 0.245IMKY_{t-1}$$

$$\underset{(9.495)}{} \qquad \underset{(4.912)}{}$$

$$R^2 = 0.982$$

$$XKY = -0.058\,\hat{FDIY} + 0.842FDIYL - 0.082\,\hat{REXL} + 1.075XKY_{T-1} \qquad (4.15)$$

$$\ \underset{(-0.259)}{} \qquad \underset{(1.865)}{} \qquad \underset{(-5.686)}{} \qquad \underset{(50.829)}{}$$

$$R^2 = 0.990$$

$$YG = -0.052FDII + 0.011FDIIL + 0.084IKY + 0.120XKG + 0.628WG + 0.303YG_{t-1} \quad (4.16)$$

$$\ \underset{(-0.952)}{} \qquad \underset{(0.181)}{} \qquad \underset{(3.290)}{} \qquad \underset{(3.671)}{} \qquad \underset{(3.724)}{} \qquad \underset{(3.949)}{}$$

$$R^2 = 0.374$$

$$CAY = SNY - IY \qquad\qquad\qquad\qquad\qquad\qquad\qquad\qquad (4.17)$$

Endogenous variables:

IY	Domestic investment/GNP (current prices)
FDIY	Inflow of foreign direct investment/GNP (dollar values converted to domestic currency, current prices)
DDCY	Change in domestic credit/GNP (current prices)
YG	Rate of growth in GNP (constant prices, continuously compounded)
SNY	National saving/GNP (current prices)
IMKY	Imports/GNP (constant prices)
REXL	Real exchange rate (domestic GNP deflator/U.S. wholesale price index)/domestic currency per U.S. dollar)
IKY	Domestic investment/GNP(constant prices)
XY	Exports/GNP (current prices)
OKY	Other capital flows/GNP (dollar values converted to domestic currency, current prices)
XKY	Exports/GNP (constant prices)
FDII	Inflow of foreign direct investment/domestic investment (dollar values converted to domestic currency, current prices)
XKG	Rate of growth in exports (constant prices, continuously compounded)

Exogenous or predetermined variables:
FDIYL   Average FDI ratio over previous five years
FDIIL   Average ratio of FDI to domestic investment over previous five years
WG   Real growth rate of OECD countries (continuously compounded)

Two factors explain the paradoxical current account simulation result. The first is that higher growth increases the saving ratio by more than it increases the investment ratio. The second is that FDI stimulates saving directly, the more so in the medium and longer runs. While the current account is improving, export growth will be above its long-run rate, so providing an extra growth-enhancing impact. All-in-all the recipients of FDI in Pacific Asia appear to have been able to have their cakes and eat them too. This serendipitous experience with FDI has not been replicated outside Pacific Asia for reasons outlined above.

The overall conclusion of this section is that both the nature and the effects of FDI flows vary significantly between different regions of the developing world. Outside Pacific Asia, FDI appears to have been used in large part as a substitute for other types of foreign flows; it has not increased aggregate domestic investment. When the control group countries attracted more FDI inflows, national saving, domestic investment, and the rate of economic growth all declined. Hence, FDI appears to have been immiserizing in these countries. In contrast, the role of FDI in Pacific Asia has been benign. In these economies, FDI financial flows have not been close substitutes for other types of foreign capital flows.

The superior efficiency of FDI in the Pacific Asian economies reflects not only less distorted financial conditions than in other parts of the developing world but also less distorted trading systems. The outward orientation of the Pacific Asian economies ensures that relative prices cannot diverge too far from world market prices. Under these conditions, there are few possibilities for FDI to find high profits in protected markets.

The favorable investment climates in the developing economies of Pacific Asia have ensured that FDI flows are readily available without the need for governments to discriminate in favor of this particular form of investment finance. Hence, these economies have avoided the two major pitfalls of FDI—namely, low or negative productivity caused by distortions in the economy and expensive discriminatory incentives provided in the mistaken belief that FDI brings externalities.

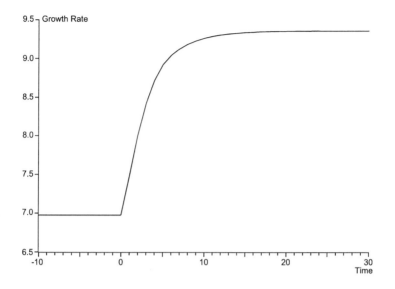

Figure 4.11. Growth effect of a ten percentage point increase in foreign direct investment

4.5.   CONCLUSION

Perhaps in no other markets is the principle of the level playing field so crucial as it is in financial markets. The government should certainly compete with other borrowers on equal terms This is exemplified in the benefits of a secondary market for government debt, which will not exist where the government forces its debt down the throats of reluctant captive buyers (Fry, 1997a). Second, a level playing field for foreign and domestically financed investment is essential for the efficient allocation of foreign capital inflows. Excessive accumulation of foreign debt can be deterred both by fiscal discipline and by resisting requests for government guarantees. Foreign direct investment contributes most to economic growth when it is attracted not by extravagant incentive packages but by a conducive investment climate. Finally, a level playing field necessitates the exclusion of uneven (insolvent) players; this is the key role of prudential supervision and regulation in the development process.

References

Agénor, P., and P. Montiel. (1996). *Development Macroeconomics.* Princeton, NJ: Princeton University Press.

Arestis, P., and P. Demetriades. (1997). "Financial Development and Economic Growth: Assessing the Evidence." *Economic Journal* 107, 783–799.

Asian Development Bank. (1985). *Improving Domestic Resource Mobilization Through Financial Development.* Manila: Asian Development Bank, Economics Office.

Bailey, M.J. (1956). "The Welfare Cost of Inflationary Finance." *Journal of Political Economy* 64, 93–110.

Barro, R.J. (1974). "Are Government Bonds Net Wealth?" *Journal of Political Economy* 82, 1095–1117.

Barro, R.J. (1989). "The Ricardian Approach to Budget Deficits." *Journal of Economic Perspectives* 3, 37–54.

Barro, R.J. (1991). "Economic Growth in a Cross Section of Countries." *Quarterly Journal of Economics* 106, 407–443.

Bencivenga, V.R., and B.D. Smith. (1991). "Financial Intermediation and Endogenous Growth." *Review of Economic Studies* 58, 195–209.

Bencivenga, V.R., and B.D. Smith. (1992). "Deficits, Inflation, and the Banking System in Developing Countries: The Optimal Degree of Financial Repression." *Oxford Economic Papers* 44, 767–790.

Brock, P. L. (1989). "Reserve Requirements and the Inflation Tax." *Journal of Money, Credit and Banking* 21, 106–121.

Bruno, M. (1985). "The Reforms and Macroeconomic Adjustments: Introduction." *World Development* 13, 867–869.

Buchanan, J.M. (1976). "Barro on the Ricardian Equivalence Theorem." *Journal of Political Economy* 84, 337–342.

Buffie, E.F. (1984). "Financial Repression, the New Structuralists, and Stabilization Policy in Semi-Industrialized Economies." *Journal of Development Economics* 14, 305–322.

Calvo, G.A., and F. Coricelli. (1992). "Stagflationary Effects of Stabilization Programs in Reforming Socialist Countries: Enterprise-Side vs. Household-Side Factors." *World Bank Economic Review* 6, 71–90.

Chamley, C., and P. Honohan. (1993). "Financial Repression and Banking Intermediation." *Savings and Development* 17, 301–308.

Cockcroft, L., and R.C. Riddell. (1991). "Foreign Direct Investment in Sub-Saharan Africa." World Bank, Working Paper 619, Washington, DC.

Cooper, R.N., and J.D. Sachs. (1985). "Borrowing Abroad: The Debtor's Perspective." In G.W. Smith and J. T. Cuddington, eds., *International Debt and the Developing Countries* (pp. 21–60). Washington, DC: World Bank.

De Gregorio, J., and P.E. Guidotti. (1995). "Financial Development and Economic Growth." *World Development* 23, 433–448.

Diamond, D.W., and P.H. Dybvig. (1983). "Bank Runs, Deposit Insurance, and Liquidity." *Journal of Political Economy* 91, 401–419.

Díaz-Alejandro, C. (1985). "Good-bye Financial Repression, Hello Financial Crash." *Journal of Development Economics* 19, 1–24.

Easterly, W.R. (1993). "How Much Do Distortions Affect Growth?" *Journal of Monetary Economics* 32, 187–212.

Fischer, S. (1993). "The Role of Macroeconomic Factors in Growth." *Journal of Monetary Economics* 32, 485–512.

Folkerts-Landau, D., and T. Ito. (1995). "International Capital Markets: Developments, Prospects, and Policy Issues." In *World Economic and Financial Surveys.* Washington, DC: International Monetary Fund.

Friedman, M. (1971). "Government Revenue from Inflation." *Journal of Political Economy* 79, 46–85.

Fry, M.J. (1978). "Money and Capital or Financial Deepening in Economic Development?" *Journal of Money, Credit and Banking* 10, 464–475.

Fry, M.J. (1979). "The Cost of Financial Repression in Turkey." *Savings and Development* 3, 127–135.

Fry, M.J. (1980). "Saving, Investment, Growth and the Cost of Financial Repression." *World Development* 8, 317–327.

Fry, M.J. (1981). *Interest Rates in Asia: An Examination of Interest Rate Policies in Burma, India, Indonesia, Korea, Malaysia, Nepal, Pakistan, the Philippines, Singapore, Sri Lanka, Taiwan and Thailand.* Washington, DC: International Monetary Fund.

Fry, M.J. (1989). "Foreign Debt Instability: An Analysis of National Saving and Domestic Investment Responses to Foreign Debt Accumulation in Twenty-Eight Developing Countries." *Journal of International Money and Finance* 8, 315–344.

Fry, M.J. (1991). "Domestic Resource Mobilization in Developing Asia: Four Policy Issues." *Asian Development Review* 9, 15–39.

Fry, M.J. (1993a). *Foreign Direct Investment in Southeast Asia: Differential Impacts.* Singapore: Institute of Southeast Asian Studies.

Fry, M.J. (1993b). "Foreign Debt Accumulation: Financial and Fiscal Effects and Monetary Policy Reactions in Developing Countries." *Journal of International Money and Finance* 12, 347–367.

Fry, M.J. (1995). *Money, Interest, and Banking in Economic Development* (2nd ed.). Baltimore: Johns Hopkins University Press.

Fry, M.J. (1996). "How Foreign Direct Investment in Pacific Asia Improves the Current Account." *Journal of Asian Economics* 7, 459–486.

Fry, M.J. (1997a). *Emancipating the Banking System and Developing Markets for Government Debt.* London: Routledge.

Fry, M.J. (1997b). "The Fiscal Abuse of Central Banks." In M.I. Blejer, and T. Ter-Minassian, eds., *Macroeconomic Dimensions of Public Finance: Essays in Honour of Vito Tanzi* (pp. 337-359). London: Routledge.

Fry, M.J. (1998a). "Macroeconomic Policy and Economic Performance in Developing Countries." *Bank of England Quarterly Bulletin* 37, 48–54.

Fry, M.J. (1998b). "Saving, Investment, Growth, and Financial Distortions in Pacific Asia and Other Developing Areas." *International Economic Journal* 12, 1–24.

Fry, M.J., Charles A.E. Goodhart, and Alvaro Almeida. (1996). *Central Banking in Developing Countries: Objectives, Activities and Independence.* London: Routledge.

Gelb, A.H. (1989). "Financial Policies, Growth, and Efficiency." Country Economics Department, PPR Working Paper WPS 202, World Bank, Washington, DC.

Gertler, M. (1988). "Financial Structure and Aggregate Economic Activity: An Overview." *Journal of Money, Credit and Banking* 20(3), 559–588.

Gertler, M., and A. Rose. (1994). "Finance, Public Policy, and Growth." In G. Caprio, I. Atiyas, and J. Hanson, eds., *Financial Reform: Theory and Experience* (pp. 13–48). New York: Cambridge University Press.

Ghani, E. (1992). "How Financial Markets Affect Long-Run Growth: A Cross-Country Study." Country Operations, PR Working Paper, Working Paper Series 843, World Bank.

Giovannini, A., and M. de Melo. (1993). "Government Revenue from Financial Repression." *American Economic Review* 83, 953–963.

Greenwood, J., and B. Jovanovic. (1990). "Financial Development, Growth, and the Distribution of Income." *Journal of Political Economy* 98, 1076–1107.

Greenwood, J., and B.D. Smith. (1997). "Financial Markets in Development, and the Development of Financial Markets." *Journal of Economic Dynamics and Control* 21, 145–181.

Harberger, A.C. (1986). "Welfare Consequences of Capital Inflows." In A.M. Choksi and D. Papageorgiou, eds., *Economic Liberalization in Developing Countries* (pp. 157–184). Oxford: Basil Blackwell.

Ize, A., and G. Ortiz. (1987). "Fiscal Rigidities, Public Debt, and Capital Flight." *International Monetary Fund Staff Papers* 34, 311–332.

Johnston, J. (1984). *Econometric Methods* (3rd ed.). New York: McGraw-Hill.

King, R.G., and R. Levine. (1993*a*). "Finance and Growth: Schumpeter Might Be Right." *Quarterly Journal of Economics* 108, 717–737.

King, R.G., and R. Levine. (1993*b*). "Finance, Entrepreneurship, and Growth: Theory and Evidence." *Journal of Monetary Economics* 32, 513–542.

King, R.G., and R. Levine. (1993*c*). "Financial Intermediation and Economic Growth." In C. Mayer and X. Vives, eds., *Capital Markets and Financial Intermediation* (pp. 156-189). Cambridge: Cambridge University Press.

Knight, M. (1998). "Developing Countries and the Globalization of Financial Markets." *World Development* 26.

Krueger, A.O. (1987). "Debt, Capital Flows, and LDC Growth." *American Economic Review* 77, 159–164.

Lanyi, A., and R. Saraco lu. (1983). "Interest Rate Policies in Developing Countries." Occasional Paper 22, International Monetary Fund, Washington, DC.

Levine, R. (1993). "Financial Structures and Economic Development." *Revista de Análisis Económico* 8, 113–129.

Levine, R. (1997). "Financial Development and Economic Growth: Views and Agenda." *Journal of Economic Literature* 35, 688–726.

Levine, R. (1998). "The Legal Environment, Banks, and Long-Run Economic Growth." *Journal of Money, Credit and Banking.*

Levine, R., and S. Zervos. (1998). "Stock Markets, Banks, and Economic Growth." *American Economic Review.*

McKinnon, R.I. (1973). *Money and Capital in Economic Development.* Washington, DC: Brookings Institution.

McKinnon, R.I. (1991). "Monetary Stabilization in LDCs." In L.B. Krause and K. Kihwan, eds., *Liberalization in the Process of Economic Development* (pp. 366–400). Berkeley: University of California Press.

McKinnon, R.I. (1993). *The Order of Economic Liberalization: Financial Control in the Transition to a Market Economy* (2nd ed.). Baltimore: Johns Hopkins University Press.

McKinnon, R.I., and H. Pill. (1996). "Credible Liberalizations and International Capital Flows: The 'Overborrowing Syndrome'." In T. Ito and A.O. Krueger, eds., *Financial Deregulation and Integration in East Asia* (pp. 7–42). Chicago: University of Chicago Press.

Metzler, L.A. (1968). "The Process of International Adjustment under Conditions of Full Employment: A Keynesian View." In R.E. Caves and H. G. Johnson, eds., *Readings in International Economics* (pp. 465–485). Homewood, IL: Irwin.

Pérez, S.A. (1997). "'Strong' States and 'Cheap' Credit: Economic Policy Strategy and Financial Regulation in France and Spain." In D.J. Forsyth and T. Notermans, eds., *Regimes Changes: Macroeconomic Policy and Financial Regulation in Europe from the 1930s to the 1990s* (pp. 169-220). Providence, RI: Berghahn Books.

Polak, J.J. (1989). *Financial Policies and Development*. Paris: Development Centre of the Organisation for Economic Co-operation and Development.

Rana, P.B., and J.M. Dowling. (1990). "Foreign Capital and Asian Economic Growth." *Asian Development Review* 8(2), 77–102.

Ricardo, D. (1817). *On the Principles of Political Economy, and Taxation*. London: John Murray.

Rojas-Suárez, L., and S.R. Weisbrod. (1995). *Financial Fragilities in Latin America: The 1980s and 1990s*. Occasional Paper 132, International Monetary Fund, Washington, DC.

Roubini, N., and X. Sala-i-Martin. (1992). "Financial Repression and Economic Growth." *Journal of Development Economics* 39, 5–30.

Sachs, J.D. (1986). "Managing the LDC debt crisis." *Brookings Papers on Economic Activity* 2, 397–431.

Sachs, J.D., ed. (1989). *Developing Country Debt and the World Economy*. Chicago: University of Chicago Press for the National Bureau of Economic Research.

Sachs, J.D., ed. (1990). *Developing Country Debt and Economic Performance* (vols. 1–3). Chicago: University of Chicago Press for the National Bureau of Economic Research.

Schumpeter, J.A. (1912). *Theorie der wirtschaftlichen Entwicklung*. (Leipzig: Duncker & Humblot). The Theory of Economic Development: An Inquiry into Profits, Capital, Credit, Interest, and the Business Cycle, translated by Redvers Opie, Cambridge, MA: Harvard University Press.

Shaw, E.S. (1973). *Financial Deepening in Economic Development*. New York: Oxford University Press.

Stiglitz, J.E. (1994). "The Role of the State in Financial Markets." In M. Bruno and B. Pleskovic, eds., *Proceedings of the World Bank Annual Bank Conference on Development Economics 1993* (pp. 19–52). Washington, DC: World Bank.

Stiglitz, J.E., and A. Weiss. (1981). "Credit Rationing in Markets with Imperfect Information." *American Economic Review* 71, 393–410.

Tobin, J. (1965). "Money and Economic Growth." *Econometrica* 33, 671–684.

Tobin, J. (1992). "Money." In P. Newman, M. Milgate, and J. Eatwell, eds., *The New Palgrave Dictionary of Money and Finance* (vol.2, pp. 770–778). London: Macmillan.

Vitols, S. (1997). "Financial Systems and Industrial Policy in Germany and Great Britain: The Limits of Convergence." In D.J. Forsyth and T. Notermans, eds., *Regimes Changes: Macroeconomic Policy and Financial Regulation in Europe from the 1930s to the 1990s* (pp. 221–255). Providence, RI: Berghahn Books.

World Bank. (1989). *World Development Report 1989*. New York: Oxford University Press for the World Bank.

World Bank. (1993). *Global Economic Prospects and the Developing Countries*. Washington, DC: World Bank.

DISCUSSION

Ross Levine
University of Virginia

During the last twenty years, a growing body of research examines why financial contracts, markets, and intermediaries arise and then traces the effects of the resultant financial system on saving and allocation decisions. While still open to further research, this body of work suggests that differences in the functioning of financial systems have important implications for economic performance. The importance of the financial system for economic activity highlights the need for policies, regulations, and legal systems that promote well-functioning financial markets and intermediaries. However, government interventions themselves often play the principal role in obstructing financial development and producing financial crises. Besides seeking to understand better the linkages between financial development and economic growth, economists must also endeavor to identify those government interventions—if any—that most effectively promote well-functioning financial systems.

Maxwell Fry's chapter provides a very useful review of some crucial policy issues associated with financial markets and economic development. Three points stand out. First, Fry stresses that financial sector policies should be viewed within the broader context of fiscal policy. Namely, to fund a given level of current fiscal expenditures, governments can directly tax agents, print money, borrow domestically at market rates, borrow internationally, or force banks to purchase government securities at below market rates. Thus, financial repression is one instrument for satisfying a particular level of current fiscal expenditures. Second, since financial sector policies are intimately linked with fiscal policy considerations, this naturally leads to a political economy framework for understanding financial reform. Specifically, relaxation of interest rate controls and directed credit requirements will be most credible when accompanied by tax reform (or by a reduction in fiscal expenditures), so that there is less pressure to use financial repression to fund current fiscal needs. Thus, policy advisors seeking to improve the functioning of the financial system may need to consider reforms to the tax system as a prerequisite for building a healthy, competitive financial system. According to this view, a reform of the tax system would reduce pressures for financial repression, which would in turn stimulate economic activity and growth. Finally, Fry argues that the empirical evidence shows that severe financial repression—measured as very negative real interest rates—and high rates of foreign borrowing negatively affect economic performance.

There are, of course, some limitations to the analysis. First, the econometric evidence needs to be qualified. Besides endogeneity issues, the paper uses annual data to investigate concepts associated with "long-run growth." Annual data may capture business-cycle fluctuations, not long-run growth. Furthermore, Fry could be more circumspect in noting the problems associated with lumping together lots of very different countries in a regression (Harberger, 1998). This is especially true for Fry, who regresses growth on either real interest rates or foreign debt without controlling for any other country characteristics.

A second limitation involves the fiscal policy perspective. While Fry perceptively highlights the importance of considering financial repression within the context of the broader fiscal policy environment, he does not illuminate some natural avenues for future research. Namely, there are interesting tradeoffs and decisions that policymakers face. Should countries delay removing restrictions that force banks to lend to the government at below market rates until they have improved their tax systems? Or are the benefits of liberalization greater than the costs of potentially higher inflation rates produced by greater use of money creation to finance a given fiscal expenditure target?

Finally, Fry's chapter implies that the critical question facing developing country policymakers today is: Should we reduce interest rate controls to foster (perhaps) marginally faster growth rates? There is considerable evidence that one should cast the net more broadly. Many factors beyond interest rate repression affect the development and functioning of the financial system. Legal, regulatory, and supervisory issues already enjoy the spot light in the policy arena, and future research should guide policymakers. In terms of financial crises, regulatory inconsistencies and ineffective supervisory systems have helped produce banking sector failures in Chile, Mexico, and Thailand. In terms of establishing a healthy financial system for long-run growth, differences in legal and accounting systems help explain differences in financial development and long-run growth (Levine, Loayza, and Beck 1998). Also, international differences in regulatory systems clearly influence the structure and performance of commercial banks (Barth, Nolle, and Rice 1996). Thus, while financial repression certainly deserves careful attention, research on the legal, regulatory, and supervisory factors underlying financial development should be a part of the profession's research agenda.

References

Barth, J.R., D.E. Nolle, and T.N. Rice. (1996). "Commercial Banking Structure, Regulation, and Performance: An International Comparison." Working Paper, Office of the Comptroller of the Currency, United States.

Harberger, A. (1998). "A Vision of the Growth Process." *American Economic Review* 88, 1–32.

Levine, R., N. Loayza, and T. Beck. (1998). "Financial Intermediation and Growth: Causality and Causes." Mimeo, University of Virginia.

Chapter 5

Institutional development and economic growth

Deepak Lal
James S. Coleman Professor of International Development Studies, University of California, Los Angeles

5.1.   INTRODUCTION

With the current worldwide move from plan to market, questions about governance and culture have come to the forefront of debates on development.[64] It is natural to think that the "habits of the heart" embodied in one's own institutions are worth emulating by others, particularly if these habits and institutions have been conjoined with the material success sought by others. As such the West has been promoting its political and economic institutions and values—democracy, the market, protecting human rights, egalitarianism—as the route to prosperity in the rest of the world. But while accepting the instrumental value of the market as a necessary economic institution to deliver prosperity, many in the rest of the world (particularly in East Asia) are resisting any attempt to have Western "habits of the heart"

---

[64] Even the Chicago school, which until recently ignored culture based on the Becker-Stigler (1977) manifesto "De Gustibus Non Est Disputandum," seems to be coming around to this view. Thus Becker (1996) now emphasizes the notion of social capital first developed by the sociologist James Coleman (1990). Becker notes that culture is part of social capital and is likely to change only slowly (p. 16), that his and Stigler's 1977 view applied only to meta-preferences, and that his later work shows "that the past casts a long shadow on the present through its influence on the formation of present preferences and choices" (p. 132). I have little quarrel with this new Chicago viewpoint. Moreover, for those who are persuaded only by cross-country regressions, a recent study by Knack and Keefer (1997) provides some evidence that social capital measured by indicators of trust and civic norms from the World Value Surveys for a sample of twenty-nine countries does matter for measurable economic performance.

thrust on them. Instead, in a neat reversal of Max Weber's famous thesis, they are claiming that it is uniquely Asian values (and the institutions they embody, such as etatist polities, and extended families) that are responsible for the East Asian economic miracles.[65] Who is right, and can we say anything useful about the institutions that promote economic growth? That is the central question I seek to answer, but inter alia I also discuss the four issues the organizers of this seminar have suggested: incorporation of institutional development in economic growth theory, influence of political factors on economic growth, institutional development and income distribution, and policy implications.

5.2.   WHAT ARE INSTITUTIONS?

There is growing agreement that the evolution of institutions is likely to be the central explanation of differing growth performances, for the present decisions of economic agents that impinge on the process of economic development will in part be constrained by their past, through various cultural and ideological norms and organizational structures (North, 1990). Institutions, broadly defined, consist of informal constraints like cultural norms or the more purposive formal ones embodied in particular organizational structures—including formal rules embodied in, for instance, the common law, which forms a spontaneous order in Hayek's sense as having evolved without any conscious design[66]—which constrain human behavior.

---

[65] The controversy about the sources of East Asian success continues unabated. Young (1994, 1995) has purportedly shown on the basis of careful growth accounting that this success could be largely explained by the growth of the primary factors of production (including human capital), with little contribution from productivity increases (a conclusion in consonance with the cross-country regressions based on the Summers-Heston data set by Mankiw, Romer, and Weil, 1992). A recent study by Klenow and Rodriguez-Clare (1997), which used a different human capital variable and sought to explain differences in growth of output per worker rather than just output, finds that productivity growth is at the center of explanations for the East Asian miracle, as it is for the differing growth performance of the Summers-Heston set of ninety-eight countries in the cross-section regressions that have become the norm. But like Young they find that neither for East Asia nor for the larger sample is the growth in human capital per worker important in explaining growth. This last conclusion is also in consonance with the evidence from the historical comparative studies of twenty-five developing countries synthesized in Lal-Myint (1996). The differences in productivity growth, of course, will reflect differences in institutions.

[66] For a game-theoretic account of how such a spontaneous order could have arisen, see Sugden (1986).

But as soon as we talk about constraining human behavior, we are implicitly acknowledging that there is some basic human nature to be constrained. While we take up this question in greater detail below, as a first cut we can accept the economists' model of Homo economicus, which assumes that human beings are motivated purely by self interest: maximizing utility as consumers and profits as producers. So as a start, the function of the rules constraining human nature, which comprise institutions must be to limit such self-seeking behavior.

This immediately points to another significant feature and reason for the existence of institutions. If Robinson Crusoe were alone on his island, he would have no reason to constrain his basic human nature. It is only with the appearance of Man Friday that some constraints on both him and Crusoe *might* be necessary for them to co-operate and thereby increase their mutual gains—by specializing in tasks in which they have a comparative advantage—over what they could each have derived from their own efforts on two separate autarkic islands. This, then immediately leads us to the notion of *transactions costs*—a concept that is even more slippery than that of institutions (Lal, 1998a).

But some help is at hand. Robin Matthews in his presidential address to the Royal Economic Society in 1986 on a subject that is close to the one I am discussing noted that, the recent economics of institutions[67] had four approaches: institutions seen as systems of property rights laid down by law, moral conventions or norms, types of contract, and authority relations. The common feature of these approaches "is the concept of institutions as sets of rights and obligations affecting people in their economic lives" (Matthews, 1986). The reason that there is a close relation between institutions and transactions costs is that, as Matthews puts it, "to a large extent transactions costs are costs of relations between people" and institutions as we have seen are par excellence ways of controlling the interactions between people.

This, however, immediately suggests why there is no hope of incorporating institutional development in economic growth theory—at least as it is conventionally understood as variations on the themes of Solow and Swan. For in the Arrow-Debreu world of our theorists, which also forms the foundations of the new endogenous growth versions, institutions as defined above would be irrelevant, apart from the ghostly Walrasian auctioneer calling out the bids in some global chamber. Within this framework, on a more eclectic view, institutions could, however, indirectly effect the efficiency of investment and in the world of *conditional convergence*

---

[67] A useful survey of this literature as it relates to developing countries is provided by Lin and Nugent (1995). But as will be apparent I am taking a very different tack in this chapter.

determine the target steady-state growth rate for a group of institutionally similar countries toward which each would be converging along its traverse. It is not surprising that all the recent flurry of interest in this area has produced is the conclusion that the level and efficiency of investment are important determinants of growth and that the efficiency of investment is in turn governed by public policy (Barro and Sala-i-Martin, 1995; Sala-i-Martin, 1994). For development economists this is old hat, and it does not need any fancy algebra or cross-country regressions to reach this conclusion.[68]

In a recent book (Lal-Myint, 1996) we tried through comparative economic histories to peel the onion a bit further to see if there were any patterns we could discern as between different polities that could explain the different policy regimes that determine these proximate causes of growth. We found that rather than the type of polity, the initial resource endowment, in particular the availability or lack of natural resources, was a major determinant of policies that impinged on the efficiency of investment and thereby the rate of growth. This was basically due to the inevitability of the politicization of the rents that natural resources yield, with concomitant damage to growth performance. In many cases natural resources proved a "precious bane" that tended to kill the goose that laid the golden eggs. No more so than in Africa, where the ethnic conflicts within artificial states created by the nineteenth century colonial scramble for the continent have made this process even more deadly.[69] Within the land abundant group, however, the polity did make a difference because of the differing extent of political dissipation of natural resource rents, with relatively autonomous polities performing better than factional ones.

In the land-scarce economies, as the only source of revenue for the state is through the development of its only available resource—human beings—they had to follow the economically virtuous path of human resource development in open economies that build on their comparative advantage in labor intensive goods. Also, unlike their land-abundant cousins, they had no conflict between the polity and the country's comparative advantage, as the latter dictated a path of factor prices over the course of

---

[68] On these cross-country regressions that have recently proliferated I sympathize with Solow's view: "I do not find this a confidence-inspiring project. It seems altogether too vulnerable to bias from omitted variables, to reverse causation, and above all to the recurrent suspicion that the experiences of various national economies are not to be explained as if they represent different 'points' on some well-defined surface" (Solow (1994). Also see Bardhan (1995).

[69] Statistical confirmation within the cross-section regression framework for the role of ethnic diversity in Africa's growth disaster is provided in Easterly and Levine (1997).

development with smoothly rising wages. In the land abundant case, however, even on the efficient development path there was a danger of declining wages if the rate of capital accumulation was not rapid enough relative to the growth rate of labor. This political danger had often led them to disastrous "big push" programs or to cycles of populism followed by authoritarianism to mediate the conflict between the polity and the country's comparative advantage. Thus by and large we found that factor endowments, not the polity, were more important in explaining growth. But this means that at the very least the political influence on economic growth has been poorly formulated as an issue. Though I have something to say on the issue of political factors and economic growth, the assumption that there is some tight connection—as some recent research suggests—is from my own work highly questionable.[70]

The last two issues—income distribution and policy implications—however, remain, and I will come to them but I hope in a somewhat surprising way. Thus I do not think the sponsors will get exactly what I suspect they were looking for—some mechanical theory linking institutions (however defined) to economic growth. The reason for this is that when thinking about institutions, the mechanical analogy doesn't work. History, not mechanics, is the proper discipline for understanding institutions and economic growth, and that in a highly condensed manner is what I do in the following sections. In this I rely on a recently completed book based on my 1995 Ohlin lectures (Lal, 1998d), in which I sought to peel the onion explaining growth performance a bit further to see whether and in what way cultural influences might effect economic performance. I deal in a cross-cultural and interdisciplinary manner with the evolution and role of three central institutions—the market, the family, and the state—which are relevant for relative economic performance.

---

[70] The most sophisticated of the recent statistical studies, which have sought a statistical link between democracy and growth, is by Helliwell (1992). Also, see Barro (1997). But the statistical proxies for the political variables used in these exercises do not inspire much confidence. Also see Deaton and Miller (1995, p. 73) who rightly note that these exercises are plagued by the econometric problem of identification: "in the absence of some influence from outside the political and economic system of each country, these political economy models remain essentially unidentified, the best they can do is to demonstrate that it is possible to use the data to tell one story or another." The Lal-Myint (1996) study based on the economic histories of twenty-five developing countries found no link between democracy and growth.

5.3.   CULTURE AND SOCIAL EQUILIBRIA

In thinking about institutions, it is inevitable that one must think about culture. The two are closely intertwined, as I hope to show. But if institutions are a murky concept, culture is even more so. I have found a definition adopted by ecologists particularly useful (Colinvaux, 1983).[71] They emphasize that, unlike other animals, the human is unique because its intelligence gives it the ability to change its environment by learning. It does not have to mutate into a new species to adapt to the changed environment. It learns new ways of surviving in the new environment and then fixes them by social custom. These social customs form the culture of the relevant group, which are transmitted to new members of the group (mainly children) who do not then have to invent these new ways *de novo* for themselves.

This definition of culture fits in well with the economist's notion of equilibrium. Frank Hahn (1973) describes an equilibrium state as one where self-seeking agents learn nothing new so that their behavior is routinized. It represents an adaptation by agents to the economic environment in which the economy "generates messages which do not cause agents to change the theories which they hold or the policies which they pursue." This routinized behavior is clearly close to the ecologists notion of social custom that fixes a particular human niche. According to this view, the equilibrium will be disturbed if the environment changes, and so, in the subsequent process of adjustment, the human agents will have to abandon their past theories, which would now be systematically falsified. To survive, they must learn to adapt to their new environment through a process of trial and error. There will then be a new social equilibrium, which relates to a state of society and economy in which "agents have adapted themselves to their economic environment and where their expectations in the widest sense are in the proper meaning not falsified".

This equilibrium need not be unique nor optimal, given the environmental parameters. But once a particular socio-economic order is established and proves to be an adequate adaptation to the new environment, it is likely to be stable, as there is no reason for the human agents to alter it in any fundamental manner, unless and until the environmental parameters are altered. Nor is this social order likely to be the result of a deliberate rationalist plan. We have known since Adam Smith that an unplanned but coherent and seemingly planned social system can emerge from the independent actions of many individuals pursuing their different ends and in which the final outcomes can be very different from those intended.

---

[71] This was the definition adopted in Lal (1988) and in Lal (1998d).

It is useful to distinguish between two major sorts of beliefs relating to different aspects of the environment. These relate to what in my recent Ohlin lectures I labeled the *material* and *cosmological* beliefs of a particular culture (Lal, 1998d). The former relate to ways of making a living and concerns beliefs about the material world, in particular about the economy. The latter are related to understanding the world around us and our place in it, which determines how people view their lives—its purpose, meaning, and relationship to others. There is considerable cross-cultural evidence that material beliefs are more malleable than cosmological ones (Hallpike, 1986; and Boyd and Richardson, 1985). Material beliefs can alter rapidly with changes in the material environment. There is greater hysterisis in cosmological beliefs, on how, in Plato's words, "one should live." Moreover, the cross-cultural evidence shows that rather than the environment it is the *language group* that influences these world views (Hallpike, 1986).

This distinction between material and cosmological beliefs is important for economic performance because it translates into two distinct types of transactions costs I have noted elsewhere (Lal, 1998a). Broadly speaking, transactions costs can be distinguished usefully as those costs associated with the efficiency of *exchange*, and those costs associated with *policing* opportunistic behavior by economic agents.[72] The former relate to the costs of finding potential trading partners and determining their supply—demand offers, the latter to enforcing the execution of promises and agreements. These two aspects of transactions need to be kept distinct. The economic historian Douglass North (1990) and the industrial organization and institutionalist theorist Oliver Williamson (1985) have both evoked the notion of transactions costs and used them to explain various institutional arrangements relevant for economic performance. They are primarily concerned with the cost of opportunistic behavior, which arises for North, with the more anonymous non-repeated transactions accompanying the widening of the market, and for Williamson from the asymmetries in information facing principals and agents, where crucial characteristics of the agent relevant for measuring performance can be concealed from the principal. Both these are cases where it is the policing aspects of transactions costs that are at issue and not those concerning exchange.

To see the relevance of the distinction in beliefs and that in transactions costs (which as we saw earlier are seen by many as important reasons for the existence of institutions) for economic performance, it is useful to briefly

---

[72] Demsetz (1964) has also used the same terms to describe what he calls the "exchange and enforcement of property rights" in the context of external effects and public goods. But I am using the distinction between *exchange* and *policing* costs in a slightly different way.

delineate how broadly speaking material and cosmological beliefs have altered since the Stone Age in Eurasia.

5.4.   EXTENSIVE AND INTENSIVE GROWTH

Before that however, there is another important distinction we need to bear in mind: that between *extensive* and *intensive* growth. Humankind has experienced extensive growth with output rising pari passu with a growing population for millennia but without any marked rise in per capita incomes.[73] Intensive growth, which implies a sustained rise in per capita incomes, has been rarer and been of two broad types. The first, I have labeled *Smithian* growth, as it is due to the widening of the market and the increased specialization that entails. This type of growth can occur even in the predominantly agrarian economy whose productivity is ultimately bounded by a fixed factor—land (Wrigley, 1988). The second is *Promethean* growth, which involves transforming a land using agrarian economy into a mineral based energy economy. This was the essence of the Industrial Revolution as Wrigley has rightly noted, and for the first time, given the relatively unbounded supply of energy available from fossil fuels, opened up the prospect for humankind of unbounded intensive growth. This in turn opens up the possibility of alleviating that mass structural poverty that has been the bane of humanity for millennia.

For the great Eurasian civilizations there is evidence for Smithian intensive growth during certain periods of their history. This was the result of the knitting together of areas of diverse resources into a larger common market. Thus there was Smithian intensive growth in India during the Pax Buddhism of the Mauryas and the Pax Hindu of the Guptas, in the Mediterranean world during the Pax Greco/Roman of the ancient world, in the areas under Pax Islam under the Abbasids, in Japan during the Pax Tokugawa, and in China during the extension of the Pax Sung to the Yangtze Valley. But in none of these civilizations with the possible exception of Sung China was there any likelihood of Promethean growth. That remains a unique event that has been called the European miracle (see Jones, 1981), whose origins still remain disputed.

The failure of the Sung to initiate Promethean growth even though they had all the resource and technological ingredients available is one of the

---

[73] The rise in human population since the Stone Age (see McEvedy and Jones, 1978) is evidence for the ubiquitousness of extensive growth, for this growing population could not have been supported at even subsistence if output growth had not kept pace.

great puzzles of history, often labeled the *Needham problem*. But it does give the lie to various technologist explanations for the European miracle.

Mokyr (1990) is the major proponent of the view that differences in technical creativity explain the different wealth of nations. But his evolutionary theory of technical creativity is not very persuasive. Furthermore, what he identifies as the West's technical creativity remains a "black box" unless as in Lal (1998d) it is identified with a unique trait that led to it, which I claim was individualism. Many of the historical puzzles Mokyr alludes to can then be more readily explained. Instead of trying to explain why something as nebulous as technological creativity was sustained in the West, the question becomes as posed in Lal (1998d) the old Weberian question: "Why did individualism uniquely arise in the West?" My answer is that Weber got his dates wrong but that the role of the Western Christian church was crucial and in surprising ways not noted by economic historians. In this context mention should also be made of White (1978) who is also a technologist but whose linkage between the West's technological exceptionalism and the medieval Christian church has resonances with the story told in Lal (1998d).

Little (1981) and Scott (1989) have rightly argued that science and technology are not an important dividing line between the West and the Rest. As Little (1981, p. 66) notes, until the eighteenth century technological

> Improvements and dissemination seem to have been almost incredibly slow. The breastplate harness of horses, which tended to throttle them, reduced their efficiency, as compared with a padded collar, from 15 manpower to 4 manpower. It took 3000 years or more for a rudimentary padded collar to evolve, and another 1000 years for it to develop and become general. It similarly took thousands of years for fore and aft rigging and a swinging boom to appear. Yet such improvements did not have to wait upon new materials, or concentrated power; nor did they require, by way of science, more than observation, wit, and ingenuity. Glancing through the 3000 odd pages of the *Oxford History of Technology*, one finds dozens of statements like "the general form of war galley had not changed very greatly 1500 years later (i.e., in A.D. 1500)", or "thus by c. 1500 B.C. three basic glass-making techniques were in use. It was not for another 1500 years or so that a new process was developed (glass blowing)."

Scott (1989) provides a more radical departure in endogenizing the role of investment in growth by making three departures from the Solow-Swan framework. First, he argues that depreciation is essentially a transfer of income from capitalists to workers in a progressive economy. Were the appreciation (in workers' income) that results not excluded, as it is in conventional national income accounting, then net investment for society as a whole is (approximately) equal to gross investment as conventionally measured and not to gross investment minus depreciation. Second, he argues that there are no diminishing returns to cumulative gross investment, but there could be diminishing returns to the rate of investment. Third, he argues there is no need to invoke any independent or exogenous technical progress to explain growth. Defining investment as costs (in terms of foregone consumption) means that all activities (including technical progress) associated with growth are covered by it. Hence in his model there is only change (growth) due to investment and population growth. He shows that the growth experience of developed countries conforms to his model, while Lal and Myint (1996) show this is also the case for the twenty-five developing countries in their sample.

Needham (1963) also argues that science and technology cannot explain the rise of the West. As he writes (1963, p. 139),

> Not to put too fine a point on the matter, whoever would explain the failure of Chinese society to develop modern science had better begin by explaining the failure of Chinese society to develop mercantile and then industrial capitalism. Whatever the individual prepossessions of Western historians of science, all are necessitated to admit that from the fifteenth century A.D. onwards a complex of changes occurred: the Renaissance cannot be thought of without the Reformation, the Reformation cannot be thought of without the rise of modern science, and none of them can be thought of without the rise of modern capitalism . . . we seem to be in the presence of a kind of organic whole, a packet of change.

An essential part of this packet, it has been claimed in different ways by both North and Thomas (1973) and Jones (1981), was the decentralization and competition among polities in the European states system, which replaced the western Roman empire and which was due to geography. This limited the natural predatoriness of the state by making it more contestable.[74] This in turn allowed intensive growth, which Jones (1988) believes is just waiting to bubble forth except for the restraints imposed by the predatory state. India, however, like medieval Europe, has also had political disunity with cultural unity (provided by the Hindu caste system in India and Christianity in Europe), but it did not obtain Promethean growth.

The essential element missing in these various explanations for the rise of the West—though each forms part of Needham's packet of explanation—is the role of cosmological beliefs. Uniquely for Eurasian agrarian civilizations

---

[74] See Lal (1988), and Lal and Myint (1996) for a model of the predatory state that uses the notion of contestability as a central analytical device.

whose common cosmological beliefs can be broadly categorized as *communalist*, medieval Europe departed from the pattern and became individualist (Dumont, 1986). This was due to the reinterpretation of Pauline Christianity by St. Augustine in the fifth century[75] in his *City of God,* which converted the other-worldly individualism of the Christian church (a trait which it shares with Hinduism) into an in-worldly one by demanding the church be put above the state (Dumont, 1986), a demand that Pope Gregory VII fulfilled in the eleventh century with his injunction "Let the terrestrial kingdom serve—or be the slave of the celestial," which led to the so-called papal revolution. But why did this lead to individualism in the West, and why did individualism promote Promethean growth? To understand these we provide a highly condensed survey of the changing material and cosmological beliefs of the Eurasian civilizations in the next section.

5.5. CHANGING MATERIAL AND COSMOLOGICAL BELIEFS

5.5.1. On human nature

Evolutionary anthropologists and psychologists maintain that human nature was set during the period of evolution ending with the Stone Age. [76]Since then there has not been sufficient time for any further evolution. This human nature appears darker than Rousseau's and brighter than Hobbes's characterizations of it. It is closer to Hume's view that "there is some benevolence, however small . . . some particle of the dove kneaded into our frame, along with the elements of the wolf and serpent." For even in the hunter-gatherer Stone Age environment, the supremely egotistical human animal would have found some form of what evolutionary biologists term *reciprocal altruism* useful. Co-operation with one's fellows in various hunter-gatherer tasks yields benefits for the selfish human that can be further increased if he can cheat and be a free rider. In the *repeated* interactions between the selfish humans comprising the tribe, such cheating could be

---

[75] This dating gets over the Max Weber problem, where as Hicks (1969, pp. 78-79) notes that one fatal objection to Weber's thesis about the Protestant origins of capitalism is that an essential element was "the appearance of banking, as a regular activity . . . This began to happen . . . long before the Reformation; in so far as the Protestant ethic had anything to do with it, it was practice that made the ethic, not the other way round." Also see Kurt Samuellson's (1961) devastating critique of the Weberian thesis.

[76] See Lal (1998d) for references. Two popular surveys of the recent developments in evolutionary biology, psychology, and anthropology are Ridley (1996) and Wright (1994).

mitigated by playing the game of tit-for-tat. Evolutionary biologists claim that the resulting reciprocal altruism would be part of our basic Stone Age human nature.[77] Also in a perceptive review of Ridley (1996), Hirshleifer (1997) points out that reciprocity cannot be sufficient to generate the virtues that are normally identified with unreciprocated generosity and that social order requires more than just reciprocity. He writes reciprocity "cannot by itself explain the extent of co-operation among non-kin. A system of exchange based on property rights must rest on more than self-defense and tit-for-tat responses. In particular, disinterested third parties have to be willing to engage in what has been called 'moralistic aggression' to defend victims and punish defectors. If so, reciprocity is not the origin of virtue. Rather, true morality—pro-social propensities motivated by principle or compassion rather than by expected compensation—must be there already if a system of trade and exchange is to be viable" (p. 58). On the origins of virtue Hirshleifer states: "morality might be a human cultural development [or the result of] . . .'group selection', a concept currently scorned by most socio-biologists . . . but to my mind the evidence [for its] power . . . seems overwhelming"(p. 58).

These views are very much in consonance with those expressed in this article. Archaeologists have also established that the instinct to "truck and barter", the trading instinct based on what Sir John Hicks used to call the "economic principle"—"people would act *economically*; when an opportunity of an advantage was presented to them they would take it"[78]—is also of Stone Age vintage(see Ridley, 1996, for references). It is also part of our basic human nature.

5.5.2. Agrarian civilizations

With the rise of settled agriculture and the civilizations that evolved around them, however, and the stratification this involved between three classes of men—those wielding the sword, the pen, and the plough—(Gellner, 1988), most of the Stone Age basic instincts that comprise our human nature would be dysfunctional. Thus with the multiplication of interactions between human beings in agrarian civilizations many of the transactions would have been with anonymous strangers who one might never see again. The

---

[77] See Axelrod (1984) and Hirshleifer and Martinez-Coll (1988) for a discussion on the restrictive assumptions on which the Axelrod results depend. For a lucid and accessible account of evolutionary game theory, see Skyrms (1996).

[78] Hicks (1979, p. 43). But as Harold Demsetz has rightly pointed out to me, of course Adam Smith said this long before Hicks.

reciprocal altruism of the Stone Age, which depended on a repetition of transactions, would not be sufficient to curtail opportunistic behavior.

Putting it differently, the tit-for-tat strategy for the repeated prisoner's dilemma (PD) game among a band of hunter-gatherers in the Stone Age would not suffice with the increased number of one-shot PD games that will arise with settled agriculture and its widening of the market.[79] To prevent the resulting dissipation of the mutual gains from co-operation, agrarian civilizations internalized restraints on such anti-social action through moral codes that were part of their religion.[80] But these religions were more ways of life as they did not necessarily depend on a belief in God.

The universal moral emotions of shame and guilt are the means by which these moral codes embodied in cultural traditions are internalized in the socialization process during infancy (Ekman and Davidson, 1994; Hirshleifer, 1987; Frank, 1988). Shame was the major instrument of this internalization in the great agrarian civilizations. Their resulting cosmological beliefs can be described as being communalist.[81]

The basic human instinct to trade would also be disruptive for settled agriculture. For traders are motivated by instrumental rationality, which maximizes economic advantage. This would threaten the communal bonds that all agrarian civilizations have tried to foster. Not surprisingly most of them have looked on merchants and markets as a necessary evil, and sought to suppress them and the market that is their institutional embodiment. The material beliefs of the agrarian civilizations were thus not conducive to modern economic growth.

5.5.3.   The rise of the West

The rise of the West was mediated by the Catholic church in the sixth and eleventh centuries (Lal, 1998d), through its promotion of individualism, first in family affairs (in Gregory I's—also known as the Great—family

---

[79] It should also be noted that though there are some evolutionary biologists and anthropologists who seek to provide an account of cultural evolution (see Boyd and Richerson, 1985), the time scale over which evolutionary processes of inclusive fitness work—about 10,000 years to produce a new species—means that the evolutionary process is unlikely to explain historical cultures. These are human creations.

[80] It might also be asked why for the cheating human animal it doesn't also pay to feign belief in moral codes? But of course it does, as Kuran (1995) in his important book on preference falsification attests. However, as he shows, if there are enough believers in particular public lies, people will conceal their private truths and follow the common norms. This is sufficient for the arguments that follow.

[81] See T.C. Triandis (1995). I have relabeled Triandis's collectivism as *communalism* to avoid confusion with collectivism as a contemporary economic system.

revolution of the sixth century) and later in material relationships, which included the introduction of all the legal and institutional requirements of a market economy as a result of Gregory VII's papal revolution in the eleventh century (Berman, 1983). These twin papal revolutions arose because of the unintended consequences of the church's search for bequests—a trait that goes back to its earliest days. From its inception it had grown as a temporal power through gifts and donations—particularly from rich widows. So much so that, in July 370 the Emperor Valentinian had addressed a ruling to the Pope that male clerics and unmarried ascetics should not hang around the houses of women and widows and try to worm themselves and their churches into their bequests at the expense of the women's families and blood relations (Lane-Fox, 1988). The church was thus from its beginnings in the race for inheritances. The early church's extolling of virginity and preventing second marriages helped it in creating more single women who would leave bequests to the church.

This process of inhibiting a family from retaining its property and promoting its alienation accelerated with the answers that Pope Gregory I gave to some questions that the first Archbishop of Canterbury, Augustine, had sent in A.D. 597 concerning his new charges (Goody, 1983). Four of these nine questions concerned sex and marriage. Gregory's answers overturned the traditional Mediterranean and Middle Eastern patterns of legal and customary practices in the domestic domain. The traditional system was concerned with the provision of a heir to inherit family property and allowed marriage to close kin, marriages to close affines or widows of close kin, the transfer of children by adoption, and finally concubinage, which is a form of secondary union. Gregory amazingly banned all four practices. Thus, for instance, there was no adoption of children allowed in England till the nineteenth century. There was no basis for these injunctions in Scripture, Roman law, or the existing customs in the areas that were Christianized.

This papal family revolution made the church unbelievably rich. Demographers have estimated that the net effect of the prohibitions on traditional methods to deal with childlessness was to leave 40 percent of families with no immediate male heirs. The church became the chief beneficiary of the resulting bequests. Its accumulation was phenomenal. Thus, for instance, in France one-third of productive land was in ecclesiastical hands by the end of the seventh century.

But this accumulation also drew predators from within and without to deprive the church of its acquired property. It was to deal with this denudation that Pope Gregory VII instigated his papal revolution in 1075, by putting the power of God—through the spiritual weapon of excommunication—above that of Caesar's. With the Church then coming into the world, the new church-state also created all the administrative and legal infrastructure that we associate with a modern polity and that provided the essential institutions for the Western dynamic that in time led to Promethean growth. Thus Pope Gregory the VII's papal revolution lifted the lid on the basic human instinct to truck and barter, and in time to a change in the traditional Eurasian pattern of material beliefs with their suspicion of markets and merchants. This in time led to modern economic growth.

But the earlier papal revolution of Pope Gregory the First, which had precipitated that of Gregory VII, also led to a change in the traditional Eurasian family patterns that were based on various forms of joint families and family values. In its quest to weaken the traditional Eurasian family bonds in its race for inheritances, the Western Christian church came to support the independence of the young: in choosing marriage partners, setting up their households, and entering into contractual rather than affective relationships with the old. They promoted love marriages rather than the arranged marriages common in Eurasia. Friar Lawrence in *Romeo and Juliet* egging on the young lovers against their families wishes is emblematic of this trend.

It has been thought that romantic love far from being a universal emotion was a Western social construct of the age of chivalry in the Middle Ages. Recent anthropological and psychological research, however, confirms that this is erroneous—romantic love is a universal emotion (see Jankowiak, 1995; Fisher, 1992). Moreover, it has a biological basis. Neuro-psychologists have shown that it is associated with increased levels of phenylethylamine, an amphetamine-related compound. The same distinct biochemicals are also to be found in other animal species, such as birds, which also evince this emotion. However, it appears that this emotion is ephemeral. After a period of attachment the brain's receptor sites for the essential neuro-chemicals become desensitized or overloaded and the infatuation ends, setting up both the body and brain for separation—divorce. This period of infatuation has been shown to last for about three years. A cross-cultural study of divorce patterns in sixty-two societies between 1947 to 1989 found that divorces tend to occur around the fourth year of marriage (Jankowiak and Fischer (1992).

An universal emotion with a biological basis calls for an explanation. Socio-biologists maintain that in the primordial environment it was vital for males and females to be attracted to each other to have sex and reproduce and also for the males to be attached enough to the females to look after their young until they were old enough to move into a peer group and be looked after by the hunting and gathering band. The traditional period between successive human births is four years, which is also the modal period for those marriages that end in divorce today. Darwin strikes again. The biochemistry of love, it seems, evolved as an inclusive fitness strategy of our species.

The capacity to love may be universal, but its public expression is culturally controlled. For as everyone's personal experience will confirm, it is an explosive emotion. Given its relatively rapid decay, with settled agriculture the evolved instinct for mates to stay together for about four years and then move on to new partners to conceive and rear new young would have been dysfunctional. Settled agriculture requires settled households. If households are in permanent flux, there could not be settled households on particular parcels of lands. Not surprisingly, most agrarian civilizations sought to curb the explosive primordial emotion, which would have destroyed their way of making a living. They have used cultural constraints to curb this dangerous hominid tendency by relying on arranged marriages, infant betrothal, and the like, restricting romantic passion to relationships outside marriage. The West stands alone in using this dangerous biological universal as the bastion of its marriages as reflected in the popular lyrical song "Love and marriage go together like a horse and carriage."

While this unleashing of Stone Age passions helped alienate the young from their families, the church also had to find a way to prevent the social chaos that would have ensued if the romantic passion its greed had unleashed as the basis for marriage had been allowed to run its course in what remained a settled agrarian civilization. First it separated love and sex and then created a fierce guilt culture based on original sin. Its pervasive teaching against sex and the associated guilt it engendered provided the necessary antidote to the animal passions that would otherwise have been unleashed by the Church's self-interested overthrowing of the traditional Eurasian system of marriage. But once the Christian God died with the scientific and Darwinian revolutions, these restraints built on original sin were finally removed. The family as most civilizations have known it became sick in the West, as the Western humanoids reverted to the family practices of their hunter-gatherer ancestors.

5.6.   THE FAMILY, THE MARKET, AND THE STATE

The above account has I hope shown that at least two of the important institutional developments that influenced the rise of the West—the legal and commercial infrastructure of the market economy and the individualism of the Western family mode—were the result of greed and circumstance. There was nothing inevitable about them, and while they have cast long shadows—a benign one concerning the market and a less benign one concerning the erosion of the family—there is no theory of institutional development that can be derived from it. At best they represent the cunning of history.

Something closer to materialist explanations can, however, I believe, be provided for the third of the triad of institutions that are relevant for economic performance—the state. Just confining our attention to historical Eurasia there is a wide variety of types of state that have existed since the rise of agrarian civilizations in the alluvial plains of Mesopotamia, Egypt, the Indus and the Yellow River. Though the most common form has been hereditary monarchy—but with important differences in its justifications—there have been democracies in ancient Greece and in the Himalayan foothills in ancient India where ecological conditions permitted (Lal, 1998d). But besides these exceptions, the common form of state was determined by a common problem faced by the agrarian civilizations: these were labor-scarce, land-abundant areas, where as Domar has shown in a sadly neglected essay that in such an economy free labor, free land, and a non-working upper class cannot co-exist. These great Eurasian agrarian civilizations were created by obtaining a surplus for use in the towns (civitas being the emblem of civilization). This predatory purpose in effect ruled out a democratic state and implied that the peasants in these land-abundant areas would have to be tied down to the land to provide the necessary labor for the fairly labor-intensive processes of plough agriculture that were feasible in these areas and that provided enough of a surplus above subsistence to support the wielders of the pen and the sword in the cities.

The wielders of the sword were also needed for another reason. The great Eurasian civilizations were sandwiched between the two great areas of nomadic pastoralism—the grasslands of the great steppe regions to the North and the semi-desert of the Arabian peninsula. The nomads of these regions had maintained many of the warlike organizations and violent habits of big game hunters of their hunter-gatherer ancestors. They constantly preyed on the more numerous but sedentary populations of the agrarian civilizations of Eurasia. In the subsequent collisions between farmers and pastoralists, the inherent military advantages the latter enjoyed because of their habits made the wielder of the sword among the farmers essential in preventing the pastoralists from conquering and exploiting them like their animals. There were thus important external exigencies for obtaining a surplus to support specialists in wielding the sword, commanded by some form of monarch.

This then meant that to extract the surplus, labor had to be tied down to the land. The means employed—the caste system in India, various forms of serfdom in Europe and China, slavery in many civilizations—were determined more by ecology than ideology. But in many cases (like the Indian caste system) an ideology—or as I have called it, a set of cosmological beliefs—became an essential instrument in maintaining the necessary social controls. Such cosmological beliefs are necessary because even the most savage predatory state ultimately has to face the question of political legitimacy.

For as Searle (1995) has recently emphasized, above all institutions unlike brute facts like mountains are *social* facts. The distinguishing features of social as opposed to brute facts Searle identifies are first, they are "observer-relative"; unlike mountains, money and the state could not exist without human beings. Second, they are based on what he calls *collective intentionality.* [82]Third, institutions are based on what he calls constitutive rules, which differ from rules that regulate some activity that already exists.[83] Thus institutional facts are a subset of social facts. For both, unlike natural facts, the *attitude* we take constitutes the fact.

These features imply that any state no matter how tyrannical and predatory must be based on some general acceptance by the populace of its legitimacy. For as is evident from the dramatic events of 1989, the role of the military or police in maintaining the institutional structures of the state is greatly exaggerated. Ultimately, like other institutions, any state also depends on general acceptance of its right to rule. As Searle notes, one cannot usually provide some rational basis for this acknowledgment. It is largely a matter of habit. But as a result it can collapse quite suddenly when people lose confidence. These conjectures have been formalized, most notably in Kuran's (1995) *Private Truths, Public Lies*, whose title gives a succinct description of its thesis. It provides a direct link between what I have called cosmological beliefs and the polity.

In my Ohlin lectures (Lal, 1998d) I provide cross-cultural evidence that these cosmological beliefs of differing Eurasian polities were determined by the ecological conditions in the areas when their ancestral states were set up. Given the hysteresis in cosmological beliefs the peoples of these areas still find political legitimacy in terms of these ancient cosmologies. A few illustrations might help to make the point.

In India, as I argued in *The Hindu Equilibrium* (Lal, 1988), Hindu civilization developed on the vast Indo-Gangetic plain. This geographical feature (together with the need to tie down the then scarce labor to land) accounts for the traditional Indian polity, which was notable for its endemic

---

[82] An example is two violinists playing in an orchestra versus two individuals playing their instruments in separate rooms who are by chance playing the same piece in a synchronized manner.

[83] Thus the rules of chess do not regulate an activity that already exists; they *create* the possibility of playing chess.

political instability among numerous feuding monarchies because of the difficulties of any one establishing hegemony over the vast plain for any sustained period given the existing means of transportation and communication. It also explains why a decentralized system based on an internalized set of cosmological beliefs embodied in the caste system developed as a way of tying labor down to land. This institution, moreover, by making war the trade of professionals saved the mass of the population from being inducted into the deadly disputes of its changing rulers. While the tradition of paying a certain customary share of village output as revenue to the current overlord, meant that the victor had little incentive to disturb the daily business of its newly acquired subjects. The democratic practices gradually introduced by the British in the late nineteenth century fit these ancient habits like a glove. The ballot box has replaced the battlefield for the hurly-burly of continuing aristocratic conflict, while the populace accepts with ancient resignation that its rulers will, through various forms of rent seeking, take a certain share of output to feather their own nests. These ancient cosmological beliefs in my view explain why unlike so many other developing countries democracy has thrived in such a vast, diverse, and poor country and has taken deep root, as was shown by Indira Gandhi's aborted attempt to stifle it during her emergency.

By contrast the Chinese polity, in its origins in the relatively compact Yellow River Valley, constantly threatened by the nomadic barbarians from the steppes to the north, developed a tightly controlled bureaucratic authoritarianism as its distinctive polity, which has continued for millennia to our day. To give some idea of the extent of this authoritarianism and its resilience over the millennia, note that from the reference manuals of a petty bureaucrat of the Chin regime in about 217 B.C. (which were discovered with his body in December. 1975 at Shuihudi in Yunmeng) it appears that the Chin regime "kept detailed, quantified central records of the state of the crops almost field by field in every county of the empire. Maintaining that sort of control would be a daunting task for a government equipped with computers and telecommunications. Doing it before the invention of paper, when all the data had to be gathered and stored on strips of wood or bamboo, would have been impossible without an enormous bureaucracy" (Jenner, 1992). Little has changed in this polity since. Thus Jenner notes the continuity between the attitudes and values of the imperial Chinese state and the contemporary Communist one. As he notes: "The communist state is in many ways a reinvention of the bureaucratic monarchy. . . . The founders of the Communist Party were products of Qing China, educated in its schools and culture and soaked its values. To them it was only natural that the state should be absolute and that a bureaucratic monarchy was the natural form it should take. . . . Attitudes to state power remain heavily influenced by traditional values. The state's power remains absolute and sacrosanct. Though it can often be got around, it cannot be challenged. Politics at the top is played by the rules of palace struggles, which owe more to the political pundit of the third century B.C. Han Fei than to Marx" (pp. 35–36).

By contrast, democracy arose in the West on the foundations of feudal societies that had grown out of the weak states succeeding the Roman empire, in which medieval lords had obtained property rights in exchange for the materiel the princes needed to maintain their highly contestable natural monopolies—their states. With the consolidation of these fragmented polities into the absolutist nation states of Renaissance Europe, "the increase in the political sway of the royal state was accompanied, not by a decrease in the economic security of noble ownership, but by a corresponding increase in the general rights of private property" (Anderson, 1978, p. 429). On this material base the Reformation provided the cosmological beliefs leading to the rise of demos.

The Reformation in England was the logical conclusion of the problem that Gregory I's family revolution had set for Henry VIII. He took the step no other medieval king had thought of taking: "and that was to cast off the authority of Rome, to keep the churches open on his own authority, and to accept papal excommunication as a permanent condition" (Southern, 1970, p. 21). Once that happened, the church-state was dead and the nation-state was born. It also meant the end of the unity of Christendom and opened up the question of political legitimacy. Until then both rulers and ruled were bound by the common law of Christendom. But after the Reformation, who represented God's law—the Catholics or the Protestants—and whose law should you obey if you were a Catholic in a Protestant kingdom or vice versa? Equally momentous was the Protestant claim of the sinfulness of the Catholic church. If the traditional interpreters of God's will appointed by the Pope were sinful, where were the true interpreters of his will to be found? "If not the church, then only the congregations" (Minogue, 1995, p. 175). These became self-governing, choosing and dismissing their pastors. But if the church is to be governed by its members why not the State? Thus were the seeds for the rise of demos sown in Northwestern Europe.

This pluralist democratic political form took immediate root in the North America of the Pilgrim fathers, where ecology further helped in creating a unique egalitarian and democratic society. We cannot go into its genesis and development on this occasion (Lal, 1998b), but it provides a striking contrast to the outcome in the southern part of the hemisphere, where it was the Southern Europeans of the Counter-reformation who established their outposts. Spain after the reconquest from the Moors had developed a patrimonial state justified in terms of the neo-Thomist ideology that saw society as a hierarchical system in which every person and group "serves the purpose of a general and universal order that transcends them" (Morse, 1964, p. 146). It was a centralizing state without the manorial system with its decentralization of rights that had developed in Northern Europe. The economic correlate of this set of cosmological beliefs and the polity they supported was corporatism.

This led to very different polities in the two parts of the New World, where even when after their independence the Iberian colonies adopted U.S. style formal constitutions, the real form was still governed by the patrimonial legacy of Philip and Isabella of Spain. The hierarchical polity justified by neo-Thomism also permitted the accommodation of the unavoidable economic inequalities engendered by the land abundance and the demands of tropical agriculture given their climate, which was only viable with some form of coerced labor.

But these inequalities arising from its ecological and political heritage create a dissonance between Latin America's social realities and its Christian cosmological beliefs emphasizing equality, which of course it shares with the North. There is no such Northern dissonance, as both for ecological and political reasons a uniquely egalitarian social and political society developed there.

In this context it is worth noting the important difference between the cosmological beliefs of what became the Christian West and the other ancient agrarian civilizations of Eurasia. Christianity has a number of distinctive features that it shares with its semitic cousin Islam but not entirely with its parent Judaism and that are not to be found in any of the other great Eurasian religions. The most important is its universality. Neither the Jews nor the Hindu or Sinic civilizations had religions claiming to be universal. You could not choose to be a Hindu, Chinese, or Jew; you were born as one. This also meant that unlike Christianity and Islam these religions did not proselytize. Third, only the semitic religions being monotheistic have also been egalitarian. Nearly all the other Eurasian religions believed in some form of hierarchical social order, which for instance in Hindu India—with its belief in reincarnation—was rationalized as resulting from the system of just deserts for one's deeds in the past life. By contrast, alone among the Eurasian civilizations the semitic ones (though least so the Jewish) emphasized the equality of men's souls in the eyes of their monotheistic deities. Dumont (1970) has rightly characterized the resulting profound divide between the societies of *Homo aequalis*, which believe all men are born equal (as the *philosophers*, and the American constitution proclaim), and those of *Homo hierarchicus,* which believe no such thing. This matters for the polity. With the rise of demos, those societies infected by egalitarianism have a greater propensity for the populism that damages economic performance than the hierarchical societies. If, as in Europe, the granting of democratic rights can be phased in with the growing economic and social equality that modern growth helps to promote, then the political effects of the dissonance between an unequal social reality and egalitarian cosmological beliefs can be avoided. In the colonial and nineteenth century patrimonial states of Latin America this dissonance was avoided by restricting the polity—in effect to the property owning classes. But if as in this century, while still in the early stages of modern growth, the polity is expanded by incorporating the "dangerous classes" with an extension of democratic rights to the whole populace, then this dissonance can, as it has, lead to political cycles of democratic populism followed by authoritarian repression as the distributional consequences of the populist phase are found unacceptable by the Haves. By contrast hierarchical societies can more easily maintain majoritarian democracies, however corrupt and economically inefficient—as the notable example of India shows—despite continuing social and economic inequalities. Thus, as many Latin American commentators (Castaneda, 1995) have noted, the historic and continuing inequalities in Latin America make democracy there insecure, largely, I would argue, because of the social and cosmological dissonance noted above.

Thus questions of income distribution, I would argue, are of relevance only in those societies and polities that have been infected by one or other monotheistic religion—in particular Christianity. [84] Egalitarianism as so many of the other of its "habits of the heart" being touted as universal values by so many in the West are no such thing: they are the culture-specific outcomes of a particular trajectory of a particular Semitic religion.

But what of the other Western institutions —the nuclear family and the institutions of the market? Are they necessary for economic growth, and what of the role of Asian values in the development of East Asia? On the role of the market in promoting development we can be brief. The market with its universal worldwide victory over the plan remains the essential instrument for promoting intensive growth. The legal and commercial infrastructure was set in place by Pope Gregory VII and can be—as it has been—copied around the world. Because of the universal recognition of its instrumental value in generating that prosperity that all governments around

---

[84] In Lal and Myint (1996) one major finding was that *equity* defined in terms of income equality between the richer and poorer sections of the population has not been a major concern, particularly in Asia. What has been of concern are distributional problems between groups that cut across the conventional notion of income equality. Thus in Malaysia it is not income inequality per se but that between the Malays and Chinese that has been of concern. In Sri Lanka income inequality between the Sinhalese and Tamils is of concern.

the globe desire, there will not be any resistance to its spread on grounds of its efficacy as part of the material beliefs of any culture. However to the extent it is seen from some cosmological viewpoints as conflicting with cosmological beliefs, there maybe resistance if it is believed that the modernization it leads to will also entail Westernization—the adoption of the cosmological beliefs of the West. But I will argue this fear is unfounded at least for the great Asian civilizations.

Nowhere does this fear impinge as strongly as in the domestic domain. The great fear of the rest of the world is that their societies will also be infected with the virus that Pope Gregory I let loose—of individualism, love marriages, a non-caring attitude to the old, and so on. Some see this as the inevitable result of the Industrial Revolution. But just as the Western family can no longer be seen as the either the cause or consequence of the Industrial Revolution (Goody, 1996), there is no reason to believe that families elsewhere will be necessarily undermined by the modernization that the market will bring.

As we have seen, the medieval Christian church had attempted to put a lid on the family breakdown that would have occurred with the unleashing of romantic passion through the creation of a fierce guilt culture. This Western morality was underwritten by the belief in the Christian God. The classic statement of this Christian cosmology was St. Augustine's *City of God*. His narrative of a garden of Eden, a fall leading to original sin, and a day of judgment with heaven for the elect and hell for the damned has subsequently had a tenacious hold on Western minds. Thus the *philosophers* of the Enlightenment displaced the garden of Eden by classical Greece and Rome, and God became an abstract cause—the divine watchmaker. The Christian centuries were the fall. The enlightened were the elect, and the Christian paradise was replaced by posterity (Becker, 1932). This seemed to salvage the traditional morality in a world ruled by the divine watchmaker. But once Darwin had shown him to be blind, as Nietzsche proclaimed from the housetops at the end of the nineteenth century, God was dead, and the moral foundations of the West were thereafter in ruins. But the death of the Christian god did not end secular variations on the theme of Augustine's heavenly city. Marxism, Freudianism, and the recent eco-fundamentalism are secular mutations of Augustine.[85] But none of them has succeeded in

---

[85] For details see Lal (1998d). Thus, for instance, in Marxism there is a garden of Eden—before property relations corrupted natural man. Then the fall as commodification leads to class societies and a continuing but impersonal conflict of material forces, which leads in turn to the day of judgment with the revolution and the millennial paradise of Communism. Similarly the deep Christian roots of eco-fundamentalism are shown in Bramwell (1989) and Lal (1995). As regards Freudianism see Webster (1995) and Gellner (1993). Thus as Gellner argues, Freud created a new faith with traditional Judaeo-Christian

providing a moral anchor to the West. Such an anchor is of importance to the economy because the policing type of transaction costs associated with running an economy are increased in its absence.[86]

There is also the growing collapse of the Western family. It was presaged by the overthrowing of the traditional family patterns of Eurasian civilizations by Gregory I's individualist family revolution (Goody, 1983). This would have destroyed the Western family much earlier were it not for the subsequent fierce guilt culture the church promoted in the Middle Ages (Delumeau, 1990), which kept the traditional morality in place. But with the exorcising of both guilt and shame as illegitimate moral emotions in the West, there are fewer moral bulwarks left to shore up the family. This is not a problem that the other shame based cultures of Eurasia face.

Another consequence of Gregory I's family revolution was that the social safety nets provided by the family in most Eurasian societies were from an early date partly provided by the state in the West (Macfarlane, 1979, 1986). This nationalization of welfare accelerated in this century, leading to vast transfer states. The accompanying erosion of traditional morality in the West is manifest in various social pathologies—such as widespread family breakdown, high levels of illegitimacy and divorce, proliferation of single parent families, soaring crime rates, and the perpetuation of an urban underclass. The most powerful statement of this position is provided by Magnet (1993), who argues persuasively that the growth of the underclass and associated social pathologies in the United States is due more to cultural than purely economic factors (also see Himmelfarb, 1994). The strongest proponent of the economic case is Murray (1984). The econometric evidence on the effects of the U.S. welfare state on incentives is summarized in Moffit (1992), who concludes: "The literature has shown unequivocal evidence of effects on labor supply, participation in the welfare system and on some aspect of family structure. . . . Yet the review has also shown that the

---

roots. The unconscious becomes a new version of original sin. The analysts form a priesthood, offering personal salvation to the faithful through the confessional of the analysts couch; the priesthood is controlled by a guild of acolytes, who preach a doctrine which though cloaked in the mantle of science, is like any religion a closed system. It is tailored to the fears of the modern West. With nature quelled, these fears concern personal relationships. "His fulfillment and contentment, and his self-respect, are at the mercy of other people: of his spouse, other close kin, and work colleagues and superiors." With God's death the Christian hell had been dismantled. Now, in Sartre's words, "Hell is other people," and the analyst now provides a bespoke morality to deal with each person's special circumstances as worked out between the patient and the analyst.

[86] Of course, there are certain moralities—for instance Robin Hood's of helping the poor, which certainly increased policing costs for those traversing Sherwood forest.

importance of these effects is limited in many respects. The labor supply effects, whilst statistically significant, are not large enough to explain the high rates of poverty among female heads. . . . In addition, the econometric estimates of family structure effects are not large enough to explain long-run declines in marriage rates and, in any case, are incapable of explaining recent upward trends in female headship because welfare benefits have been declining" (pp. 56–57).

But the rest (except possibly Islam) do not have to fear this outcome—at least as long as they are not forced to create their own welfare states at the urging of do-gooders and moralizers from the West. Their moralities are based on religions that are ways of life that do not depend on a belief in God, so that the death of God that could follow their modernization does not entail giving up traditional morality. This (as Hume had also commended for the West) is based neither on reason nor a belief in God but on the "necessary habits" inculcated in the traditional socialization processes of the young through shame. Attempts to found a morality based on reason are open to Nietzsche's (1881/1982, p. 220): fatal objection in his aphorism about utilitarianism: "moral sensibilities are nowadays at such cross purposes that to one man a morality is proved by its utility, while to another its utility refutes it"). Kant's attempt to ground a rational morality on his principle of universality—which harks back to an ancient Biblical injunction—founders on Hegel's two objections: it is merely a principle of logical consistency without any specific moral content, and worse, it is as a result powerless to prevent any immoral conduct that takes our fancy as long as we are willing to make it universal. The subsequent ink spilt by moral philosophers has merely clothed their particular prejudices in rational form.

As long as their traditional families are not undermined, the rest will not have to create the vast transfer states of the West, which are required to substitute public for private social safety nets to deal with the ubiquitous risks associated with living. Combined with the workings of a majoritarian democracy, such public transfers have tended to corrupt the polity, with competing politicians showing their compassion by indiscriminately buying votes with other people's money. The different but indubitable corruption that currently also exists in the rest will by contrast be increasingly controlled both by the restraints on dirigisme that the spread of the market, and the globalization and increased openness that the ongoing communications revolution are promoting.

Moreover, the traditional family is likely to have a comparative advantage in the emerging international division of labor, whereby the West will increasingly have virtual factories that take orders for and design bespoke products tailored to the particular tastes of individual consumers, and then produce these by placing orders with the most efficient production facilities they can find around the globe (Rosecrance, 1996). The computer and Federal Express—at least for the least bulky goods—ensure that differentiated tastes can be catered for in a timely and efficient manner through global mass production (Gates, 1995). As this brave new world of virtual factories in the West demands flexible production structures in the rest to meet the needs of bespoke mass production, the family enterprise—as demonstrated spectacularly by the performance of the Chinese family enterprises in both mainland China and the lands of its diaspora—will come into its own (Whyte, 1996).

This raises the question of Asian values. I cannot go into details, but there is enough evidence (Lal, 1998d) to support Jenner's (1992) assertion that the success of the purported neo-Confucian societies on the East Asian edge has little to do with China's past but with "European economics, commercial law, science, and technology" (p. 172). Where 'values' may have helped is in the continuing strength of their traditional families, which have allowed them to avoid both the economic and cultural costs of public welfare systems.

This raises the final question that this paper has been leading to. Will the rest be forced to change their cosmological beliefs as a result of the modernization that they all seek because of the prosperity that it brings and that is being accelerated by the communications revolution? This is an old question in development studies. Will Westernization follow modernization, and in fact can—as some claim—modernization occur without Westernisation? There has been an influential body of thought that has claimed this necessary connection. [87] It is also the basis of the current belief in the West, reflected in its global moral crusades concerning so called human rights, democracy, and saving Spaceship Earth, that with the success of the market its own values will also be adopted worldwide. But this is to assume that material beliefs determine cosmological beliefs. [88]There is little to support this assumption even though in the rise of the West the two sets of beliefs were conjoined. The important case of a modernized but non-Westernized Japan has shown this is not a necessary connection. [89]The rest do not have to make the Faustian compact of the West, where the instrumental rationality promoted by its individualism led to the Industrial Revolution but in the process destroyed its Christian soul. It is often argued that the evidence from church attendance and the professions of religious

---

[87] This was identified with the work supported by the Committee on Comparative Politics of the Social Science Research Council in the United States during the 1960s. The most important work in this genre remains Almond and Coleman (1960).

[88] A belief shared equally by Marxists and Chicago school economists.

[89] This is argued forcefully by Waswo (1996). Also see Eisenstadt (1996).

belief in the united States would contradict this. Thus Bellah et al. (1986) note "some 40 percent of Americans attend religious services at least once a week (a much greater number than would be found in Western Europe or even Canada) and religious membership is around 60 percent of the total population" (p. 219). But if other aspects of current American behavior concerning Christian moral injunctions are taken into account—against adultery and divorce for instance—to an outsider, these figures for professed religious belief appear to be merely a sign of hypocrisy or a manifestation of the fractured American self outlined by Macintyre discussed below. Of course, there maybe some—for instance, President Clinton from recent reports in the U.S. media—who might claim that they are still faithful Christians but that their purported forms of extra marital sex do not constitute adultery as defined by the Bible.

There are also those of a Polyannish tendency best represented by Lipset (1996) who claim that even the signs of social decay such as the growth of the American underclass does not matter as it is statistically insignificant. The underclass, he claims, only amounts to about 1 to 2 percent of the U.S. population, which makes it about 2 to 3 million people. This is, of course, a larger number than the U.S. armed forces. If the latter, though about 1 percent of the population, were let loose in the inner cities as invading armies often were in the bad old days, even Lipset might view this prospect with some trepidation.

Japan has been able to alter its material beliefs by adopting the institutions of the market. But it has kept its ancient hierarchical social structures—by basing them on acquired rather than ascribed status through the fierce meritocratic competition based on educational attainment—rather than abandon them for the social egalitarianism espoused by the West. It has also not had to give up its traditional forms of family or its other cosmological beliefs based on shame. The same opportunity is open to the rest to adopt the West's material but eschew its cosmological beliefs.

5.7.   CONCLUSIONS

I have argued that institutions and culture are closely linked. Of the two aspects of culture I have identified, cosmological beliefs have been as important as material beliefs in determining economic outcomes. Material beliefs can change rapidly as can the institutions based on them, such as systems of property rights, with changing factor and commodity prices (for examples, see Demsetz, 1967, and Feeny, 1988). Cosmological beliefs influence the polity. The initial resource endowments of the ancestral states of Eurasian civilizations governed the form of their polities and engendered cosmological beliefs, which provided political legitimacy. There is great hysterisis in cosmological beliefs and in transferring one type of polity into a region with a differing cosmology. But, paradoxically, the multiplicity of political forms, as long as they do not represent an "enterprise association" in Oakeshott's (1993) sense, in themselves do not hinder economic growth. Thus a particular political form such as democracy is not essential for development. After all, it was hereditary monarchy and not democracy that delivered the Industrial Revolution. What matters for intensive growth is that the market should be allowed to function. Here the sages of the Scottish Enlightenment were clear-headed about the link between the polity and the economy.

They recognized the importance of good governance, which for them was provided by a government that promoted opulence through promoting natural liberty by establishing laws of justice that guaranteed free exchange and peaceful competition. The improvement of morality was left to non-government institutions. But they were quite undogmatic about the particular form to use to promote these characteristics of the state seen as (Oakeshott calls it) a "civil association." According to this view, the state is not seen as the custodian of laws that seek to impose a preferred pattern of ends (including abstractions such as the general (social) welfare, or fundamental rights), but that merely facilitates individuals to pursue their own ends.

But as Oakeshott emphasizes, this classical liberal view that goes back to ancient Greece has been challenged in Western political thought and practice by a rival conception of the state, which has its roots in Judeo-Christian tradition, and views the state as a enterprise association. The state according to this view is seen as the manager of an enterprise seeking to use the law for its own substantive purposes, and in particular for the legislation of morality. Since the truce declared in the eighteenth century wars of religions, the major substantive purposes sought by states seen as enterprise associations are nation-building and the promotion of some form of egalitarianism. In our time Khomeni's Iran represents the religious version of an enterprise association of another semitic religion.

In the developing nations both nation-building and egalitarianism were the aims of the leaders who saw the state as an enterprise. As in the past this led to dirigisme and the control of the market. The nation-building aim was particularly badly served as the dirigisme it entailed led as in eighteenth century Europe—where the mercantilist system of the post Renaissance absolutist states was established for similar motives—to national disorder (see Hecksher, 1955). For dirigisme bred corruption, rent seeking, tax evasion, and illegal activities in underground economies. The most serious consequence for the state was erosion of its fiscal base and the prospect of an un-Marxian withering away of the state. In both cases economic liberalization was undertaken to restore the fiscal base, and thence government control over ungovernable economies. In some cases the changeover could only occur through revolution—most notably France (see, Lal, 1987, and Lal and Myint, 1996).

Egalitarianism, as I have been at pains to emphasize, is a value unique to Christendom. It was incorporated into the polities of the non-Christian Eurasian civilizations by Westernized elites infected with its various variants (Fabian socialism in India and Marxist communism in China). But with the inevitable economic failure of the dirigisme it promoted, these great Eurasian civilizations are eschewing these imported creeds and turning back to their traditional polities—which were concerned with maintaining some form of civil association and social order rather than promoting some enterprise. Though the political forms these take could diverge—for the reasons given earlier—they are more likely to be closer to the old classical notion of the state seen as a civil association than the various enterprise versions promoted by variations on the theme of St. Augustine's City of God.

Given the uneasy tension in Western thought and action between these two rival conceptions of the state, it is those regions of the developing world (Latin America, Africa) that are outposts of Christianity where the problems of governance pace Smith and Hume are likely to be most acute. The problems in Africa have been compounded by the artificiality of the states created, which has pitted tribe against tribe within and without the arbitrary boundaries resulting from the European scramble for Africa. Following the logic of my argument that traditional political forms have a legitimacy (that imported ones do not) as they are in consonance with the people's cosmological beliefs and that in themselves political forms do not matter for economic performance, the best outcome for Africa would be to create states that coincide with tribal homogeneity with a polity ruled as in the past by some form of tribal chief.

This suggests that the *institutional development* of the title of this chapter set me by the sponsors is a misnomer, suggesting as it does that there is some technocratic template to design institutions most likely to promote development. There is no such template except for the well worn legal and commercial infrastructure of Pope Gregory VII's papal revolution. Institutional development is a form of cultural evolution—not well understood. Thus I am led to conclude that the implication for policies towards the state in developing countries is by and large to let well alone—a conclusion that is even stronger for policies like the welfare state which impinge on the traditional family. The welfare state is a Western necessity because of the long shadow cast by Pope Gregory I's family revolution. It should not be wished on or thrust on the non-Christian rest.

Which leaves the market. This is now spreading spontaneously throughout the world because of its instrumental value. The greatest threats to its worldwide spread now come in fact from the West, where the traditional fear of pauper labor imports that have been used to justify protectionism in the past are being refurbished in the guise of human rights, environmental protection, and other aspects of so-called ethical trading (Lal 1998c). This political moralism represents a continuing threat to the prosperity of the developing world. But as I have tried to show, it is not something new, nor is the ethics being promoted universal. It is the culture-specific, proselytizing, universal, and egalitarian ethic clothed in secular garb of what remains at heart Western Christendom. The rest, as I have argued, have seen the utility of the market and can adopt it and the prosperity it brings without the need to adopt the two other Western institutions—its family or its polity.

References

Almond, G.A., and J.S. Coleman, eds. (1960). *The Politics of the Developing Areas.* Princeton, NJ: Princeton University Press.

Anderson, P. (1978). *Passages from Antiquity to Feudalism.* London: Verso.

Axelrod, R. (1984). *The Evolution of Co-operation.* New York: Basic Books.

Bardhan, P. (1995). "The Contributions of Endogenous Growth Theory to the Analysis of the Development Process: An Assessment." In J. Behrman and T.N. Srinivasan, eds., *Handbook of Development Economics* (vol. 3B). Amsterdam: North Holland.

Barro, R.J. (1997). "Determinants of Economic Growth — A Cross-Country Empirical Study." Development Discussion Paper 579, Harvard Institute of International Development, Cambridge, MA.

Barro, R.J., and X. Sala-i-Martin. (1995). *Economic Growth.* New York: McGraw Hill.

Becker, G. (1996). *Accounting for Tastes.* Cambridge, MA: Harvard University Press.

Becker, G., and G. Stigler. (1977). "De gustibus non est disputandum." *American Economic Review* 67, 76–90.

Becker, C.L. (1932). *The Heavenly City of the Eighteenth Century Philosophers.* Yale, New Haven.

Bellah, R.N., R. Madsen, W.M. Sullivan, A. Swidler, and S.M. Tipton. (1986). *Habits of the Heart.* New York: Perennial, Harper and Row.

Berman, H.J. (1983). *Law and Revolution.* Cambridge, MA: Harvard.

Bork, R.H. (1996). *Slouching towards Gomorrah.* New York: Harper-Collins.

Boyd, R., and P.J. Richerson. (1985). *Culture and the Evolutionary Process.* Chicago: Chicago University Press.

Bramwell, A. (1989). *Ecology in the Twentieth Century — A History.* New Haven: Yale University Press.

Castaneda, T. (1992). *Combating Poverty.* San Francisco: ICS Press.

Coleman, J.S. (1990). *Foundations of Social Theory.* Cambridge, MA: Harvard University Press.

Colinvaux, P. (1983). *The Fates of Nations.* London: Penguin.

Deaton, A., and R. Miller. (1995). "International Commodity Prices, Macroeconomic Policies, and Politics in Sub-Saharan Africa." *Princeton Studies in International Finance* 79, Princeton University, Princeton, NJ.

Delumeau, J. (1990). *Sin and Fear: The Emergence of a Western Guilt Culture 13-18th centuries.* New York: St. Martin's Press.

Demsetz, H. (1964). "The Exchange and Enforcement of Property Rights." *Journal of Law and Economics* 8, 11–26.

Demsetz, H. (1967). "Toward a Theory of Property Rights." *American Economic Review*, 347–359.

Demsetz, H. (1970). "The Private Production of Public Goods." *Journal of Law and Economics* 13, 293–306.

Demsetz, H. (1968/1988). "The Costs of Transacting." *Quarterly Journal of Economics* 82, reprinted in H. Demsetz, *Ownership, Control and the Firm* (pp. 63–81). Oxford: Blackwell.

Domar, H. (1970). "The Causes of Slavery or Serfdom: A Hypothesis." *Journal of Economic History* 30 (March), 18–32.

Dumont, L. (1970). *Homo Hierarchicus.* London: Weidenfeld and Nicholson.

Dumont, L. (1986). *Essays on Individualism.* Chicago: Univ. of Chicago Press.

Easterly, W.R., and R. Levine. (1997). "Africa's Growth Tragedy: Policies and Ethnic Divisions." *Quarterly Journal of Economics*, 1203–1249.

Eisenstadt, S.N. (1996*). Japanese Civilization — A Comparative View.* Chicago: Chicago University Press.

Ekman, P., and R.J. Davidson, eds. (1994*). The Nature of Emotion.* New York: Oxford University Press.

Feeny, D. (1988). "The Development of Property Rights in Land: A Comparative Study." In R.H. Bates, ed., *Toward a Political Economy of Development.* Berkeley: University of California Press.

Fischer, S. (1977). "Long Term Contracting, Sticky Prices, and Monetary Policy: Comment." *Journal of Monetary Economics* 5.

Fisher, H. (1992). *Anatomy of Love: The Natural History of Monogamy, Adultery and Divorce.* New York: Norton.

Frank, R. (1988). *Passions Within Reason.* New York: Norton.

Gates, B. (1995). *The Road Ahead.* New York: Viking.

Gellner, E. (1988). *Plough, Book and Sword: The Structure of Human History.* Collins Harvill, London.

Gellner, E. (1993). *The Psychoanalytic Movement — The Cunning of Unreason.* Evanston, III, Northwestern Univ. Press.

Goody, J. (1983). *The Development of the Family and Marriage in Europe.* Cambridge, MA.

Goody, J. (1996). "Comparing Family Systems in Europe and Asia." *Population and Development Review* 22, 1–20.

Hahn, F. (1973). *On the Notion of Equilibrium in Economics.* Cambridge, MA: Cambridge Univ. Press.

Hicks, J.R. (1969). *The Theory of Economic History.* Oxford: Oxford University Press.

Hicks, J.R. (1979). *Causality in Economics.* Oxford: Blackwells.

Himmelfarb, G. (1994). *The Demoralization of Society.* New York: Knopf.

Hirshleifer, J. (1980). *Price Theory and Applications* (2nd ed.). Englewood Cliffs: Prentice Hall.

Hirshleifer, J. (1987). "On the Emotions as Guarantors of Threats and Promises." In J. Dupre, ed., *The Latest on the Best: Essays on Evolution and Optimality.* Cambridge, MA: MIT Press.

Hirshleifer, J. (1997). "Good Genes." *Reason* (November), 56–59.

Hirshleifer, J., and J.C. Martinez-Coll. (1988). "What Strategies Can Support the Evolutionary Emergence of Co-operation." *Journal of Conflict Resolution* 32, 367–398.

Hallpike, C.R. (1986). *The Principles of Social Evolution.* Oxford: Clarendon Press.

Hecksher, E. (1955). *Mercantilism* (2 vols.). London: Allen and Unwin.

Helliwell, J. (1994). "Empirical Linkages between Democracy and Economic Growth." *British Journal of Political Science* 24, 225–248.

Hume, D. (1740/1985). *A Treatise on Human Nature.* London: Penguin Classics.

Jankowiak, W., ed. (1995). *Romantic Passion: A Universal Experience?* New York: Columbia Univ. Press.

Jankowiak, W., and E. Fischer. (1992). "A Cross-Cultural Perspective on Romantic Love." *Ethnology* 31(3), 149–155.

Jenner, W.J.F. (1992). *The Tyranny of History.* London: Penguin.

Jones, E.L. (1981). *The European Miracle.* Cambridge, MA: Cambridge University Press.

Jones, E.L. (1988). *Growth Recurring.* Oxford: Oxford University Press.

Klenow, P.J., and A. Rodriguez-Clare. (1997). "The Neoclassical Revival in Growth Economics: Has It Gone Too Far?" In B.S. Beranke and J.J. Rotenberg, eds., *NBER Macroeconomics Annual 1997.* Cambridge, MA: MIT Press.

Knack, S., and P. Keefer. (1997). "Does Social Capital Have an Economic Payoff? A Cross-Country Investigation." *Quarterly Journal of Economics*, 1252–1287.

Kuran, T. (1995). *Private Truths, Public Lies.* Cambridge, MA: Harvard University Press.

Lal, D. (1983, 1997). *The Poverty of Development Economics.* London: IEA.

Lal, D. (1987). "The Political Economy of Economic Liberalization." *World Bank Economic Review* 1, 273–299. Reprinted in Lal (1993).

Lal, D. (1988). *The Hindu Equilibrium.* Oxford: Clarendon Press.

Lal, D. (1993). *The Repressed Economy, Economists of the Twentieth Century Series.* Elgar, Aldershot.

Lal, D. (1994). *Against Dirigisme.* San Francisco: ICS Press.

Lal, D. (1995). "Eco-Fundamentalism." *International Affairs* 71, 515–528.

Lal, D. (1998a). *Unintended Consequences: The Impact of Factor Endowments, Culture and Politics on Long Run Economic Performance.* The Ohlin Lectures. Cambridge, MA: MIT Press.

Lal, D. (1998b). *The Communications Revolution, Transactions Costs, Culture, and Economic Performance.* Mimeo, UCLA.

Lal, D. (1998c). *The Political Economy of Reform in Latin America.* Mimeo, UCLA.

Lal, D. (1998d). "Social Standards and Social Dumping." In H. Giersch, ed., *The Merits of Markets.* Berlin: Springer.

Lal, D., and H. Myint. (1996). *The Political Economy of Poverty, Equity and Growth.* Oxford: Clarendon Press.

Lane-Fox, R. (1988). *Pagans and Christians.* London: Penguin.

Lewis, B. (1982). *The Muslim Discovery of Europe.* New York: Norton.

Lin, J.Y., and J.B. Nugent. (1995). "Institutions and Economic Development." In J. Behrman and T.N. Srinivasan, eds., *Handbooks of Development Economics* (vol. 3A). Amsterdam: North Holland.

Lipset, M. (1996). *American Exceptionalism —A Double Edged Sword.* Norton, New York.

Little, I.M.D. (1981). "Comment on Kuznets 'Driving Forces of Economic Growth: What Can We Learn from History?" In H. Giersch, and J.C.B. Mohr, eds., *Towards an Explanation of Economic Growth*. Tubingen.

Macfarlane, A. (1979). *The Origins of English Individualism*. Oxford: Blackwell.

Macfarlane, A. (1986). *Marriage and Love in England: Modes of Reproduction, 1300-1840*. Oxford: Blackwell.

Macintyre , A. (1990). "Individual and Social Morality in Japan and the United States: Rival Conceptions of the Self." *Philosophy East and West* 40, 489–497.

Magnet, M. (1993). *The Dream and the Nightmare: the Sixties Legacy of the Underclass*. New York: Quill/Murrow.

Mankiw, N.G., D. Romer, and D.N. Weil. (1992). "A Contribution to the Empirics of Economic Growth." *Quarterly Journal of Economics* 107, 407–437.

Matthews, R.C.O. (1986). "The Economics of Institutions and the Sources of Growth." *Economic Journal* 96, 903–918.

McEvedy, C., and R. Jones. (1978). *Atlas of World Population History*. London: Penguin.

Minogue, K. (1995). *Politics*. Oxford: Oxford Univ. Press.

Moffitt, R. (1992). "Incentive Effects of the US Welfare System: A Review." *Journal of Economic Literature* 30, 1–61.

Mokyr, J. (1990). *The Lever of Riches*. New York: Oxford University Press.

Murray, C. (1984). *Losing Ground: American Social Policy 1950-1980*. New York: Basic Books.

Morse, R.M. (1964). "The Heritage of Latin America." In L. Hartz, ed., *The Founding of New Societies*. New York: Harcourt, Brace and World.

Needham, J. (1963). "Poverties and Triumphs of the Chinese Scientific Tradition." In A.C. Crombie, ed., *Scientific Change*. London: Heinemann.

Niehans, J. (1987). "Transactions Costs." In Eatwell, Milgate and Newman, eds., *The New Palgrave- A Dictionary of Economics* (pp. 676–679). New York.

Nietzsche, F. (1881/1982). *Daybreak: Thoughts on the Prejudices of Morality*. Cambridge, MA: Cambridge University Press.

North, D.C. (1981). *Structure and Change in Economic History*. New York.

North, D.C. (1990). *Institutions, Institutional Change and Economic Performance*. Cambridge, MA: Cambridge University Press.

North, D.C., and R.P. Thomas. (1973). *The Rise of the Western World*. Cambridge, MA: Cambridge University Press.

Oakeshott, M. (1993). *Morality and Politics in Modern Europe*. New Haven: Yale Univ. Press.

Ridley, M. (1996). *The Origins of Virtue*. Viking. London: Penguin.

Rosecrance, R. (1996). "The Virtual State." *Foreign Affairs*.

Sala-i-Martin, X. (1994). "Cross-Sectional Regressions and the Empirics of Economic Growth." *European Economic Review* 8, 739–747.

Samuelsson, K. (1961). *Religion and Economic Action*. New York: Basic Books.

Scott, M.F. (1989). *A New View of Economic Growth*. Oxford: Clarendon Press.

Searle, J.R. (1995). *The Reconstruction of Social Reality*. New York: Free Press.

Skyrms, B. (1996). *Evolution of the Social Contract*. Cambridge, MA: Cambridge University Press.

Solow, R.M. (1994). "Perspectives on Growth Theory." *Journal of Economic Perspectives* 8, 45–54.

Southern, R.W. (1970) *Western Society and the Church in the Middle Ages*. New Haven: Yale University Press.

Sugden, R. (1986). *The Economics of Rights, Cooperation and Welfare*. Oxford: Blackwell.

Triandis, T.C. (1995). *Individualism and Collectivism*. Boulder, Colorado: Westview Press.

Waswo, A. (1996). *Modern Japanese Society, 1868-1994*. Oxford: Oxford University Press.

Webster, R. (1995). *Why Freud was wrong*. London: Harper-Collins.

White, L. (1978). *Medieval Religion and Technology*. Berkeley: University of California Press.

Whyte, M.K. (1996). "The Chinese family and Economic Development: Obstacle or Engine?" *Economic Development and Cultural Change* 45, 1–30.

Williamson, O.E. (1979). "Transactions Cost Economics: The Governance of Contractual Relations." *Journal of Law and Economics* 22.

Williamson, O.E. (1985). *The Economic Institutions of Capitalism*. New York: Free Press.

Wright, R. (1994). *The Moral Animal*. New York: Pantheon.

Wrigley, E.A. (1988). *Continuity, Chance and Change*. Cambridge, MA: Cambridge University Press.

Young, A. (1994). "Lessons from the East Asian NIC's: A Contrarian View." *European Economic Review* 38, 964–973.

Young, A. (1995). "The Tyranny of Numbers: Confronting the Statistical Realities of the East Asian Growth Experience." *Quarterly Journal of Economics* 110, 641–680.

DISCUSSION

Aristomene Varoudakis

Senior Economist, OECD, Paris

The focus of Deepak Lal's chapter is on the interaction between culture and three kinds of institutions (the family, the market, and the state) in the process of economic development. This is an important and, at the same time, very difficult and controversial issue. Lal's thought-provoking chapter is of interest not only to economic historians but also to theorists and to policy-oriented applied economists.

Economists have always been reluctant to explicitly incorporate the cultural dimension in their theories of economic development. Issues related to cross-country differences in attitudes toward personal achievement, in the influence of religion, or in the hierarchy of social values have been dismissed from most systematic studies of economic development and institutional change (see, for example, North, 1981).

In his analysis of the way cultural influences may affect economic performance, Lal provides a paradigm—well documented by historical examples—that , taking the risk of some simplification, can be summarized in three points:

1. Particular forms of institutions (the family, the legal infrastructure of markets, the state) develop to solve mainly problems of resource allocation. These problems are closely related to the relative human and natural resource endowments of various geographical areas.

2. These particular institutions need political and social legitimacy. This is provided by what Lal calls the material and cosmological beliefs, which are embodied in a society's culture. Therefore, one might say that countries get the economic and political institutions they need and, accordingly, the culture they deserve. Material beliefs are reflected by the ranking of values, which determine individual attitudes toward the market and the organization of economic activities. As stressed by Lal, material beliefs can be altered rapidly with changes in the material environment. Cosmological beliefs relate to individual's understanding of their place in the world and their relationships to others. They include ideology and religion, and they change much more slowly than material beliefs.

3. According to the proposed paradigm, changes in cosmological beliefs are an important neglected factor in understanding some major puzzles of economic history—namely, the rise of the West starting from the later Middle Ages, as well as the relative backwardness of China, despite its technological advance over Europe up to the foreteenth century (the well-known Needham problem).

It is claimed that, contrary to other Eurasian civilizations whose cosmological beliefs were broadly communalist, in Western Europe cosmological beliefs became progressively individualist under the influence of a twin revolution:

• The reinterpretation of Christian dogma by St. Augustine in the fifh century.

• The family revolution promoted by the church in the eleventh century. In its race for bequests, it is claimed, the church promoted a weaker pattern of family ties, which replaced the extended nets of the oriental family. At the same time, the church set up the institutional infrastructure for contractual exchange that was necessary for these new kind of social arrangements.

The induced change in cosmological beliefs paved the way for a gradual change in material beliefs towards a friendlier attitude to markets and industrial activities. This, in due time, made it possible for Western societies to benefit from opportunities arising from technological change, leading to the Industrial Revolution of the late eighteenth century.

According to this paradigm, political forms (which are the third pillar of institutions, together with the family and the contractual arrangements of the market) have legitimacy derived from society's cosmological beliefs. They do not really matter for economic performance. After all, as stressed by Lal, the Industrial Revolution took place under political regimes of hereditary monarchy. What really seems to matter for economic performance is good governance, not democracy.

Going one step forward—and bringing the analysis from history to the current policy debate—Lal concludes that, to ensure sustained growth, Asia and other developing countries do not necessarily need to adopt all Western institutions. Models of weak families and Western egalitarian democracy are deeply rooted in Western cosmological beliefs. They are not suitable to Asian hierarchical culture or to African tribal tradition.

What seems to be important for prosperity is the smooth functioning of the market mechanism, and this is what Asian or African countries should make sure to adopt among Western institutions.

Although I find Lal's approach appealing, I feel (as an outsider to the professional field of economic history) that his emphasis on the exclusive role of cosmological beliefs, behind institutional change and relative economic performance, might be somewhat restrictive. Moreover, this raises some doubts with regard to his argument about the irrelevance of Western political institutions (namely, modern democracy) for economic development outside the West.

Starting from history, the proposed paradigm competes successfully with alternative explanations of the Needham problem (the rise of the West against the decline of medieval China). However, it might not be entirely suitable to explain other historical puzzles, related to episodes of near-economic take-off, which came to a halt. Economic historians seem to agree as to the trial-and-error character of the Industrial Revolution. The necessary technological conditions to start what Lal calls "Promethean growth" seem to have existed in various places and times before England at the end of the eighteenth century. These include Hellenistic Alexandria, medieval China, and various places in Europe in the high Middle Ages.

An especially disturbing case, discussed by the French historian Fernand Braudel (1979), is Milan and the region of Lombardy in the sixteenth century. Thanks to an efficient agriculture, Lombardy had not experienced serious damage from plague during the two preceding centuries. Moreover, thanks to the great Renaissance engineers, all of the inventions that subsequently paved the way to the first Industrial Revolution were already around. It is also well known that high farming historically started in Lombardy. On top of that, Milan had already successful manufacturing industries, as well as a prosperous middle class to promote capital accumulation.

Why then the Industrial Revolution did not start two and a half centuries earlier in Northern Italy? It seems to me that Lal's paradigm of changes in cosmological beliefs is not well suited to understand a paradox internal to the rise of the Western world.

Should we revert to Max Weber and to his emphasis on Protestant ethics as a vehicle of capitalist development? I don't think so, and it seems to me that Lal would agree. I have much sympathy for the conceptual framework developed by Mokyr (1990), to explain medieval China's relative backwardness and other economic history puzzles. Actually, I think that many of Lal's arguments fit well in this framework and could give rise to a useful synthesis, having more explanatory power.

According to Mokyr, what matters for economic take-off is an acceleration of technological progress, through an efficient combination of invention and innovation activities—*innovation* meaning the implementation of new technologies. Although many societies have been inventive (such as the Hellenistic and Chinese ones), few have managed to maintain at the same time a steady level of innovation. Societies that were able to exploit the complementarity between invention and innovation, have been characterized by technological creativity. These societies have been able to enjoy economic take-off.

Invention—a game against nature—depends on factors that affect directly individual behavior. However, innovation—a game against other players—is related more to the social environment—that is, to institutions, incentives, and attitudes around people who struggle to implement new technologies.

Among factors that directly affect individual behavior toward invention and innovation one can list life expectancy (which determines time preference), health status, and attitudes toward risk. Willingness to take risks seems of particular importance. It depends on the possibilities for efficient risk diversification (related, of course, to the development of financial intermediaries) but also on the structure of families—which is a factor also strongly stressed in Lal's paradigm. As argued by Mokyr, heads of extended families can be less willing to take risks than heads of weaker families, since more people depend on the extended family net. The transformation of the Western family, induced by the twin revolutions of the church, fits therefore quite well in this framework, which explains the technological creativity of Western societies.

Among social factors that affect individual creativity, the most important seem to be the following:

- Religion and the cosmological beliefs it involves,

- Hierarchy of values (that is, material beliefs),

- Extent of the market,

- Form of the political system, and

- Existence of secure property rights.

The importance of having well-defined property rights being widely agreed, I briefly comment on the remaining four factors.

- With regard to religion and cosmological beliefs, it can be argued that the anthropocentric character of Judeo-Christian religions enhances attitudes to challenge the physical environment. The cosmological beliefs embodied in the Indian caste system, with the resulting propensity toward preserving the existing status quo, could hardly be conducive to technological creativity.

- With regard to the ranking of values by societies, a low ranking of economic activities can hardly be expected to be conducive to technological creativity. What seems to be important for the ranking of material beliefs is the incentive system provided by the economy. These incentives form the rules of the game that direct the behavior of most talented people. Some insights on that have been provided by Baumol (1990). In ancient Rome, participation in industry or commerce was not seen as a suitable activity to individuals with a honorable social status. In medieval China, entering the imperial administration was the avenue to success for educated people. The bias against industry was of course reversed in places where the industrial revolution has got deep roots.

- With respect to the extent of the market, it can be argued that this is a powerful factor that governs the incentives to implement new technologies—which involves incurring some form of sunk costs. According to Braudel, this could explain why Lombardy and Milan did not succeed in starting an Industrial Revolution in the sixteenth century. Contrary to England in the late eighteenth century, Milan lacked direct access to overseas markets. At that time, the maritime route to the East was controlled by Venice, while the route to Spain and the West was under the control of Genoa.

- With regard to the political system, I think we can agree that what really matters is good governance—not just egalitarian democracy. Democracy, in some circumstances, can also lead to populism. This can hinder attitudes toward personal achievement and restrict meritocracy. Lack of good governance usually shows up as a high level of corruption, which of course increases uncertainty and hampers innovative activity. Although there is not yet definite evidence on these issues, it seems that political competition and democracy can promote accountability—which is necessary to provide some checks on corruption (Bardhan, 1997).

Summarizing, it seems to me that Lal's paradigm could be usefully cast in a more eclectic scheme of economic development, allowing an interplay of a larger set of economic, cultural and political factors.

On the policy level, my view is that the conclusion on the irrelevance of Western social and political institutions for economic development outside the West might not be warranted. Clearly, democracy has not been and cannot be at the origin of economic take-off. However, having democratic institutions can conceivably strengthen economic growth, by promoting good governance and leading to less-distorted economic policy-making.

I must admit that on the second pillar of 'Western institutions—namely, the Western family—I would be ready to endorse Lal's conclusions. My doubts come from casual inspection of recent events in East Asia, where nepotism, strong hierarchical ties, and family networks have been singled out as possible factors of public and private sector mismanagement and crisis.

References

Bardhan, P. (1997). *The Role of Governance in Economic Development: A Political Economy Approach*. Paris: OECD Development Centre.

Baumol, W.J. (1990). "Entrepreneurship: Productive, Unproductive, and Destructive." *Journal of Political Economy* 98, 893–921.

Braudel, F. (1979). *Civilisation matérielle, économie et capitalisme, XVe-XVIIIe siècle* (vol. 3). Paris: Armand Colin.

Mokyr, J. (1990). *The Lever of Riches. Technological Creativity and Economic Progress*. Oxford: Oxford University Press.

North, D.C. (1981). *Structure and Change in Economic History*. New York: W.W. Norton & Co.

DISCUSSION

Theo van de Klundert
Catholic University of Brabant, Tilburg

The chapter by Deepak Lal covers a broad spectrum of social sciences. It is fascinating to read about the emergence of economic communities, the role of the state, the destruction of the Christian soul, and so many other things, especially so when written in a slightly provocative manner. By doing so the author is vulnerable to criticism from different angles. As an economist who has grown up with the idea that modeling helps to understand a part of the real world I want to make a few points.

The thing that struck me most is Lal's observation that "there is no hope of incorporating institutional development in economic growth theory." Therefore, in his view history has to take the place of theory or mechanics, as he prefers to call it. By raising objections to this statement I run the risk of starting an unproductive methodological discussion. To avoid this I do two things. First, I shall isolate a number of concepts in Lal's chapter that can be used as building stones for models on institutions, allocation and growth. Second, I discuss two examples of such models from the recent literature.

The definition of institutions as the formal and informal constraints on human behavior, which goes back to Douglas North (1990), is a useful starting point for each attempt to get some grip on the matter. The idea of transaction costs comes next, but as Lal notes that may be a very slippery concept. But models are an ideal way to make clear what one is thinking of in case transaction costs need to be related to the rules of the game. This is illustrated later on. Culture is another important aspect to take into account. This gives rise to a distinction between material beliefs and cosmological beliefs in the chapter. Material beliefs can be changed more rapidly so that the institutions based on them can be adapted to different circumstances. Cosmological beliefs, which are to a large extent path-dependent, correspond in my view to the concepts of *trust* in Fukuyama (1995) and *confiance* (trust) in Peyrefitte (1995). Therefore, institutions come in layers. In a recent paper Williamson (1998) distinguishes four levels of economic institutions, with customs, traditions, norms, and religion in the top level and formal rules of the game (polity, judiciary, bureaucracy) in the second level seen from the top. Institutions at the top have a lasting grip on society, but change only slowly—Williamson thinks on the order of centuries or millennia. So far there seems to be sufficient agreement between different scholars taking part in the debate.

The situation becomes somewhat trickier if the role of the state is introduced. Lal sees a direct link between cosmological beliefs and the polity. This may give rise to different forms of the polity without immediate implications for the economy. So long as the state functions as a "civil association" the economy may flourish. In such a civil association the state merely facilitates individuals to pursue their own goals. If the state acts as an 'enterprise association' it may suppress economic freedom to pursue moral ends. These typologies of the state may be useful in political theory, but there is also another aspect as becomes clear in Section 5.6 of the chapter. There it is stated that a materialist explanation for the existence of the state seems warranted. This brings me to the first example of model building I want to discuss.

In a recent paper under the biblical title "Make Us a King" Grossman (1997) shows that a proprietary state is better than anarchy for everyone in the economy even though the proprietary state maximizes the consumption of a ruling elite. The model distinguishes producers and predators who can appropriate a fraction of the consumption good supplied by producers. This assumption delineates the constraints on the economic activity of producing goods. However, producers can spend resources to guarding against predators. Although the concept is not explicitly introduced, one could say that guarding costs and appropriation constitute transaction costs. Individuals are allowed to choose between becoming a producer or becoming a predator. In an anarchic general equilibrium the allocation between occupations and the distribution of income are determined by a parameter that shows the effectiveness of predation. The introduction of a state means several things. First, there is an irreversible collective choice of guarding. Second, the state taxes producers to finance the expenses for guarding. Third, the state maximizes the consumption of a ruling elite. The result is that all people are deterred from choosing to be predators because the tax base is highest with everyone producing. The more interesting outcome is that for a sufficient large effectiveness of predators everyone is better off than under anarchy even though the consumption of a ruling elite is maximized, which implies excessive taxation.

In the Grossman model the ruling elite is not connected with producers. This is different in the second paper I discuss, which is by Vega-Redondo (1993) and published in the *Journal of Evolutionary Economics* under the title "Technological Change and Institutional Inertia: A Game-Theoretic Approach." There are different sectors producing a homogenous consumption good. Each sector has its own productivity level (labor is the only production factor). Inventions lead to productivity improvements.

Invention is modeled as the outcome of a stochastic process, but the amount of resources in a sector has a positive impact on the "invention draws" obtained. The allocation of labor across sectors is driven by differences in pay-offs but takes the form of a so-called epidemic process. Institutions emerge out of a process of social bargaining over the distribution of output. Coalitions can be formed, and the bargaining power of a coalition is induced by the relative output that it initially commands. Vega-Redondo refers to "institutions" themselves as the matrix of sectorial taxes that results from the bargaining process. The outcome depends on a parameter indicating the percentage of the output individuals can destroy when threatened by "confiscation". This crucial parameter is conceived as reflecting relatively stable "meta-institutions," which underlie the more variable institutions in the form of taxation. It is interesting to note that this idea of "meta-institutions" is reminiscent of the concept of culture in the chapter by Lal.

It is shown by Vega-Redondo that sooner or later the economy will enter a situation of "institutional deadlock" with probability one if innovation is sufficiently gradual and meta-institutions are severe enough. In such a situation one sector levies a tax on all other sectors, which are then unable to innovate because they operate below a threshold level that represents the minimum scale necessary for innovation. A situation of institutional deadlock can be broken by contact with another dynamic economy if such a contact entails technological diffusion with a time lag.

My defense of theory and model construction does not imply that history has no role to play. On the contrary, history in the form of case studies and theory are complements. Economic theory shows how to look at the past, while economic history may provide the flesh on the theoretical bones. For instance, many of the descriptions presented by Mokyr (1990) in his well-known book on the history of technological development fit remarkably well in the theoretical framework of Vega-Redondo.

There is another question in Lal's chapter that somewhat puzzles me. The rise of the west is connected with the mediating role of the Catholic church. According to Lal the popes Gregory I in sixth century and Gregory the Great in the eleventh century have paved the way for the market economy. However, as shown by Peyrefitte (1995) the church was rather hostile toward capitalism in the Middle Ages. There was the prohibition of interest on loans forcefully maintained by Pope Alexander III and other clerical leaders. Exceptions were sometimes allowed, but there was always regulation in the capital market in one way or another. Moreover, profits were condemned by the church. The whole idea of the fair price (*justum pretium*) introduced by Thomas of Aquino was meant to regulate trade. These constraints on economic behavior have been detrimental to innovation and economic growth.

The Reformation opened the possibility of sustained growth in countries where Protestants gained a majority. This led to the first example in history of something resembling Promethean growth in the Republic of the Seven United Provinces (The Netherlands) from 1580 to 1700. GDP per work-hour rose structurally as appears from estimates presented by Maddison (1991). A change in cosmological beliefs may not be the only factor in explaining economic growth in the Golden Age, but it certainly was an important element. These ideas on the relevance of the Reformation and the Counter-reformation are confirmed in many studies confronting economic growth in Northwestern Europe with that in the Latin countries even in modern times (e.g. Desdoigts, 1997).

Last but not least, I want to say something on the relation between material beliefs and cosmological beliefs. Lal denies that the former determines to some extent the latter. He calls that view "belief shared equally by Marxists and Chicago school economists" (n. 25). I would say "bien etonné de se trouver ensemble," but apart from that I think that there *is* a relation. The counter-example of Japan does not convince me because I do not think that the Japanese culture is not deeply influenced by Western values. There may be marked differences, but there is also some kind of convergence. As a consequence I guess that the value system in the rest of the world will come under pressure if the economies in that part of the world become more affluent. On the other hand, the moral anchor the West threatens to loose may be reinstalled by cross-cultural influences from outside. In that case everyone will have the best of two worlds.

References

Desdoigt, A. (1997). *Patterns of Economic Development and the Formation of Clubs.* Université d'Evry-Val d'Essone.

Fukuyama, F. (1995). *The Social Virtues and the Creation of Prosperity.* London: Hamish Hamilton.

Grossman, H.I. (1997). "'Make Us a King': Anarchy, Predation and the State." Working Paper 6289, November, NBER.

Maddison, A. (1991). *Dynamic Forces in Capitalist Development. A Long-Run Comparative View.* Oxford: Oxford University Press.

Mokyr, J. (1990). *The Lever of Riches. Technological Creativity and Economic Progress.* Cambridge, MA: Oxford University Press.

North, D.C. (1990). *Institutions, Institutional Change and Economic Performance.* Cambridge, MA: Cambridge University Press.

Peyrefitte, A. (1995). *La societé de confiance: essai sur les origines et la nature du développement* ("The society of trust: essay into the origin and nature of development"). Paris: O. Jacob.

Vega-Redondo, F. (1993). "Technological Change and Institutional Inertia: A Game-Theoretic Approach." *Journal of Evolutionary Economics* 3, 199–224.

Williamson, O.E. (1998). "Transaction Cost Economics: How It Works; Where It Is Headed."
    De Economist 146(1), 23–58.

Chapter 6

Human capital and growth: The cost of rent seeking activities

Jean-Claude Berthélemy,[*] Christopher Pissarides,[**] and Aristomene Varoudakis[***]
*Director, Centre d'Etudes Prospectives et d'Information Internationales, Paris, ** London School of Economics, *** Senior Economist, Development Centre, OECD, Paris*

6.1. INTRODUCTION[*]

The existence of a positive impact of human capital on economic growth is not controversial at the theoretical level. In the neoclassical growth model, human capital can be considered as an additional production factor, alongside physical capital and unskilled labor. In the new growth theory, it is assumed that human capital plays a role as an engine of growth that increases total factor productivity (TFP), in particular within R&D activities that produce innovations.

What is controversial is the empirical existence of its positive impact on economic growth or at least its robustness and intensity. Moreover, casual observations in a number of developing economies suggest that investment in education by governments does not always seem beneficial. This is a serious issue, since investment in education can be costly, accounting for several percentage points of GDP each year, and these expenses compete with a number of other public expenditures in a context of tightened budget constraints.

* The research reported in this chapter has been supported by the OECD Development Centre, where J.C. Berthélemy was Head of Research at the initial stage of this project. The OECD Development Centre support is gratefully acknowledged, without implying any responsibility of the OECD on the opinions expressed in this chapter. Helpful comments by Shanta Devarajan, Howard Pack, and Lant Pritchett are gratefully acknowledged.

Recently, a number of studies have attempted to test the impact of human capital on economic growth, with variable success. Although there is a growing consensus on the way these tests are specified, following a seminal paper by Mankiw, Romer, and Weil (1992), the results obtained in these studies are not very robust. It seems in particular that the elasticity of economic growth to human capital varies strongly depending on the national context.

One very simple reason why human capital might have only a poorly significant impact on economic growth is that skilled labor may be employed in unproductive activities. This happens frequently in a number of developing countries, where graduates are more often employed in the civil service than in production activities. In this chapter, we attempt to provide a theoretical formulation of this idea, through modeling rent seeking activities in the context of an economy where these activities are stimulated by distortions imposed by government policies. We then use data on the distribution of labor force to evaluate the empirical pertinence of our framework. It appears that, according to our estimates, a significant share of human capital is likely to be wasted in rent seeking activities.

In Section 6.2, we summarize the standard formulation used to test the positive impact of human capital on growth. In Section 6.3, we develop a model of rent seeking activities, which is used in Section 6.4 to discuss, in a neoclassical production model, the impact of rent seeking on the link between human capital and economic efficiency. Section 6.5 provides a similar analysis in an endogenous growth model. In Section 6.6 we propose estimates to measure the empirical relevance of our theory. Section 6.7 concludes with some policy implications.

6.2.   STANDARD FORMULATIONS OF THE ROLE OF HUMAN CAPITAL IN EMPIRICAL GROWTH EQUATIONS

We know from initial growth accounting exercises that human capital accumulation can be considered as a significant factor explaining growth performances of an economy. In recent years, a number of contributions have explored again this question and have provided new evidence on the role of human capital in the growth process.

The issue at stake is more empirical than theoretical. Both Solowian growth analysis and new growth theories admit that human capital is a key factor to economic growth. In the new growth theory, the most important argument has been provided by Romer (1990). In his paper, endogenous growth is introduced through R&D activities, which are highly intensive in skilled labor (we will use such a framework in Section 6.5). According to Romer's model, the steady-state growth rate of an economy can be directly linked to its total endowment in human capital.[90]

Following the growing literature on endogenous growth theory, empirical tests have been developed, in particular to show the impact of human capital on long-run growth. This empirical literature has been deeply influenced by an article by Barro (1991), which has shown, using cross section data, that there was no absolute convergence among countries, but that some conditional convergence could be observed. Human capital (measured through school-enrollment ratios) was found to be one of the key conditioning variables in Barro's growth equation. This result has been interpreted as an indication that the neoclassical growth model, which predicted absolute convergence, had a limited validity. More important for our subject, human capital was found to be one of the key determinants of long-run growth.

The specification proposed in Barro's style equations has been, however, questioned both on empirical and on theoretical grounds.

On the empirical side, the stability of the relationship between human capital indicators and economic growth has been tested, among others, by Berthélemy and Varoudakis (1996). They have shown that the human-capital, economic-growth relationship is nonlinear. Their test is based on a standard stability test of a growth equation similar to the equation estimated by Barro (1991). It is shown that the parameters of this equation are unstable and depend particularly on the level of human capital. As a result, two groups of countries with two separate sets of parameters can be identified. The first group consists of countries with low levels of skilled labor endowment (with a ratio of secondary school enrollment below 6 percent) for which the level of human capital has no impact on growth. In the second group of countries, which are better endowed in skilled labor, human capital has, on the contrary, a positive impact on growth. In other words, the first set of countries would be in a sort of poverty trap, in which their education efforts have no impact on growth. Only above a certain level of educational development, such investments could be profitable. These empirical results

---

[90]   There are other ways of introducing human capital accumulation as an engine for growth. Lucas (1988) assumed that the production of human capital was a CRS function of human capital, introducing therefore endogenous growth in the educational sector. Berthélemy, Herrera, and Sen (1995) assumed, in a neoclassical framework, the existence of some substitutability between skilled labor and unskilled labor in production. In such a framework, if education investments are high enough, human capital outgrows the natural growth rate of the economy, and steady-state growth is endogenous and equal to the growth rate of skilled labor.

can be interpreted in a multiple equilibria framework such as the one developed by Azariadis and Drazen (1990). In the end of this chapter, we suggest another explanation, based on our results regarding the demand of skilled labor in rent seeking activities.

On theoretical grounds, the above-mentioned literature has been criticized for omitting to consider that the existence of a positive impact of human capital on economic growth could be consistent with an extended version of the neoclassical growth model. This has been shown by Mankiw, Romer, and Weil (MRW) (1992) in a now standard extension of the Solow growth model that includes human capital as a production factor. Most of the new empirical research has been based on their specification, which is a log-linear approximation around the steady state of an augmented Solow model. This approximation can be written as follows:

$$\ln(y/y_{-1}) = \alpha - \beta \ln(y_{-1}) + \gamma_K \ln(s_K) + \gamma_H \ln(s_H) -$$
$$(\gamma_K + \gamma_H) \ln(\delta + g^* + n), \tag{6.1a}$$

where y is real income per capita, y_{-1} its initial level (measured at the beginning of each time period if the data set has a time dimension), s_K is the rate of savings in physical capital, s_H the rate of saving in human capital, g^* the rate of exogenous technical progress, and n the population growth rate. δ is the depreciation rate of physical capital,[91] α, β, γ_K, and γ_H are parameters.

The issue of measurement of s_H is particularly difficult to solve. Some authors have used as proxy the secondary school enrollment ratio, weighted by the share of the corresponding age group (age fifteen to nineteen) in the working-age population (e.g., Mankiw, Romer and Weil, 1992). This view has been challenged by Prichett (1996), who has shown that enrollment ratios were negatively, not positively, correlated with the rate of growth of human capital.

In absence of a good proxy for s_H, one can conversely estimate a modified version of (6.1a), in which the steady-state human capital (h^*) appears instead of s_H (see, for example, Islam, 1995). Under the assumption that the current human capital stock (h) is a good proxy for h^*, one can then replace (6.1a) by (6.1b):

$$\ln(y/y_{-1}) = \alpha - \beta \ln(y_{-1}) + \gamma_K \ln(s_K) +$$
$$\gamma_H \ln(h) - \gamma_K \ln(\delta + g^* + n). \tag{6.1b}$$

---

[91] Following Mankiw, Romer, and Weil (1992), and Islam (1995), we assume that $g^* + \delta$ is equal to 0.05.

There is no strong theoretical reason for preferring one of the flow or stock variables rather than the other, since both are very crude proxies of what one intends to measure.

There are yet other possible reasons to enter a human capital stock variable as an explanatory variable of the growth rate in a neoclassical framework. We can extend the idea developed by D. Cohen (1995), who assumed that producing human capital requires using a mix of factors different from the mix of factors used to produce equipment goods. Consequently, the preceding equation is transformed through the addition of a term measuring the physical capital availability in the economy:

$$\ln(y/y_{-1}) = \alpha - \beta \ln(y_{-1}) + \gamma_K \ln(s_K) + \gamma_H \ln(s_H) -$$
$$(\gamma_K + \gamma_H) \ln(\delta + g^* + n) + \varepsilon \ln(y/k), \qquad (6.2)$$

where k is the stock of physical capital per head. Since in this model y is a function of k and h, the preceding equation can easily be re-written by introducing h rather than k in the right-hand side. This variable will have a positive effect on growth provided that the education sector is more intensive in human capital (relative to physical capital) than the capital goods sector. In such a framework, therefore, both the flow (enrollment) and stock (attainment) of education enter as explanatory variables in the growth equation.

This discussion suggests that it is hard to disentangle the neoclassical and new growth theories on the role of human capital by simply comparing the performances of regressions that would alternatively incorporate human capital flows or stock variables. Introducing capital stocks rather than flows or growth rates as explanatory variables in a growth equation is not very useful to test an endogenous growth theory against the neoclassical one.

The recent empirical literature based on the MRW specification does not provide more robust evidence than Barro's style equations of the role of human capital in economic growth, be it measured on a stock or flow basis. Although in cross-section regressions, human capital, or school enrollment, does seem to have a positive and significant impact on economic growth, this result has been challenged by several authors.

First, Pritchett (1996) has found a negative, not positive, correlation between economic growth and human capital growth, a result that does not fit in the neoclassical framework. He has also found similar results when trying to explain TFP growth with human capital growth.

Second, a number of authors have attempted without much success to estimate MRW models with panel data. Basically, the issue appears on the time dimension of the available observations: on panel data sets, LSDV (least squares with dummy variables) estimators of a MRW equation do not show any significant impact of human capital (or of school enrollment) on economic growth. More sophisticated estimators, based on generalized moments methods (GMM) that take account of the endogeneity of explanatory variables linked to the dynamic nature of the MRW equation, give the same results, as shown by Knight, Loayza, and Villanueva (1993) and Islam (1995).

A possible explanation is that the positive impact of human capital on economic growth depends on other variables. In particular, it has been shown in cross-section equations (Gould and Ruffin, 1995) and in panel data equations (Berthélemy, Dessus, and Varoudakis, 1997) that the impact of human capital on economic growth depends positively on the trade openness of the economy. Berthélemy, Dessus, and Varoudakis (henceforth BDV) use a varying parameter method to show that the elasticity of growth to human capital is positively related to the ratio of foreign trade to GDP. In other words, in rather open economies, human capital has a positive impact on growth, while in rather closed economies this positive link disappears. As a matter of fact, when the MRW equation is estimated on a panel data set made of OECD member countries only, a positive link between economic growth and human capital can be observed. This result is however a partial one, since it is obtained only with human capital stocks. If, alternatively, human capital growth or enrollment ratios are considered, no similar significant result is obtained. This would suggest that new growth theories work better than the neoclassical growth theory, but, as explained before, such a result does not provide enough evidence to reject the neoclassical growth theory.

Two explanations are possible. A first one would be consistent with Benhabib and Spiegel (1994), who argued that total factor productivity in developing countries can be related to a technological imitation process. In this process, achieved progress depends on three characteristics of the economy: its technological backwardness, its human capital stock, and its openness to the rest of the world. As a matter of fact, it could be reasonably argued that the speed of convergence to the total factor productivity level of the leading countries depends on the success of foreign technology imitation by the home country, which in turn depends both on the level of education and on the outward orientation of the trade regime. On the one hand, a high level of education enhances the ability of the economy to imitate and implement technologies discovered in the leading countries. According to Benhabib and Spiegel (1994), this speeds up the convergence process and leads to a higher rate of growth. On the other hand, the more a country trades with its partners, the more it knows about the state of the technology in the leading countries. Improving management of existing technologies and expanding the set of known technologies, which can potentially be imitated, increases the probability of success of the imitation process and speeds up convergence. These ideas have been formalized by Pissarides (1995) through a North-South extension of the innovation-induced growth model of Romer (1990). In this theoretical framework, TFP in the North grows at an exogenously given rate that is the long-run rate of growth of the world economy. The rate of growth of TFP in the South during the process of convergence is determined by the imitation technology: it depends, first, on the available amount of human capital, and, second, on the degree of trade openness that determines the set of known technologies.

In the next sections, we provide a second, complementary, theoretical interpretation of the BDV result. A closed economy can be considered as characterized by heavy distortions, which pave the way for the development of rent seeking activities. Assuming that rent seeking activities are human capital intensive, this means that closed economies will waste part of their human capital in rent seeking activities. Hence, the positive impact of total human capital on growth will be affected by trade barriers and, more generally, by all kind of distortions that can be created by government policies. As suggested by Pritchett (1996), this kind of interpretation is consistent with the fact that, although there is no robust positive relation between human capital and growth at the macro level, a positive link exists between education and individual wages at the micro level. In some countries demand for educated people comes from rent seeking activities, which are privately remunerative but socially wasteful.

An early theoretical analysis of the implications for growth of the allocation of human capital among rent seeking and productive activities was provided by Murphy, Shleifer, and Vishny (1991). In their model (hereafter MSV)—which follows insights by Baumol (1990)—when talented people become entrepreneurs, they improve technology and, as a result, promote productivity and income growth. On the contrary, when they become rent seekers, they tax implicitly profits of the productive sector, so that their private returns come from wealth redistribution rather than from wealth creation. In the MSV model the allocation of talent depends on the relative returns that the ablest people are being offered in the rent seeking and the productive sectors of the economy. These returns depend on the size of the market, on the technology in the two sectors (extent of diminishing returns), and on the attractiveness of compensation contracts (secureness of property rights).

Although our theoretical model bears some similarity with MSV, there is an important difference. Whereas in MSV rent seeking is just an implicit tax on profits of productive activities, in our model (as it will be explained in the next section) there is a pecuniary counterpart to rent seeking. In our framework rent seeking arises in response to policy-induced distortions in economic activity, which amount to an implicit taxation of productive activities. Rent seekers reduce the impact of distortions on the productive sector. This gives rise to demand for their services and to a potentially beneficial side effect on economic growth. At the same time, however, as in the MSV model, the fact that able people are diverted from the productive (or R&D) sector into the rent seeking sector can be harmful for growth. In our model the overall impact of rent seeking on growth is endogenously determined, as is the rate of implicit taxation of economic activity resulting from the combination of rent seeking and policy-induced distortions.

6.3.   RENT SEEKING AS AN ECONOMIC ACTIVITY

Rent seeking is defined as an economic activity that contributes both to private and social output. It takes place in response to policy distortions, such as taxes, price controls, red tape, and trade restrictions. The rent seeker reduces the effects of the distortion on the private producer, and so the private producer is prepared to pay for the service. Therefore, the rent seeker plays a useful social function, but only because there is a policy distortion that hinders the free functioning of the market. When there are more distortions, more resources are diverted into rent seeking and so fewer into other activities that could add to national output.

Thus, an economy that is characterized in equilibrium by much rent seeking is likely to be one that performs less than one that is characterized by less. Given, however, that rent seeking is endogenously determined, what makes the former economy less efficient is not the rent seeking per se but the policy distortions. Without rent seeking, the economy would be even less efficient.

Rent seeking is most often carried out by skilled individuals. They are the accountants who find ways of reducing tax payments, the lawyers who find ways of using the law to one's own financial gain, and the traders who manage to find a way round the restrictions on prices and trade. Thus, in a model economy with two types of labor, skilled and unskilled, rent seeking uses more skilled labor relative to the production sector of the economy. We take this assumption to its logical conclusion and assume that the only input into rent seeking is human capital.

We assume that the labor force of the country is L and the available human capital H. We shall talk as if L and H were two separate factors of production. The aggregate production function depends on the input of both L and H. Rent seeking, however, depends only on the input of H.

Policy distortions influence economic activity in a variety of ways. In an aggregate analysis, however, we need to take a short cut. We assume that distortions reduce the efficiency of the production process in a neutral way: they act as a proportional shadow tax on output. We let T denote the level of the tax, so if Y is output in the absence of the distortions, output with distortions but without the rent seekers is $(1-T)Y$.

The rent seekers reduce the effect of the distortions on output. If the quantity of human capital employed in rent seeking activities is H_S, the effective tax due to the distortion is $z(H_S)T$. The rent seeking function $z(.)$ satisfies the properties $z'(.) \leq 0$ and $z''(.) \geq 0$—that is, although there are diminishing returns to rent seeking, the more human capital that is transferred to rent seeking activities, the less the effect of the distortion on output. We also assume that both T and $z(.)$ lie between 0 and 1, and $z(0) = 1$ and that it is never possible to get rid of all the distortions through rent seeking—that is,

$$\lim_{H_S \to H} z(H_S) > 0 \tag{6.3}$$

for any finite H.

The rewards from rent seeking are equal to the marginal product of the human capital employed in rent seeking. The quantity of human capital employed in rent seeking is chosen to maximize profit and depends on T. Given our definitions, if there are no distortions ($T = 0$) there will be no rent seeking.

6.4. THE IMPACT OF RENT SEEKING ON ECONOMIC OUTPUT

We first solve a simple model with no capital and no growth but with two factors of production, unskilled labor and human capital. The purpose of this model is to further explain the role of rent seeking in the economy. As before, the only input into rent seeking is human capital, but both human capital and unskilled labor are needed in production. We ignore capital and assume that the total supply of labor and human capital, respectively denoted by L and H, are both fixed.

Let the production function be

$$Y = BH_y^\alpha L^\beta, \tag{6.4}$$

where B is a constant, H_Y is the human capital employed in the genuine production process, and L is the entire labor force, which can only be employed in production. The coefficients α and β sum to a number not larger than 1.

The wage rate of human capital is w_H and the wage rate of unskilled labor w_L. The rate of return to human capital is measured by their ratio, w_H/w_L. With the definition of rent seeking given in the preceding section, profit is given by

$$\pi = \left[1 - z(H_S)T\right]Y - w_H\left(H_Y + H_S\right) - w_L L. \tag{6.5}$$

This expression is maximized subject to (6.4) and the restrictions on the rent seeking function, $z'(H_S) \leq 0$, $z''(H_S) \geq 0$. The firm takes prices as given.

The first-order maximization conditions with respect to L, H_Y and H_S are, respectively,

$$\beta\left[1 - z(H_S)T\right]\frac{Y}{L} - w_L = 0 \tag{6.6}$$

$$\alpha\left[1 - z(H_S)T\right]\frac{Y}{H_Y} - w_H = 0 \tag{6.7}$$

$$-z'(H_S)TY - w_H = 0. \tag{6.8}$$

Second-order conditions are satisfied by the assumptions on the production function and the rent seeking function.

In order to solve for market rates of return we assume that both factors are fully employed, so the allocation of human capital satisfies

$$H = H_S + H_Y. \tag{6.9}$$

Combining equations (6.7), (6.8) and (6.9), we find an implicit equation that determines H_s:

$$\frac{\alpha\left(1 - z(H_S)T\right)}{-z'(H_S)} = T(H - H_S). \tag{6.10}$$

The LHS of this equation is an increasing function of H_s (the LL curve) in Figure 6.1), while the RHS decreases with H_s (the RR line in Figure 6.1A, B and C). Therefore, this equation determines H_S, as a function of H and T. As shown in Figure 6.1, this equation has two interesting properties.

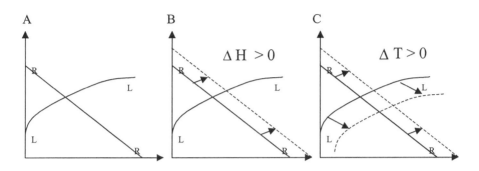

Figure 6.1.

When H increases, H_S increases, but less than proportionately (Figure 6.1B). Therefore, H_Y (and consequently labor productivity) still remains an increasing function of the total human capital available H.

When T increases, H_S increases as well (Figure 6.1C). This means that more distortions will stimulate more waste of human capital into rent seeking activities. The positive effect of human capital on output is therefore lowered by the distortions.

Assuming that this rent seeking activity is entered into a MRW model, one has here a straightforward explanation of why human capital accumulation has a reduced impact on growth in a distorted economy.

6.5. RENT SEEKING AND GROWTH IN AN ENDOGENOUS GROWTH MODEL

Let us turn now to a model that allows for endogenous growth, linked to human capital endowment. For that matter, we work out a simplified Romer's style model, where human capital is used in two sectors: R&D and rent seeking.

There are three sectors: final goods, (differentiated) capital goods, and R&D. In the final good sector, producers employ unskilled labor (L) and capital goods ($x(i)$). Production is given by:

$$Y = L^\alpha \int_0^A x(i)^{1-\alpha} \, di.$$ (6.11)

We assume, as before, that a quantity H_S of human capital is devoted, in the final good sector, to rent seeking activities that reduce the effect of distortions on profit. Thus, the profit of an entrepreneur in this sector is

$$\Pi = \left(1 - z(H_S)T\right)Y - w_H H_S - w_L L - \int_0^A p(i)x(i) \, di,$$ (6.12)

where $p(i)$ is the price of capital good i.

Capital goods are produced with a CRS technology using capital goods, with a unit cost equal to 1. Their production depends on the availability of a blueprint (i), produced by the R&D sector. For the sake of simplicity, we assume that this activity is not directly affected by distortions and rent seeking. As usual in this type of model, the producer of each variety exerts a monopoly power, based on the demand function that can be derived from the maximization of π with respect to $x(i)$:

$$\left(1 - z(H_S)T\right)(1 - \alpha)L^\alpha x(i)^{-\alpha} - p(i) = 0.$$ (6.13)

Solving for the profit maximization problem of the producer of the variety (i) leads to

$$p(i) = \frac{1}{1 - \alpha}.$$ (6.14)

$p(i)$ is the same for all variety and will be noted p. Consistently, $x(i)$ is independent of the variety (i) and noted x.

The production of blueprints is described by the following technology:

$$\dot{A} = \lambda H_R A,$$ (6.15)

where λ is a parameter and H_R measures the quantity of human capital allocated to the R&D activity.

If r is the real interest rate, the total present value of the profit generated by a blueprint (i) is equal to $(px - x)/r$, which is equal to $(\alpha/1 - \alpha)(x/r)$. As a consequence, the wage rate w_H of skilled labor employed in the R&D sector is

$$w_H = \lambda A \frac{\alpha}{1-\alpha} \frac{x}{r}. \tag{6.16}$$

In order to solve the model for H_S, equation (6.16) is combined with equation (6.17), which equates w_H and the marginal productivity of rent seeking, obtained through a maximization of π with respect to H_S:

$$w_H = -z'(H_S)YT. \tag{6.17}$$

Combined with equations (6.11), (6.13) and (6.14), this gives:

$$\lambda\alpha(1-\alpha)\frac{1-z(H_S)T}{-z'(H_S)} = r. \tag{6.18}$$

Assuming a standard iso-elastic intertemporal utility function with δ equal to the rate of time preference and ρ equal to the inverse elasticity of the utility function, the real interest rate r can be linked, at the steady state, to the real growth rate g through the Keynes-Ramsey condition

$$g = \frac{r-\rho}{\sigma}. \tag{6.19}$$

Knowing from (6.15) that at the steady state g is also equal to λH_R, one obtains therefore from (6.18) and (6.19) an equation, which determines H_S:

$$\lambda\alpha(1-\alpha)\frac{1-z(H_S)T}{-z'(H_S)} = \rho + \sigma\lambda(H - H_S). \tag{6.20}$$

The LHS of equation (6.20) is increasing with H_S (and represented as the LL curve in Figure 6.2), while the RHS is decreasing, and represented as the RR line.

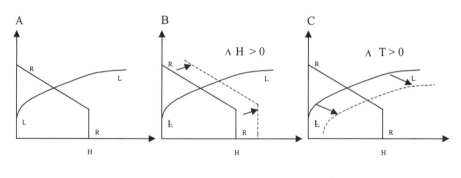

Figure 6.2..

Figures 6.2B and 6.2C exhibit the same properties as Figures 6.1B and 6.1C in the preceding model: H_S increases with H (but less than proportionately) and decreases with T. Therefore, the steady-state equilibrium growth rate increases with human capital and decreases with distortions.

Moreover, the marginal impact of human capital on growth is a negative function of T. This can be seen from equation (6.21), where we have computed the derivative of H_S with respect to H:

$$\frac{dH_S}{dH} = \frac{-z'\sigma\lambda T}{-z'\sigma\lambda T + (\rho + \sigma\lambda(H - H_S)T)z'' - z'\alpha(1-\alpha)\lambda T}, \qquad (6.21)$$

which is increasing in T.

Another interesting feature of this model is that above a certain threshold of distortions, growth will disappear. This will happen when the solution H_S of equation (6.20) tends to H, in which case no human capital is available for R&D, and consequently the engine of endogenous growth disappears. This threshold, called τ, is equal to

$$\tau = \frac{1 + \rho z'(H)/\lambda\alpha(1-\alpha)}{z(H)}. \qquad (6.22)$$

Of course, above this threshold, there is no room for R&D activity, and all human capital is allocated to rent seeking, which means that the RR line is kinked and becomes vertical.

These theoretical results are consistent with the econometric findings of BDV, assuming that trade openness is correlated with the level of distortions. The positive impact of human capital on growth decreases when distortion increases and can completely disappear in a highly distorted economy.

It is worth observing, also, that τ increases with H, which means that in a country that is poorly endowed in human capital, distortions will more likely inhibit growth (by generating rent seeking activities) than in better endowed countries.

6.6.   EMPIRICAL ASSESSMENT: EVALUATING HUMAN CAPITAL DEVOTED TO RENT SEEKING ACTIVITIES

Our econometric exercise consists of trying to measure the amount of human capital devoted to rent seeking activities, assuming (consistently with the theoretical model) that this specific human capital has no impact on growth. Even this simple question is not easy to solve, since we do not have any direct statistical measure of employment in rent seeking activity. By nature, rent seeking activities are spread over all sectors. Therefore, all attempts to find an accurate proxy of human capital engaged in rent seeking are bound to be imperfect. In their empirical work, MSV used data on college enrollment in law as a measure of talent allocated to rent seeking and data on college enrollment in engineering as a measure of talent allocated to entrepreneurship. These two variables have been found to have, respectively, a negative and positive influence on growth in a cross-section of countries over the 1970 to 1985 period.

Here we start with the assumption that, anyhow, there is one sector in which rent seeking activities are more observable than anywhere else: the government sector.[92] Of course, not all civil servants are rent seekers. However, most rent seeking activities are carried out in interaction with civil servants: policy distortions are, according to our definition, the principal incentive of rent seeking activities and are necessarily implemented by government officials.

Therefore, we assume that the amount of time spent in rent seeking activities in the whole economy is proportional to the number of civil servants who are in a position to administer policy distortions. We define this category, called L_G, as civilian (central and local) government employees, excluding those who are working in the education and health sectors. We use for that matter data collected by the World Bank (Schiavo-

---

[92] A similar approach was pursued by Gelb, Knight, and Sabot (1991) in their CGE modeling of the effect of rent seeking on growth.

Campo, de Tomasso, and Mukherjee, 1997), which provides information on government employment for eighty to 100 countries in the early 1990s.

We suppose that the amount of rent seekers is proportional to L_G. Assuming all rentseekers are, consistently with our theoretical model, skilled people and that all human capital is in the non-agricultural sector of the economy (where employment is denoted by L_{NA}), the proportion of human capital employed in rent seeking activities should be proportional to the ratio $l_G = L_G/L_{NA}$, with a proportionality parameter called θ.

Assuming that human capital plays a role in growth (either as a factor of production or as a factor utilized in innovation processes), the relevant variable to enter in our model is not the total human capital stock H but the amount of human capital that remains after deduction of the skilled labor force employed in rent seeking activities, called H_N, which is defined as

$$H_N = H(1 - \theta \frac{L_G}{L_{NA}}).$$ (6.23)

More specifically, we estimate the following modified MRW equation:

$$\ln(y/y_{-1}) = \alpha - \beta\ln(y_{-1}) + \gamma_K \ln(s_K)$$
$$+ \gamma_H \ln(h(1 - \theta l_G)) - \gamma'_K \ln(\delta + g^* + n).$$ (6.24)

Our goal, in doing so, is of course not to test the MRW model versus, for instance, an endogenous growth model but to specify a growth equation where the impact of human capital net of rent seeking can be empirically tested. Working with the human capital stock (rather than its flow) is certainly here the easiest way to enter our corrective term that takes account of rent seeking. As explained before, this has not necessarily any strong meaning in terms of choice between a neoclassical and an endogenous growth model. At any rate, we do not pretend to test the validity of endogenous versus neoclassical growth theories.[93]

This equation is tested for a cross-section data set of fifty-four countries for which the necessary data are available, where economic growth is measured from 1985 to 1995 on a PPP basis, y_{-1} is the 1985 PPP level of GDP per capita, the investment ratio s_k is measured over the 1986 to 1990 period (for lack of complete data after 1990), n is the annual population

---

[93] Besides, we do not state in this equation that the elasticity of growth to the investment ratio and to $\delta+$ the natural growth rate are equal. This restriction, which is based on a strict MRW specification, is not satisfied in our estimations. However, we obtain similar results when such a restriction is imposed.

growth rate (1981 to 1995), and h accounts for the human capital stock per head, measured as the average number of years of education in active population. All these data are from the World Bank.[94]

With a nonlinear least-square method, we obtain the following result with t-statistics in brackets:

$$\ln(y/y_{-1}) = \underset{(5.75)}{-2.47} \underset{(6.78)}{-0.23} \ln(y_{-1}) + \underset{(6.44)}{0.44} \ln(s_K)$$

$$\underset{(5.84)}{-1.07} \ln(\delta + g^* + n) + \underset{(2.88)}{0.22} \ln(h(1 - \underset{(4.27)}{1.71} l_G)) \qquad (6.25)$$

$$n = 54$$

$$\overline{R}^2 = 0.68$$

This equation is significantly better than the equivalent MRW equation estimated on the same sample assuming that θ is equal to zero:

$$\ln(y/y_{-1}) = \underset{(6.34)}{-2.87} \underset{(5.52)}{-0.20} \ln(y_{-1}) + \underset{(6.58)}{0.49} \ln(s_K)$$

$$\underset{(5.47)}{-1.10} \ln(\delta + g^* + n) + \underset{(2.01)}{0.17} \ln(h) \qquad (6.26)$$

$$n = 54$$

$$\overline{R}^2 = 0.62$$

Not only is the adjusted R^2 better in (6.25), but also the elasticity of growth to human capital is estimated more precisely and more robustly than in (6.26). In particular, it appears that this elasticity is no longer significant in (6.26) when OECD member countries are excluded from the sample, while it still is significant in (6.25).[95]

Introducing specification (6.25), where one attempts to estimate the size of the skilled-labor force, which is wasted in rent seeking activities, gives therefore some empirical relevance to our theoretical model.

In order to check the robustness of this result, a second proxy for the human capital devoted to rent seeking activities is attempted. Again, it is assumed that H_S is proportional to human capital in civil service (excluding education and health services), but we now assume that the wage income

---

[94] World Bank Development Indicators 1997 and World Bank Capital Stock Data 1950 to 1990.

[95] In the latter case, the t-student associated to this parameter falls to 0.8 when estimated on the non-OECD sample, while it remains close to 2 in the former case.

received by these people is an indicator of their human capital. More precisely, we now assume that H_S is a proportion of the wage bill of the civil service in the total wage bill. However, since we do not have information about the total wage bill in the economy, we will consider the ratio of the (non-education and non-health) civil service wage bill in total GDP, ω_G, as a proxy for H_S.[96] The corresponding equation, which is estimated for a sample of forty-four countries only (because of data availability constraints) is the following:

$$\ln(y/y_{-1}) = -\underset{(5.43)}{2.62} - \underset{(5.62)}{0.22}\ln(y_{-1}) + \underset{(6.34)}{0.49}\ln(s_K)$$
$$-\underset{(5.02)}{1.07}\ln(\delta + g^* + n) + \underset{(2.23)}{0.20}\ln(h(1 - \underset{(2.54)}{8.69}\omega_G)) \qquad (6.27)$$

$$n = 44$$

$$\overline{R}^2 = 0.69$$

Equation (6.24) and (6.26) have very similar properties. In particular, they exhibit almost the same elasticity of growth to net human capital.

Assuming that equations (6.25) and (6.27) identify accurately the amount of available human capital, net of rent seeking skilled labor, one can compare the size of this net human capital with the size of total human capital. This is what is done in Table 6.1 for equation (6.25) and in Table 6.2 for equation (6.27) below, where we report averages for five main regions: OECD members (excluding Turkey), Asia, Latin America, Middle East, and North Africa including Turkey (MENA) and Sub-Saharan Africa. We also report in these tables the amount of economic growth which is wasted due to rent seeking activities for these five regions, according to equations (6.25) (Table 6.1) or (6.27) (Table 6.2).

Table 6.1. Human capital and economic growth lost due to rent seeking (equation 6.25)

Region	Total human capital available (H)	Proportion of H in rent seeking (percent)	Corresponding lost growth (1985-1995)
OECD	9.0	20.6	5.1
Asia	5.2	19.8	4.9
Latin America	6.2	17.7	4.3
MENA	4.4	31.7	8.4
Sub-Saharan Africa	4.2	32.9	8.8

[96] This ratio is computed as the ratio of the total civil service wage bill over GDP, multiplied by the ratio of non-education and non-health employees over total civil service employment.

Table 6.2. Human capital and economic growth lost due to rent seeking (equation 6.27)

Region	Total human capital available (H)	Proportion of H in rent seeking (percent)	Corresponding lost growth (1985-1995)
OECD	9.2	25.1	5.8
Asia	5.5	20.8	4.7
Latin America	6.4	22.0	5.0
MENA	4.4	38.8	9.8
Sub-Saharan Africa	4.4	34.8	8.6

Note: The average H differs in Table 6.1 and 6.2 because they are not computed on the same sample.

These two tables provide very similar results. It appears that the proportion of human capital wasted in rent seeking activities is highest in the MENA and Sub-Saharan Africa regions, where the total human capital available is the lowest. This result is consistent with casual observations of widespread rent seeking behavior in countries in these two regions. Since these two regions are particularly poorly endowed in human capital, the cost of their rent seeking behaviors is maximum: it accounts for 0.8 to 0.9 percentage point of growth yearly, which is twice as much as in OECD, Asian, and Latin American economies. These estimates show that the waste of human capital in rent seeking activities is a serious issue. This may explain, in particular, why heavy investments in education made by some countries have had apparently only minor effects on their economic growth.

6.7. CONCLUSION

Rent seeking is a serious obstacle to economic growth and prosperity. This issue has been already discussed in the recent economic literature, particularly by Murphy, Shleifer, and Vishny (1991,1993). What is new here is that we discuss the specific impact of rent seeking on human capital allocation. In our model, we interpret rent seeking as the rational outcome of the existence of distortions. We show how such rent seeking behavior can affect long-term growth through a serious misallocation of human capital, within an endogenous growth framework. In this framework, it appears that this issue of rent seeking is particularly serious when human capital is scarce: in such situations, rent seeking can pass a threshold that eliminates any growth potential for the economy.

A natural extension of our theoretical framework would be to consider distortions T not as an exogenous variable but as the result of another sort of socially wasteful activity, which consists in lobbying to obtain income redistributions through such distortions. In a sense, such activities can be considered as rent seeking but are of a different nature since the corresponding benefits are collective (for a specific group of agents) rather than individual. Modeling such lobbying activities to endogenize T would therefore require a somewhat different kind of theory, which would be usefully considered in future works.

Our theoretical framework suggests that rent seeking is particularly costly in economies that are poorly endowed in human capital. Our empirical results show also that rent seeking is more pervasive in such countries than in OECD or emerging economies. Therefore, when human capital is particularly scarce (Sub-Saharan Africa and MENA regions), it is also particularly wasted. This means that for low levels of human capital, the impact of this human capital on growth might be minimal, creating a sort of low equilibrium trap. Such an interpretation is fully consistent with the existence of convergence clubs observed by Berthélemy and Varoudakis (1996).

This poverty trap scenario is, however, not inevitable. In the end, the amount of human capital that is wasted is directly related to the amount of distortions imposed by government policies. There is a way out of this vicious equilibrium, through a reduction of distortions. Another policy recommendation that emerges from this chapter is that education investments should be encouraged, even though human capital is not fully productive: the higher the level of education, the more human capital waste in rent seeking activities can be afforded without blocking growth. But when a government decides to increase its effort in education, it must make sure, at the same time, that the new graduates that will be produced by the education system will not have incentives to work in rent seeking activities. In particular, it must certainly not provide graduates with a guarantee of employment in the public sector, as it has been done in some sub-Saharan Africa (such as Senegal) or MENA (such as Egypt) countries.

A further empirical investigation in which indicators of distortions would be introduced as explanatory variables of the number of rent-seekers, in an instrumental variable model, could usefully complement our results. This would in particular provide more lessons for policymakers on the kind of distortions that are responsible for the lack of development effectiveness of education policies.

References

Azariadis, C., and A. Drazen. (1990). "Threshold Externalities in Economic Development." *Quarterly Journal of Economics* 105, 501–526.

Barro, R.J. (1991). "Economic Growth in a Cross Section of Countries." *Quarterly Journal of Economics* 106, 407–443.

Baumol, W.J. (1990). "Entrepreneurship: Productive, Unproductive, and Destructive." *Journal of Political Economy* 98, 893–921.

Benhabib, J., and M. Spiegel. (1994). "The Role of Human Capital in Economic Development: Evidence from Aggregate Cross-Country Data." *Journal of Monetary Economics* 34, 143–173.

Berthélemy, J.C., S. Dessus, and A. Varoudakis. (1997). "Capital humain et croissance: le rôle du régime commercial." ("Human capital and growth: The role of the trade regime"). *Revue Économique* 48, 419–428.

Berthélemy, J.C., R. Herrera, and S. Sen. (1995). "Military Expenditure and Economic Development: An Endogenous Growth Perspective." *Economics of Planning* 28, 205–233.

Berthélemy, J.C., and A. Varoudakis. (1996). "Economic Growth, Convergence Clubs, and the Role of Financial Development." *Oxford Economic Papers* 48, 300–328.

Cohen, D. (1995). "Tests of the Convergence Hypothesis: Some Further Results." Working Paper 9509, CEPREMAP, Paris.

Gelb, A.H., J.B. Knight, and R.H. Sabot. (1991). "Public Sector Employment, Rent Seeking and Economic Growth." *Economic Journal* 101, 1186–1199.

Gould, D.M., and R.J. Ruffin. (1995). "Human Capital, Trade, and Economic Growth." *Weltwirtschaftliches Archiv* 131, 425–445.

Islam, N. (1995). "Growth Empirics: A Panel Data Approach." *Quarterly Journal of Economics* 110, 1127–1170.

Knight, M., N. Loayza, and D. Villanueva. (1993). "Testing the Neoclassical Theory of Economic Growth: A Panel Data Approach." *IMF Staff Papers* 40, 512–541.

Lucas, R.E. Jr. (1988). "On the Mechanics of Economic Development." *Journal of Monetary Economics* 22, 3–42.

Mankiw, N.G., D. Romer, and D.N. Weil. (1992). "A Contribution to the Empirics of Economic Growth." *Quarterly Journal of Economics* 107, 407–437.

Murphy, K.M., A. Shleifer, and R.W. Vishny. (1991). "The Allocation of Talent: Implications for Growth." *Quarterly Journal of Economics* 106, 503–530.

Murphy, K.M., A. Shleifer, and R.W. Vishny. (1993). "Why is Rent seeking so Costly to Growth?" *American Economic Review* 83, 409–413.

Pissarides, C. (1995). "Trade and the Returns to Human Capital in Developing Economies." Mimeo, London School of Economics, October.

Pritchett, L. (1996). "Where has all the Education Gone?" Policy Research Paper 1581, World Bank.

Romer, P.M. (1990). "Endogenous Technological Change." *Journal of Political Economy* 98 (Supp.), 71–102.

Schiavo-Campo S., G. de Tommaso, and A. Mukherjee. (1997). "An International Statistical Survey of Government Employment and Wages." Policy Research Working Paper 1806, World Bank.

DISCUSSION

George J. Borjas
Harvard University

This chapter analyzes how rent seeking activities affect economic growth—particularly through their effect on the country's "effective" human capital stock. Here Berthélemy, Pissarides, and Varoudakis (henceforth BPV) argue that rent seeking activities distort how human capital is used in the production process. Because rent seeking activities are conducted mainly by skilled workers, rent seeking activities may well dissipate some of the productive benefits of an increase in the human capital stock.

The authors' study is motivated by the fact that human capital variables in the typical cross-country economic growth regression model have not been robust. The typical regression model in this literature is given by

$$\log (y/y_{-1}) = \alpha \log y_{-1} + \gamma_h \text{ human capital} + \lambda \text{ other variables,} \qquad (1)$$

where y gives per capita income at some point in time, and y_{-1} gives per-capita income at some initial period in the past. The human capital variable is often measured in terms of school-enrollment rates or in terms of mean-numbers-of-years of schooling in the economically active population.

In Barro's (1991) study, the human capital variable was significantly positive. Moreover, Barro also found that the coefficient α turned negative and significant (as opposed to being essentially zero) when the regression controlled for human capital and other variables. Barro called this result a type of "conditional convergence." The per capita incomes of countries that start out with roughly the same level of human capital tend to converge over time.

Subsequent investigations of this regression model by many authors have shown that the estimated impact of human capital on the rate of economic growth is very sensitive to the specification of the model—depending on how the human capital variable is measured and on whether the data forms a cross-section or a panel of countries (Islam, 1995). Often the coefficient γ_h is positive, but sometimes it is zero or negative. This sensitivity in the results has led to a related debate on whether the finding of conditional convergence is consistent with Solowian models of economic growth or requires the use of an endogenous growth model.

The current chapter enters the debate by attempting to provide a partial explanation of why the human capital variable might not work in the expected way—with a positive coefficient—in cross-country regression models like the one in equation (1). BPV tell the following story. Suppose that the government of a particular country pursues a set of policies that distort the economy and reduce national income by an amount T below its maximum potential. These policy distortions include taxes, price controls, and so on. These policies effectively enact barriers on trade that create opportunities for economic participants to come in and "grease the wheels" of the market to facilitate some of these exchanges. In BPV's view, the rent seekers are like middlemen who reduce "the effects of the distortion on the private producer and so the private producer is prepared to pay for the(ir) services." The authors make the key assumption that rent seeking activities are skill intensive—in other words, the persons who can facilitate the exchanges tend to be skilled workers. The theoretical development, however, does not elaborate on the possibility that different types of skills—such as those possessed by lawyers or engineers—might play very different roles in rent seeking activities. The empirical work of Murphy, Shleifer, and Vishny (1991), in fact, shows that enrollments in law schools and engineering schools have very different effects on economic growth: more lawyers reduce growth, while more engineers increase growth. Although the theoretical model does not take into account that different types of skills affect economic growth in different ways, the empirical model does take some of these differences into account (although in a very extreme way).

In the BPV analysis, the rent-seeker plays a socially useful role by facilitating economic exchanges that allow the economy to recover at least part of the T dollars that are squandered because of inefficient government policies. This approach leads to a number of interesting—and empirically relevant—implications. The greater the loss suffered by the economy from the distortions (that is the larger T), the greater the incentives for rent-seekers to arise. As a result, the greater the likelihood that highly skilled persons become rent seekers. This effect serves to diminish the productive impact of human capital on economic growth.

Although the BPV hypothesis is interesting, it is not the only approach to rent seeking that one could pursue in the context of growth models. A great deal of economic activity in modern governments, after all, involves the redistribution of resources. Some subset of the population is taxed, and another subset of the population is subsidized. One could easily postulate that a new class of persons—call them rent-seekers—arise to ensure that the redistribution of resources in modern welfare states flow in the direction of the rent-seekers (or in the directions of the principals who employ the rent seekers).

This type of rent seeking activity would not help the economy recover part of the T dollars that are wasted because of government-enacted inefficiencies. In other words, this type of rent seeking activity is not productive. Instead, rent seeking plays a purely redistributive role. It would be useful if BPV investigated this alternative viewpoint further. Even though both approaches imply that the impact of human capital on economic growth is distorted by rent seeking behavior, it would be useful to empirically identify the type of rent seeking behavior that a society engages in and to measure the relative impacts of the two types of rent seeking behavior.

The empirical analysis in BPV uses the generic regression model:

$$\log (y/y_{-1}) = \alpha \log y_{-1} + \gamma_h \log h(1 + \theta I_G) + \lambda \text{ other variables}, \quad (2)$$

where h gives the human capital stock at the initial point in time, as measured by the average number of years of schooling in the economically active population; and I_G gives the fraction of the non-agricultural work force that is employed by government (again at the initial point in time). The variable I_G is the empirical variable that BPV use to measure rent seeking activities. In the BPV analysis, rent seeking affects economic growth solely because it affects the "effective" amount of human capital that is available for "productive" purposes. The parameter θ thus estimates the extent to which allocating workers to the government sector reduces effective human capital in the overall economy—assuming, of course, that government employment is a good proxy for these rent seeking activities. The theoretical framework predicts that the parameter θ should be negative. The authors estimate equation (2) using nonlinear least squares. The empirical evidence indeed suggests that rent seeking activities (as measured by I_G) do indeed seem to reduce the effective human capital in the country.

It is instructive to linearize equation (2) by using the approximation $\log (1 + x) \approx x$, for small x. In particular, let $\log (1 + \theta I_G) \approx \theta I_G$. We can then rewrite the regression equation as

$$\log (y/y_{-1}) = \alpha \log y_{-1} + \gamma_h \log h + \gamma_h \theta I_G + \lambda \text{ other variables}. \quad (2)$$

The nonlinear regression estimated by BPV is roughly equivalent to a simple linear regression where the explanatory variables include the log of the human capital stock (years of schooling) and the percentage of the workforce that is employed by the government sector. What the BPV model does is to *impose* a particular structural interpretation on the coefficients of these two variables. In particular, the coefficient of the government employment variable should be equal to the coefficient of the human capital variable times the factor θ.

Interpreted in this fashion, it is a bit easier to make sense of (and question) the econometric evidence. In terms of equation (2), it is evident that the key empirical result is that countries where governments employ a large fraction of the workforce have lower economic growth, holding human capital constant. This "cleaner" interpretation of the empirical evidence raises a number of interpretative problems for the analysis.

For instance, the empirical finding that θ is negative may have nothing to do with rent seeking, but it's just a fact that government workers simply produce a type of output that is not well measured in national income accounts. Consider, for example, the output produced by the government bureaucrats that grant driver licenses. What exactly is the value of these bureaucrats to economic growth? And is this value properly measured in the national income accounts? Moreover, many government bureaucrats are engaged in running redistribution programs. How does their output enter into the calculations of economic growth?

Moreover, even if government employment is a measure of rent seeking, there is something incomplete in both the theoretical and empirical analyses. Countries do not randomly choose a particular level of government employment. The size of the government sector is endogenous to social, political, and economic conditions—and surely varies across countries and over time. In view of this endogeneity, I am not sure that I can interpret international differences in government employment—or even within-country changes in government employment—as a measure of rent seeking activities. I would have preferred a more reduced-form type of analysis, where the country's rate of economic growth is related to the presence or absence of particular policies that create the incentives for rent-seekers to arise. This approach would also provide a much more helpful policy prescription because it would help to identify which government policies are most likely to lead to the dissipation of human capital through rent seeking behavior.

The BPV chapter develops a nice hypothesis and presents empirical evidence suggesting that rent seeking activities may be playing an important role in economic growth—particularly in the less-developed countries where government employment makes up a large fraction of the work force. The empirical results are interesting, and the underlying question is clearly important. This line of research, therefore, will probably lead to very fruitful insights in the future.

References

Barro, R.J. (1991). "Economic Growth in a Cross Section of Countries." *Quarterly Journal of Economics* 106, 407–443.

Islam, N. (1995). "Growth Empirics: A Panel Data Approach." *Quarterly Journal of Economics* 110, 1127–1170.

Murphy, K.M., A. Shleifer, and R.W. Vishny. (1991). "The Allocation of Talent: Implications for Growth." *Quarterly Journal of Economics* 106, 503–530.

Berthélemy, J.C., S. Dessus, and A. Varoudakis. (1997). "Capital humain et croissance: le rôle du régime commercial" ("Human capital and growth: The role of the trade regime"). *Revue Economique* 48, 419–428.

Chapter 7

Recent advances in economic growth. A policy perspective

Robert Lensink and Gerard Kuper
Department of Economics, University of Groningen

7.1.   INTRODUCTION

Understanding long-run economic growth and explaining differences between rates of growth among countries is one of the most important questions in economics. Yet during the 1970s growth theory was dormant. This was partly due to the emphasis on short-run fluctuations, but the limitations of the standard neoclassical theory also played a role. The traditional Solow-Swan neoclassical model leaves the main factor in economic growth unexplained, which is indicated by growth-accounting exercises. These studies suggest that a main part of growth variations had to be attributed to a rest factor—say technological progress—which is exogenous in the traditional Solow-Swan model. This implies that economic policies, apart from those that increase technological progress, have no effect on long-run growth. This is unsatisfactory from the standpoint of policymakers.

Since the mid-1980s, due to the seminal contributions of, for example, Baumol (1986), Romer (1986) and Lucas (1988), the study of economic growth and its policy implications re-entered the research agenda quite vigorously. According to *The Economist*: "The [economic] profession has chosen for once to have one of its most vigorous debates about the right subject" (May 25, 1996, p. 29). The new growth theory emphasizes issues that played only a marginal role in the traditional growth theory, such as the accumulation of knowledge, human capital, increasing returns to scale, externalities, learning-by-doing, and research and development.

Many new growth theorists try to explain long-run growth *within* their model. That is, economic growth is influenced by decisions made by economic agents and is not merely the outcome of an exogenous process as it is in the *old* literature. This important subgroup of new growth models is indicated by the term *endogenous growth models*.

The endogenous growth models are able to show that certain economic policies may have lasting effects, which is important for the potency of domestic policies. Moreover, even in the case where the paradigm of optimizing rational consumers and firms is adopted, the new growth theory shows that a role for the government may exist. This is the result of its emphasis on externalities and spillover effects, which deters a decentralized economy without government interventions from being Pareto optimal.

Economic growth theory is primarily based on a production function approach. This approach, in line with the microeconomic theory of the firm, assumes that economic growth on an aggregate level can be related to factor inputs and technology. More in particular, changes in output are said to be caused by changes in the physical capital stock, labor, human capital, and technology. Therefore, most growth studies try to examine the contribution of different factor inputs and technology on economic growth. In the taxonomy of Maddison (1995), these growth-inducing factors are called *proximate* causes of growth since they have an immediate impact on economic growth. However, factor accumulation and technology will only contribute to economic growth in the case where the institutional setting in which markets operate is reasonably good. The institutional setting refers to issues like property rights, laws, political stability, income distribution, financial markets, and so on. In the taxonomy of Maddison, these are the underlying, or *ultimate* causes of growth, which may even be more important for economic growth than the proximate causes of economic growth.

In this chapter, we review the recent literature on economic growth from a policy perspective.[97] More in particular, we try to answer the following question: what can economic policy learn from the recent wave of theoretical and empirical studies on economic growth? We use the taxonomy of proximate and ultimate causes of growth to organize the chapter. Sections 7.2, 7.3, and 7.4 focus on the proximate causes of growth. Section 7.2 provides a general discussion of some of the main traditional growth models. This section explains the basic differences between an exogenous and an endogenous growth model. It also deals with the impact of the accumulation of the stock of physical capital on economic growth according to different

---

[97] The relationship between growth and the physical environment is not discussed here. However, problems of sustainable development become more and more important in the growth literature.

growth theories. Section 7.3 deals with human capital. Since human capital is the result of learning and education, this section summarizes the importance of learning and education—with an emphasis on the latter—for economic growth. Section 7.4 provides a general discussion of the role of technology and the related importance of stimulating research and development. Improvements in technology can also be the result of international technological spillovers. Therefore, the role of external trade in technology is discussed as well. The ultimate causes of economic growth are discussed in Sections 7.5 and 7.6. Section 7.5 explains the importance of well-developed financial markets and the role of external capital flows. Only in the case where financial intermediaries function well, an efficient reallocation of production factors (the proximate causes) can be brought about. Moreover, if financial markets do not function perfectly, countries may be faced with (domestic) financial constraints, so that the availability of external financial flows become important for economic growth. Section 7.6 provides a more general discussion of the role of institutions, and discusses the importance of income equality and political stability. While the Sections 7.2 up to and including 7.6 mainly refer to theory, section 7.7 focuses on empirical studies. Section 7.8 concludes the chapter.

7.2.   GROWTH THEORY: SOME BASIC CONCEPTS

The most influential neoclassical growth model is the model due to Solow (1956) and Swan (1956). The appearance of the Solow-Swan model was of great importance for the theory of economic growth and for economic policy. Since the times of David Ricardo, economists emphasized the importance of physical capital formation, and hence increasing investment, for economic growth. The dominant theory of economic development, often indicated by the term *capital fundamentalism*, argued that differences in long-term economic growth were mainly due to differences in capital stocks.[98] Therefore, during the first decades after World War II economic policies, in particular in developing countries, were characterized by an emphasis on large-scale industrialization, which had to be brought about by government interventions. The theoretical backing to this idea was provided by a number of seminal articles in the development literature, such as the articles on balanced growth and on the inferior role of the agricultural sector. The theory of balanced economic growth emphasizes the importance of a minimum volume of the investment program, also known as the Big Push

---

[98]   For a discussion of capital fundamentalism and economic growth, see King and Levine (1994).

(Rosenstein-Rodan, 1943) and the importance of balanced development of the various sectors of the economy (see Nurkse, 1953). The literature on the inferior role of the agricultural sector in the process of economic development emphasizes that the agricultural sector is less productive than the industrial sector and has fewer linkages to other sectors. The article of Lewis (1954) is particularly important in this respect. Most important, both types of literature stress the significant role of capital accumulation and government interventions for economic growth. Underlying these theories a Harrod-Domar production function was assumed in which GDP is proportional to the capital stock, and hence GDP growth directly relates to the investment share, through savings.

The neoclassical economists challenged the assumed importance of physical capital accumulation for economic growth by showing that investment does not affect the long-run equilibrium growth rate. The long-run per capita growth rate in the traditional neoclassical model is affected only by labor-augmenting technological progress, which is assumed to be exogenous. Since long-run economic growth in this model is affected only by exogenous variables, the model is sometimes referred to by the term *exogenous growth model*. The impact of physical capital accumulation on economic growth is restricted to the adjustment period to the long-run equilibrium of the economy (the *steady state*). More in general, the idea that government interventions by means of large-scale industrialization would stimulate economic growth is rejected by the neoclassical economists by referring to the advantages of free markets.

Neoclassical economists not only doubt the long-run effect of physical capital accumulation for economic growth, they also argue that the short-run effect of capital formation on economic growth is small. Using a growth accounting framework, based on the Cobb-Douglas production function, it is argued that growth in output per worker is primarily explained by the residual (see Krugman, 1993, for a simple example). The main reason behind this modest effect of capital formation is that neoclassical economists assume that the elasticity of output with respect to capital equals the capital share in GDP, which is usually only about one-third.

The standard neoclassical exogenous growth model is based on a neoclassical production function, which assumes substitutability between labor and capital. One of the most important implications of this model concerns the so-called *convergence* hypothesis. The model implies that a country's per capita growth rate decreases the closer it approaches its long-run equilibrium level. If all countries had the same long-run equilibrium of per capita production, this would imply that a poor country would grow faster than a rich country, since the former is further away from the common long-run equilibrium level. This is the famous absolute convergence paradigm of the neoclassical model. However, due to, for example, differences in domestic savings rates, population growth, and production technology, it might well be the case that long-run equilibrium levels of per capita production differ among countries. If this is the case, the neoclassical model predicts *conditional* convergence, which implies that a country grows faster when it is further away from its own long-run equilibrium level.[99]

The long-run exogeneity of economic growth, as well as the convergence implications of the traditional neoclassical growth models, stem from the important assumption that the amount of extra output from an extra unit of capital, holding constant the other production factors, decreases the greater the amount of capital. Economists refer to this as *diminishing marginal returns to capital*. If there are diminishing returns to capital, the growth effects of additional capital, brought about by saving and hence investment, become smaller if the capital stock increases. In other words, growth effects of additional saving come to an end during the process to the long-run equilibrium level.

However, if it would have been assumed that an extra amount of capital would always increase production by the same amount (*constant returns to capital*), the conclusions regarding the exogeneity of long-run growth and the convergence hypotheses drastically change. The simplest (endogenous growth) model that satisfies these assumptions is the AK-model,[100] which uses the same production function as in the old-fashioned Harrod-Domar model. In this model, the marginal productivity of capital is constant and hence independent of the size of the capital stock. This implies that there is no adjustment process, so that the short and long run growth rates are equal. For this reason, changes in, for example, the savings rate have lasting effects on economic growth and hence a process of endogenous growth takes place. The absence of an adjustment path in which per capita production growth becomes smaller and smaller also implies that the standard endogenous growth model does not predict (conditional or absolute) convergence of growth rates among different countries.[101]

---

[99] Although this may hold for some groups of countries, it seems to be refuted by the data for developing countries (Renelt, 1991). However, it should be noted that there is still much discussion about this issue. See, for instance, Barro and Sala-i-Martin (1995).

[100] The AK-model finds its existence in the standard Cobb-Douglas production function: $Y = AK^aL^{(1-a)}$ in which $a = 1$ and therefore $Y = AK$.

[101] For a general discussion of endogenous growth models we refer to the Policy Forum in The *Economic Journal* of 1992 and to the contributions on endogenous growth in the *Journal of Economic Perspectives* of 1994. In particular, we refer to Dowrick's (1992) contribution on catch up and divergence in *Economic Journal* and to Romer (1994) and Pack (1994). Furthermore, we refer to Durlauf (1996), Sala-i-Martin (1996), Bernard and Jones (1996), Quah (1996), and Galor (1996) in *Economic Journal*.

7.3.   EDUCATION AND HUMAN CAPITAL

In the previous section, it has been stated that the mechanism that makes economic growth endogenous is the elimination of the neoclassical assumption of diminishing returns to capital in the long run. In the endogenous growth theory, this has been done either by including human capital or by discovering new ideas by profit-driven entrepreneurs (R&D-type models). This section deals with human capital, while R&D-type models will be addressed in the next section.

The accumulation of human capital can be brought about by on-the-job-training—in other words by *learning by doing* (cf. Arrow, 1962) or by education. For reasons of space we focus in this section primarily on the role of education. Development theory has always regarded education as an important engine for economic growth. Traditionally, studies concerning the importance of human capital especially relate to the micro level. Schultz (1961, 1988) developed the human capital theory. This theory makes a cost-benefit analysis of investments in human capital and calculates rates of return of investments in education. These studies come up with some important results for economic policy. Most of them conclude that the rate of return of investments in human capital is higher than that of investments in physical capital. Moreover, the rates of return for primary education are almost always higher than for secondary and tertiary education (see Szirmai, 1994, ch. 6).

Despite the importance of human capital in the old development theories, the traditional Solow-Swan neoclassical growth model does not pay any attention to human capital. The Solow growth model considers exogenous labor augmenting technological progress. However, this is not the same as human capital. Labor augmenting technological progress refers to inventions that allow producers to generate the same amount of output with relatively less labor input, whereas human capital is the general skill level of a worker.[102]

Mankiw, Romer, and Weil (1992) reformulate the Solow neoclassical model by taking human capital into account. In their model, human capital is an additional production factor in the standard neoclassical production function. The main contribution of Mankiw, Romer, and Weil is that they firmly challenge the idea of most endogenous growth theorists that the neoclassical model along the lines of Solow cannot explain cross-country

---

[102] Another difference is that technology can be used freely over many activities, while human capital is mostly restricted to one activity because it is related to a particular worker. Hence, human capital is a rival good. For the same reason, unlike knowledge and technology, human capital is, to some extent, an excludable good (see Barro and Sala-i-Martin, 1995, ch. 5).

differences in economic growth. Estimates with respect to the original Solow model point at a much too high implied value for the capital share in GDP. However, the value of the capital share becomes reasonable when human capital is included in the capital measure. Therefore, Mankiw, Romer, and Weil argue that a simple extension of the Solow growth model with human capital does a good job in explaining cross-country economic growth differences. This certainly confirms the importance of human capital in explaining economic growth.[103]

The endogenous growth literature has always paid much attention to the role of education in stimulating economic growth. Aghion and Howitt (1998) distinguish two types of endogenous growth models in which the relationship between education and growth is considered. The first approach, in line with the Mankiw, Romer, and Weil model, takes human capital as input in the production function and emphasizes the importance of the *accumulation* of human capital for economic growth. According to this type of analysis, cross-country differences in economic growth are mainly due to differences in the *growth rates* of human capital accumulation. An unrealistic implication of these models is that education, and thus the change in human capital, will always have a positive effect on economic growth, even when the technology is stagnant. In the other types of models, which are based on a Schumpeterian analysis, this is not the case. These models emphasize that countries with a higher stock of human capital are better able to create new products and technologies and hence to innovate. Moreover, a country with a higher *stock* of human capital is better able to adapt to new technologies and hence to improve the diffusion of technology throughout the economy (Aghion and Howitt, 1998). Hence, these models suggest that differences in growth rates can better be explained by differences in the stock of human capital than by differences in its growth rates.

One of the most well known endogenous growth models based on the first approach is the model due to Uzawa (1965) and Lucas (1988). In these models, only a part of human capital is used for producing goods. The accumulation of human capital takes place since the part of human capital not used for current production goes to school and becomes educated. A special feature of the model is the existence of an externality, which is taken into account by spillover effects of human capital accumulation. The idea is that individual workers, given their own skill level, are more productive when other workers have more human capital. The introduction of externalities is a common approach in endogenous growth models to avoid

---

[103] The model of Mankiw, Romer, and Weil forms the basis of many recent growth regressions, which we will describe in Section 7.7. It should be noted, that there is a lot of discussion on this model, though (see, for instance, Obstfeld and Rogoff, 1996, p. 439).

the diminishing returns to capital assumption from the traditional neoclassical model and hence to obtain a model which reproduces a process of endogenous growth.[104] The externality with respect to human capital implies that the social optimum cannot be reached in a competitive market without government interventions. Due to the fact that private agents do not take into account the external effect of human capital accumulation, investment in human capital will be sub-optimal when governments do not intervene. The policy implication is that a subsidy on education could help to improve economic growth substantially.

Barro and Sala-i-Martin (1995, ch. 5) provide some interesting analyses concerning the behavior of the Lucas model during the adjustment process. In particular, they consider what would happen if the ratio between human and physical capital is not at its optimal level. It appears that a sort of a neoclassical convergence process starts when the initial human capital, physical capital ratio is above its optimal level. In that case, the growth rate will increase with the amount of the imbalance. On the other hand, if there is too little human capital, growth rates will decrease with the amount of the imbalance. This implies that a country would have much more difficulties to recover when it has a shortage of human capital than when it has a shortage of physical capital, so that a brain drain will do much more harm for economic growth than a war, which destroys only physical capital.

There is another class of endogenous growth model in which education and development of human capital plays an important role. In this type of models, a threshold level of human capital is specified (see, for instance, Azariadis and Drazen, 1990). These models formulate the old-fashioned *poverty trap* idea, which is often applied to developing countries. A good example is given by Rebelo (1991). He uses a model in which a threshold level of human capital is specified. If the level of human capital is below the threshold, the economy is characterized by a neoclassical growth model without sustained economic growth. However, if the level of human capital is above this threshold, the economy behaves as an endogenous growth model, and hence a situation of lasting long-run economic growth is reached. The obvious policy implication is here to try to increase human capital above the threshold level since then a continuous process of economic growth starts.

---

[104] In the model of Lucas the spillover effect is taken into account by introducing the *average* level of human capital as an additional factor-input in the production function for physical goods. In most other endogenous growth models, like the seminal model of Romer (1986), the externality is taken into account by introducing *aggregate* values of particular variables, such as the capital stock. A drawback of the latter approach is that it leads to *scale* effects, which implies that large countries always perform better (see Barro and Sala-i-Martin, 1995, pp. 151–152).

7.4. TECHNOLOGY, R&D, AND TRADE

As explained in Section 7.2, the Solow model assumes an exogenous rate of technological progress. However, in practice most technological improvements are due to deliberate actions, such as research and development (R&D) carried out in research institutes or firms. In the new growth theory there is considerable attention to the modeling of R&D and hence the endogenizing of technological progress.[105]

R&D evolves new ideas and designs and is used by firms in search for blueprints of new varieties of products or higher quality products. R&D is not directly productive but will contribute to the expansion of the so-called *frontiers of knowledge*. The accumulation of knowledge will generate growth, which in turn will stimulate capital accumulation and not the other way round (Romer, 1990). Hence, technological change emerges from technical innovations generated by research and development, patenting and software, and productivity-enhancing developments in the fields of education, management, and marketing.

In R&D-type models elements of invention and learning by doing are combined into models with economic uncertainty, new varieties of products, and creative destruction. Creative destruction refers to the effect that an incumbent innovator, being replaced by a new innovator, loses his or her monopoly rents. Schumpeter (1934) was the first to identify and define technological change clearly. He defined technological change in a very broad sense as the "carrying out of new combinations," which generate growth along qualitative changes of economic variables.

Technological advances involve the creation of new ideas, which are not restricted to one activity (that is, it is non-rival) and are (partially) non-excludable and therefore have characteristics of public goods.[106] The existence of nonrivalry and non-excludability implies increasing returns and spillovers through, for instance, learning, which conflicts with the neoclassical assumption of perfect competition. This would imply a role for the government since the return on investment in R&D only partly accrue to the original investors. Otherwise, as has been assumed in most R&D models, the assumption of imperfect competition makes it profitable for firms to introduce new varieties and to continue if other competitors enter the market. In this analysis a Schumpeterian idea returns—namely, that of a profit-

---

[105] This section draws heavily on Rensman (1996).

[106] *Non-rivalry* refers to the fact that consumption of a good does not influence consumption of the same good by others. Here it implies that a new idea can be used by several agents at the same time. *Non-exclusive* means that it is almost impossible to exclude individuals from using new ideas once these new ideas have been supplied to some other individuals.

seeking entrepreneur generating growth by his purposive activities, which are stimulated by market imperfections (Romer, 1990).

However, monopoly power will bring some distortions in the market, so governments will have a task to create a Pareto optimal long-run growth rate (Mankiw, 1995). The monopoly profits are earned by the discoverers. Because imitation is in general cheaper than innovation, other agents will copy the technology, and their activities will generate technological diffusion. This diffusion leads to a form of convergence.

Romer (1990) is one of the most well-known endogenous growth models in which an R&D sector is introduced, in combination with monopolistic elements and spillovers. Romer (1990) makes three premises. First, technological change is the driving force of growth. Second, R&D is responding to market incentives such as profits. This means that R&D is at least partially excludable. Third, technology research generates spillovers in knowledge, which can be used without additional costs. Thus R&D is nonrival, what implies that knowledge can be accumulated without bound, whereas human capital cannot be accumulated infinitely. The importance of the Romer (1990) model comes from the fact that there are two sources of increasing returns: product differentiation and research spillovers, both of which are important. An R&D model would force economists to think carefully about technology and knowledge and offer a broader perspective (Romer, 1995). Moreover, knowledge differences do exist in the real world because of interfirm differences.

Some other more recent models in line with this are Aghion and Howitt (1992, 1996) and Young (1993a, 1993b). Aghion and Howitt (1992) present a model, which captures the creative destruction process of Schumpeter. A separate research sector generates endogenous innovations, which intertemporarily cause changes in productivity growth. Different equilibria are possible in this model. The growth rate is dependent on inventive activity, education, productivity of research, and (negatively) on the rate of time preference. The average growth rate might not be socially optimal because of conflicting distortionary effects. Growth may be too high or too low to maximize welfare because of different externalities. It depends on whether the positive externalities or the negative externalities of research dominate. The positive externalities are the appropriability (excludability) effect and the intertemporal spillover effect as discussed in Romer's (1990) model. The negative effect is the business-stealing effect: innovations destroy the social returns from previous innovations and researchers do not internalize the loss of these rents, taking the size of innovations as given. If this size is endogenized, innovations may be too small.

The Aghion and Howitt (1996) model explores a structural aspect of growth—namely, that of competition.[107] Competition and growth are inversely related in the recent elementary Schumpeterian models: more competition reduces monopoly rents for successful innovators, which in turn lowers the incentive to innovate. As a result growth is reduced. However, evidence does not support this result. Aghion and Howitt (1996, p. 43) demonstrate that a more competitive market structure can contribute to growth. The model suggests that "competition in research, as opposed to market competition, is almost likely to be favorable to growth." The argument is as follows: if production workers can more easily switch from producing old products to producing new products, then this increased adaptability of workers induces a higher level of research, which favors growth. Furthermore, the impact of market competition on growth may be positive in subgroups of the economy.

Young (1993a, 1993b) explores other extensions of the Aghion and Howitt (1992) model. The Young (1993a) model combines invention (like Romer, 1990, and Grossman and Helpman, 1991) and learning by doing (like Arrow, 1962, and Lucas, 1988). Young assumes that the ability to learn is "bounded": after introduction of a new technology, the inherent physical limit on its productivity slows down learning, unless a new innovation is made. Young founds this assumption on historical evidence, which indicates that pre-industrial economies experience long-run technical stagnation. As Crafts (1995) argues, the role of learning as opposed to R&D or invention is understated. Historical examples also support the statement of Young (1993b), that the Schumpeterian model of creative destruction "forgets" the possibility of new technologies complementing older ones, which create rents instead of destroying them.

Griliches (1994) argues that the estimations of R&D spillovers affecting productivity growth are real but that their magnitudes are modest. The same is true for studies that try to embody technological change in capital accumulation. Griliches concludes that there is no real decline in relative expenditures on R&D but that there is a widening gap between social and private returns, due to the internationalization of R&D, increased competition, and the change in the exchange rates. Before we analyze the role of trade, especially in R&D, we first digress a bit on traditional theories of trade.

There is a vast amount of literature on the advantages and disadvantages of trade openness for economic growth. Traditionally, mostly the neoclassical trade theory has been used to explain why external trade is

---

[107] Other aspects are the difference between fundamental and secondary research, business cycles, waves of technological change, and unemployment.

advantageous. The simplest version of this theory, the model of Ricardo, argues that each country will profit if it specializes in goods that offer a comparative advantage. The neoclassical trade theory assumes that production factors are fully employed—that is, there is no unemployment. This is not the case in practice. However, as is explained by the vent for surplus theory, also with unemployed resources, trade may be beneficial since it enables countries to bring otherwise unemployed resources into use. Trade, by extending the market on which products can be sold, may lead to the use of production factors, which are otherwise wasted. So the gains from trade according to the neoclassical trade theory stem from a better allocation of the fully employed production factors, whereas the gains from trade according to the vent for surplus theory are the result of an increase in the amount of factors employed.

The gains from trade, however, are not undisputed. Especially with respect to developing countries many arguments against trade openness are brought forward. These arguments include, for instance, the negative terms-of-trade effects and the short-term gains from protection due to an infant industry argument. While the traditional theories and discussions with respect to trade openness are important, we will confine the analysis here to trade of R&D. The new growth theory especially deals with this. However, in the section on growth regressions some more attention will be given to more traditional growth inducing effects of trade-openness.

Some models, which are closely related to the R&D models as described above, emphasize the international technological spillovers. The Romer (1990) model can easily be extended by modeling two economies producing and trading different intermediate products. If there is a single final-goods sector, there are scale effects because of trade of intermediate products raising output of final goods. If ideas are being traded as well, the stock of ideas increases as well. This increases the productivity of labor devoted to research and the growth rate of output. How ideas are being traded is still an open question. Here we discuss the importance of foreign know-how and the effects of globalization and localization.

The knowledge that a firm possesses is obtained from various internal and external sources. Internal sources are R&D of the firm itself and experiences in production or learning by doing. Schooling and training are needed to adopt knowledge. So human capital investment is essential (see Section 3). By diffusion the firm can acquire external knowledge. It can, possibly supported by the government, buy patents or licenses from abroad and use external services. Nowadays, interfirm agreements are even more important. The firm can also procure equipment and intermediates in which new knowledge is embodied. Finally, free exchange of knowledge in informal relationships between researchers will spread knowledge across firms, sectors, and nations. The firm must, however, be able to adopt this knowledge, and this is dependent on the social capability of its environment (SER, 1995). All this can be linked up with the distinction between foreign and domestic knowledge. Domestic research generates new ideas that can be patented and enhances the adoption of foreign R&D. The capability to adopt is very important for the diffusion and exploitation of knowledge in a profitable way. Foreign knowledge can be acquired directly by licenses or learning and indirectly via importing embodied knowledge. Evidence shows that for small countries foreign know-how is very important and that open economies benefit more from productivity-enhancing spillovers from abroad than closed economies. International technology spillovers are thus crucial and should earn more attention in studies on growth differences between countries. Through international spillovers the world economy's knowledge is becoming more and more a general knowledge pool, accessible for many at (nearly) zero cost. The growth of this pool accelerates because the path-dependency of technological progress causes cumulation of ideas that are "built on the giants' shoulders" (Caballero and Jaffe, 1993).

The globalization of the world economy in the last decades is reflected in international trade. This development is caused by different factors, among which two are the most important. These are deregulation of finance and political developments, which enhance liberalization of international trade, and technological progress, which increases the pressure in global competition. These developments have various consequences. For instance, international investments become more important than international trade itself. Furthermore, international capital flows have been increased strongly and multinationals have gained economic power, which was inconceivable before. The relation between capital flows and growth is discussed later. According to Guile and Brooks (1987) the concept of a competitive nation with a particular endowment is less applicable now because of the globalization. In traditional theories a "national system of innovation" determines the growth differential with other countries. By now international technological spillovers between countries are so large that little economic advantage can be acquired by applying common technologies. Nevertheless, Porter (in OECD, 1992) argues that a national structure remains important for firms because an economy exists of a mix of connected clusters of firms, of which the specific features reflect the economy's comparative advantage. Empirical studies show that international polarization takes place, where the relative position of countries in disaggregated fields is still marked by growing divergence and specialization (Archibugi and Pianta, 1992). The divergence is caused by the differences in nature and institutions of the national innovation system as well as in the social capability. Comparative advantage has to be obtained by specialization at the sectoral level.

Sustained comparative advantage at a sectoral level can be acquired from the interaction between the determinants in the environment. Because of the specific features of this environment and the path-dependency of the technological development in a cluster, the innovation system will be difficult to copy by foreigners. The easiest and cheapest way to develop specific technological knowledge is to collaborate within clusters with other firms, which possess relevant knowledge and are prepared to share it, because of the large capital investments, which are required. The exploitation of economies of scale and scope in one particular field, whatever this field will be, appears to be important to obtain non-zero profits in a market with product differentiation and imperfect competition.

Marshall (1920) already predicted clustering to enhance efficiency in production. According to Krugman (1991) chance plays a large role in the development of such clusters. Which location and technology will be used is the consequence of coincidence and not of taste, technological development, or factor endowments. An example is Silicon Valley in the United States. Such core industries will, however, form the spearheads in international competition. Inter- and intrasectoral differences reflect the complexity of economic patterns. These differences are caused by the coexistence of different technology systems and by the uneven rates of diffusion and exploitation of technologies in different sectors. According to the OECD (1992) the productivity of firms depends more on innovations elsewhere than their own innovations. Archibugi and Pianta (1992) show this trend very clearly. Industries are also unequally affected by spillovers. Industries with relatively high R&D shares show a positive relationship between their own R&D and rival innovations. Own research enhances the capability to adopt ideas from abroad. If the firms only purchase innovations, this has less impact on economic efficiency.

Above the role of location is already touched on briefly. Griliches (1994) advocates the approach used in Jaffe, Trajtenberg, and Henderson (1993). They observe that various studies are carried out on the relationship between R&D expenditures (own or imported) and productivity growth but that these studies do not analyze the geographical localization of the knowledge spillovers. In the growth literature of the 1980s knowledge was assumed to spill over within a country but not between countries. Only when Grossman and Helpman (1991) explicitly recognized the importance of international technological spillovers, the interest in localization was renewed. Jaffe, Trajtenberg, and Henderson (1993) find significant effects of localization gradually fading over time, but they do not find strong evidence of differences in localization around universities and firms.

One of the consequences of international spillovers in technology is that comparative advantage, which is assumed to be given in each point in time in the traditional neoclassical trade theory, now becomes endogenous. The new growth theory emphasizes the simultaneous determination of technology and comparative advantage. The endogeneity of comparative advantage is one of the main contributions of the new trade theory. This theory, for example, shows that it can be profitable for a country to protect the economy for a certain period of time and try to develop a comparative advantage in a sector with considerable growth-inducing possibilities. What we learn from the empirical studies focusing on the international aspects of R&D is discussed in Section 7.7.

7.5.   FINANCIAL MARKETS AND CAPITAL FLOWS

The discussion so far has focused primarily on the *proximate* causes of economic growth. One of the underlying assumptions of the growth enhancing effects of changes in the production factors and of technology is that financial markets function reasonably well. In a world without a well-developed financial sector, growth-enhancing effects of trade policies, improvements in technology, and so on, will probably not take place.

Pagano (1993) surveys the mechanisms by which financial growth may affect real growth. He shows that financial intermediation can boost real growth by improving the allocation of resources and hence the productivity of capital, by increasing the savings rate, and by reducing the proportion of savings lost in the process of financial intermediation.

Financial intermediaries primarily improve economic growth by allocating resources to investment projects that provide the highest returns. In the absence of banks, agents can protect themselves from uncertain liquidity shocks only by investing in liquid assets that can be converted very easily in a medium of exchange. This implies that investments in more illiquid, but also more productive, projects would not take place when banks do not exist. Therefore, an important function of banks is the providing of liquidity insurance (Diamond and Dybvig, 1983). Banks offer deposits, and are thereby able to pool risks of different investors. Since risks are shared, banks are better able to invest in the more productive illiquid investment projects than individual investors. Financial intermediaries also improve the productivity of capital by providing information on the expected rate of return on different investment projects and by monitoring entrepreneurs. In a world with imperfect information, especially when high fixed costs are involved with monitoring, individual savers may have difficulties in identifying the investment projects with the highest returns. Since financial institutions are able to spread the monitoring costs over a group of investors, the existence of fixed costs provides an incentive for financial institutions to

market integration induces external capital to flow from rich to poor countries: in poor countries the capital stock is lower than in rich countries. Assuming a neoclassical production function with diminishing returns to capital, this implies that the productivity of capital should be higher in developing countries. Thus, once all impediments on the capital market are removed, capital would flow from rich to poor countries. On the other hand, the endogenous growth theorists, by emphasizing external economies to capital accumulation, assume that the marginal return to capital is (nearly) constant. In this case there is no incentive for external capital to flow from rich to poor countries. It may then even be that the return on capital is higher in rich countries so that capital market integration induces external capital to flow from the poor to the rich countries.

Before concluding this section it is useful to discuss recent contributions to the foreign-aid growth literature. Those are the studies of Boone (1994, 1996) and Burnside and Dollar (1996). These studies are unique in the aid-growth literature, since they derive an empirical model for examining the effects of aid on saving and investment by explicitly using a neoclassical intertemporal optimizing framework. Moreover, in the empirical application, they use instruments instead of actual data on foreign aid, so that the simultaneity problem (that is, aid causes growth and growth causes aid) is addressed. The main conclusion from Boone's studies is that for the group of countries where the aid to GNP ratio is below 15 percent, aid does not have a significant effect on investment. His studies suggest that aid here mainly finances consumption. The main contribution of Burnside and Dollar is that they try to examine whether effects of aid differ in the presence of good or bad economic policies. They conclude that aid in general has not much effect. However, aid positively affects economic growth in countries with good economic policies. While the papers of Boone and Burnside and Dollar are welcome new contributions to the aid-growth literature, it remains unclear how robust their results are. It would be very interesting to see how robust the results of Boone and Burnside and Dollar are for changes in the set of explanatory variables.

7.6.   INSTITUTIONS AND INEQUALITY

Factor accumulation and technological progress are proximate causes of growth. Besides proximate causes, the underlying, or ultimate, causes are important. According to North (1990), institutions are the main underlying determinant of the long-run performance of countries. He defines institutions as the framework within which human interactions take place. In other words, institutions provide the setting in which markets work.[109] Institutions may be formal, such as property rights or laws, but also informal, such as behavioral codes. If markets operate perfectly, as is assumed by the neoclassical economists, institutions do not play a separate role in explaining growth. However, in practice, markets do not perform in a way as is assumed in the neoclassical world, for instance, due to the absence of perfect information, so that institutions may play an important role in reducing uncertainty and thus transaction costs.

To stimulate long-term economic growth, the development of efficient institutions that motivate individuals to act in a way that contributes to social welfare is extremely important (see North and Thomas, 1973). The development of efficient institutions will however not take place automatically: the existence of growth harming institutions that were developed to enrich the rulers of a country may have lasting negative effects due to *path dependency*. An important example of an efficient institution is the existence of well-defined property rights. The absence of well-defined property rights may imply that individuals do not acquire the revenues related to their activities, so that probably a social sub-optimum results. For instance, intellectual property rights (patents) are needed to induce new innovations, and individual land rights are needed to stimulate more productive and less polluting production methods.

Although almost all economist agree on the importance of well defined institutions for long-term economic development, one of the main limitations of the old and the new (formal) growth theory is the lack of attention to institutions (Van de Klundert, 1996; Aghion and Howitt, 1998). Apart from some emphasis on the role of patent protection in R&D models, the impact of institutions, in the sense of North, on economic growth has been analyzed only in descriptive studies.[110] However, there are some empirical growth studies in which the importance of well-defined institutions for economic growth is examined. In these studies, institutional instability is often measured as expropriation risk and the degree of enforceability of contracts. For a recent empirical study on the effects of institutional uncertainty on investment, see Brunetti and Weder (1997). This study concludes that in

---

[109] According to North (1990) institutions are "the rules of the game in a society or, more formally, are the humanly devised constraints that shape human interaction." (North, 1990, p. 3). North makes a clear distinction between organizations and institutions: "Institutions, together with the standard constraints of economic theory, determine the opportunities in a society. Organizations are created to take advantage of those opportunities" (North, 1990, p. 7).

[110] For an extensive discussion of the role of institutions in economic development, and vice versa, we refer to Lin and Nugent (1995).

particular the absence of credible rules and the existence of corruption (which they see as institutional uncertainty) are harmful for investment.

An issue that is closely related to the absence of efficient institutions is social inequality. An unequal distribution of land rights, as well as unequal access to education may cause extreme income inequalities. The relationship between income inequality and economic growth is already for a long time an important field of research. Traditionally, many authors have argued that economic growth increases when incomes are more unevenly distributed. One of the reasons is that investments are indivisible, so that a concentration of wealth is needed to induce investments. On the other hand, authors like Myrdal (1968) argue that social inequality hurts economic development by having a negative effect on productivity.

Aghion and Howitt (1998, ch. 9) provide an interesting discussion of the effect of inequality on economic growth by using a simple AK-model. They show that inequality and hence also redistribution policies do not affect economic growth when capital markets are perfect. In that case, there are no credit constraints so that each individual can borrow what he or she wants to borrow. The result is that the optimum capital stock is equal for all individuals and hence that all individuals, the poor and the rich, ultimately produce the same amount of goods and have the same income. Therefore, redistribution policies will have no effect on economic growth. However, this result will drastically change when the capital market functions imperfectly (see Benabou, 1996). In that case, individuals cannot borrow the amount of money they want to. For this reason, investments will differ across individuals. Redistribution policies, leading to a reduction in income inequality, will lead to a decline in investments by the rich and an increase in investments by the poor. This will have a positive effect on economic growth due to the assumed decreasing returns to capital. This assumption implies that the decline in output due to the decline in investments by the rich is smaller than the increase in output due to the increase in investments by the poor. For an empirical study on the effect of income inequality on growth we refer to Perotti (1996). Based on reduced-form growth equations, he concludes that reducing inequality (measured as the share of output that goes to the middle class) can raise growth. In his view, the reduction of the inequality comes from better education, lower fertility rates, more political stability and less spending of governments. The negative relation between inequality and growth may be caused by policies that do not protect property rights and do not allow full private appropriation of returns from investment (Persson and Tabellini, 1994) or by conflict over distribution of income and land (Alesina and Rodrik, 1994).

There is also an important literature on the effect of growth on inequality. Based on experience of America, Britain, and Germany, Kuznets concluded that growth in poor countries would initially raise the gap between rich and poor. Only as economies become richer would the gap close (inverted-U relationship). Deininger and Squire (1995), looking at the relationship between inequality (measured by Gini coefficients) and growth for both rich and poor countries, come up with rather ambiguous results. Recently, Galor and Tsiddon (1996) derived a general equilibrium model that captures the inverted-U relationship between income inequality and per capita output. The model seems to be consistent with the stylized facts that output growth is accompanied in the early stage of development by a widening wage differential between skilled and unskilled labor. In later stages of development this wage differential declines. The model is strictly theoretical, but it shows that an economy that faces a trade-off between short-run equity and long-run prosperity might be trapped at a low equilibrium without ever reaching prosperity if it implements a redistribution of income too early. Education (or human capital) is the magic word. Investment in human capital of the upper segments of the economy increases inequality and the aggregate level of human capital. This accumulated human capital is beneficial for the lower segments as well. So, in the end, human capital and income will be distributed more evenly.[111]

Finally, we refer to a somewhat related literature dealing with the effects of political factors, in general, and political instability, in particular, on economic growth. This literature is mainly empirical. In these studies political instability is measured as the number of revolutions and political assassinations, the frequency of strikes, riots, and coups (see Aghion and Howitt, 1998; De Haan and Siermann, 1996). We return to some of these results in the next section.

7.7. EMPIRICAL STUDIES

A drawback of the theoretical endogenous growth framework is that almost all economic policies can be shown to have a positive effect on long-run growth. Ultimately, empirical studies should give more insights into the relationship between a certain policy and economic growth.

Broadly speaking, we can distinguish two approaches in the empirical literature on economic growth: those based on growth accounting and those based on regression analysis. The latter can again be subdivided in two groups. The first subgroup is studies looking for variables that explain growth, usually in a cross-country setting. The second subgroup, following

---

[111] More recently, the same conclusion is reached by Chiu (1998).

the new growth theory, estimates the impact and efficiency of R&D. The emphasis in these studies is on inter- and intrasectoral spillovers from R&D.

The objective of growth accounting is to decompose the growth rate of GDP into contributions from different factor inputs. Most growth-accounting studies work within the neoclassical tradition of Solow (1956). The growth accounting tradition is then to search for data on the labor and capital shares, the growth of labor, the growth of capital, and production growth. The part of the growth rate of GDP, which can be explained by the factor inputs capital and labor, can now be calculated. The remaining part is called the unexplained *Solow residual*. A common outcome of the growth-accounting studies is the high share of the unexplained residual. For a survey, see Chenery (1986) and Barro and Sala-i-Martin (1995). A cross reading of the studies suggest that total factor productivity (the unexplained residual) accounts for forty to fifty percent of total growth.

To try to explain the unexplained residual several authors add additional explanatory variables in the basic framework. These variables are assumed to be important for economic growth and proxy for disequilibrium effects, so that it implies a move away from the standard neoclassical framework. Moreover, many studies try to make adjustments for changes in quality. Famous examples of this tradition are Denison (1967) and Maddison (1987, 1995). However, even after these adjustments in the basic framework, the unexplained residual remains substantial.

Finally, although the traditional neoclassical model does not deal with human capital, early growth accounting exercises based on the neoclassical growth model done by, for example, Denison (1967), also point at the possible great importance of the development of human capital since these studies found that a large part of growth could not be explained by physical capital formation or by population growth. The *unexplained* part of growth was substantial and might be explained for an important part by improvements in the quality of the factor inputs, such as human capital.

Following the seminal paper of Barro (1991), there is now a sizable literature in which economic growth in a cross-section of countries is regressed on a group of explanatory variables. Unfortunately, theory does not provide a clear guidance with respect to the explanatory variables that should be taken into account. Dependent on the aim of the study, and the insights or beliefs of the author, different explanatory variables are included in the regression equation and different variables are found to be significant. A clear drawback of this approach is that almost any explanatory variable can be shown to have a significant effect on economic growth, while it actually is caused by common causalities, or spurious regressions. This may especially occur when no other variables are included in the regression, which are closely related to the variables under consideration. This problem is clearly illustrated by Renelt (1991, p. 17), who states in his review of the literature that "about 50 separate independent variables are included in at least one study and most are shown to have statistically significant partial correlations with growth."

A way around this problem is to apply stability checks on the explanatory variables, as has been done by Levine and Renelt (1992). They use Leamer's extreme bound analysis to test the robustness of a set of explanatory variables. We confine the analysis to a description of the main results. Levine and Renelt (1992) test a huge amount of variables on their robustness in explaining economic growth. These variables include proxies for fiscal, trade, monetary, and political-instability indicators. The conclusion of the entire study is that only a few variables—such as the investment share, the secondary school enrollment rate, and the initial level of income—robustly affect economic growth when a stability analysis is applied. It also appears that exports as a percentage of GDP has a robust impact on economic growth when the investment share is not included in the regression. This suggests that trade affects growth through higher physical investment and not through improved resource allocation what is normally concluded from the theoretical analyses.

It is useful to give some more explanation on some of the variables that do robustly affect economic growth in Levine and Renelt (1992), since these variables appear to be significant in almost all growth regression studies. The initial level of real GDP per capita is included to test for the *conditional convergence* hypothesis (see Section 7.2). The conditional convergence hypothesis is accepted when the coefficient on GDP per capita appears to be negative, since this implies that a higher GDP per capita leads to a lower per capita growth rate. This happens to be the case in any growth regression. An interesting test with respect to the speed of convergence has been done in a recent study by Sachs and Warner (1997). They found evidence for the fact that open economies converge faster than closed ones, which confirms the idea that the international mobility of capital helps to accelerate the transition to the long-run equilibrium level of per capita income. The secondary-school enrollment rate proxies for human capital. Human capital, and hence indirectly the role of education, is also often tested by the primary-school enrollment rate. However, many studies show that the primary-school enrollment rate, in contrast to the secondary-school enrollment rate, does not have a robust effect on economic growth. This seems to be in contrast to the micro studies on the effectiveness of education (see Section 7.3). The latter show that the rates of return on primary education are larger than those on secondary education. A word is also in order with respect to the inclusion of the investment share in most growth regressions. If the investment-to-GDP ratio is introduced as an additional variable in a growth regression, the interpretation of the coefficients for the other variables in the equation changes.

In a later study, King and Levine (1993) test whether financial indicators have a robust effect on economic growth. To test this relationship, King and Levine construct several financial ratios, which proxy for specific characteristics of the financial sector found to be important from the theoretical literature. The study shows that the financial indicators have a significant and robust effect on economic growth. Moreover, they also robustly affect the rate and efficiency of physical capital accumulation. This is a clear indication of the importance of financial sector development for economic growth.

Sala-i-Martin claims that the extreme bound analysis test is too extreme and would lead to the conclusion that almost none of the possible explanatory variables would have a robust effect on economic growth. Sala-i-Martin (1997a, 1997b) selects sixty-two variables for his sensitivity test, among which some proxy for human capital, openness, financial development, and institutions but none for R&D.[112] Not surprisingly, he finds many more variables that have a robust impact on GDP growth than Levine and Renelt (1992). Variables found to be significant by Sala-i-Martin (1997a) include regional variables (belonging to a certain region), political variables, religious variables, and types of economic organization. He also finds a significant long-run growth effect of openness and market distortions. In line with the Levine and Renelt study, none of the government spending variables or inflation proxies are significant. In contrast to King and Levine (1993), financial development does not significantly affect growth in the study of Sala-i-Martin. Finally, the study suggests that, given a constant aggregate level of investment, more public investment is bad.

An important drawback of the reduced-form growth regressions is that the variables that are supposed to induce growth, such as education, technology, and financial development, are assumed to be exogenous. However, one of the main messages of the new growth theory is that technological progress is endogenous with R&D playing an important role. However, assessing the impact of R&D on production is difficult, since R&D is not directly productive. Furthermore, there is a large uncertainty surrounding the pay-offs that R&D is supposed to generate. Moreover, how do we measure technological change? Schmookler already in 1966 used patents as a proxy for inventions. But one has to bear in mind that not all inventions are patented, that some inventions are not measured, and that

---

[112] There are only a few studies in which R&D variables are included in growth regressions, such as Birdsall and Rhee (1993). R&D variables, in particular, are subject to measurement problems (Aghion and Howitt, 1998).

there are differences in quality of inventions. Griliches (1994) uses data on R&D to indicate the development of technology, not because they are such a good indicator but because our understanding "is constrained by the extent and quality of the available data" (p. 2). In Griliches's opinion part of the difficulty in estimating the impact of variables on productivity growth is due to the misinterpretation of data caused by "inadequate attention to how they are produced" (p. 2).

Nadiri (1993) explores various studies to find evidence on R&D investment. He concludes that one can neither say that there are diminishing returns on innovation nor that there are no diminishing returns because the used yardsticks of patent numbers and R&D are inadequate and cause measurement problems (this point is already mentioned above). However, most empirical studies show that the rates of return to own R&D are high and that there are significant spillover effects from R&D (Coe and Helpman, 1993; Fagerberg, 1995; and Rensman and Kuper, 1998). Furthermore, R&D affects the growth rates of output and total factor productivity (TFP) positively and strongly, although the magnitude of its impact varies. Moreover, R&D investments interact with other inputs. The average rates of return on R&D vary among the studies between 20 to 30 percent at firm level and between 10 to 30 percent at industry level. Evidence also demonstrates that since the 1970s, TFP growth have slowed down and R&D expenditures decreases. With respect to R&D spillovers, Nadiri finds significant international spillover effects, growing over time. On average, the social rate of return is 50 percent. Within the OECD, many technology transfers take place, especially via multinationals. Finally, spillovers also induce changes in structures of production and rate of profitability, next to productivity growth. R&D spillovers account for more than half of TFP growth. Wolff and Nadiri (1993) study the relationships between R&D, technological change, and intersectoral linkages. They find that R&D embodied in capital stock generates sizable spillovers among all sectors. Furthermore, suppliers and purchasers in manufacturing experience close links in their growth rates of TFP. Sectors, which are strongly linked, also show relatively higher R&D expenditures and higher TFP growth rates. Finally, Wolff and Nadiri conclude that private R&D provides stronger spillover effects than total (embodied) R&D, which includes governmental R&D. Lichtenberg (1992) draws the same conclusion about the difference in returns on governmental and private R&D. In this respect, Fagerberg (1995) concludes that the (indirect) spillover effects are at least as important as the direct effects of R&D, which makes a case for subsidizing R&D.

More recently, Keller (1997) predicted that technology, in the form of product designs and created through R&D investments, is transmitted to other domestic and foreign sectors by being embodied in differentiated intermediate goods. Using data from thirteen manufacturing industries in eight OECD countries for the period 1970 until 1991, he finds a positive relation between productivity levels and R&D expenditures. The elasticity of TFP with respect to own-industry R&D is somewhere between 7 percent and 17 percent. Industries also benefit from technology investments in other industries by trading embodied technology. The benefit from foreign R&D in the same industry is about 50 to 95 percent of the productivity effect of own R&D. Domestic outside-industry R&D is one-fifth to one-half as effective in raising productivity as own-industry R&D. Summarizing: industries benefit more from foreign technology in the same industry than from domestic technology created in other industries, which clearly deviates from the findings of OECD (1992).

7.8.   CONCLUSIONS

Now we have completed the literature survey, without claiming to be exhaustive, we come back to the question asked in the introduction of this chapter: What can policymakers learn from recent growth contributions? Our immediate answer would be, not that much.

The new growth analyses have provided an important theoretical contribution by embellishing the theoretical modeling of the impact of certain economic policies. However, while we do not intend to underrate the importance of better theoretical foundations, we would like to emphasize that almost all fundamental ideas already existed in the *old* development literature. Hence, "old wine in new bottles". We doubt whether policymakers can learn much from these analyses because the main insights were known already for a long time. The main contribution of the new growth theory probably is that some ideas considered to be old-fashioned are now put once again on the agenda and that a better microeconomic justification is given for a certain degree of government interventions.

With respect to the empirical contributions we doubt the relevance of many of the growth regressions, which has come to the fore in recent years. In our opinion, one should be cautious in interpreting results coming from growth regressions without stability tests on the variables of interest. Therefore, the contributions of Levine and Renelt and of Sala-i-Martin are certainly important steps forward. However, also these studies do not give a definitive answer to the growth effects of certain economic policies. One of the main problems remains how to measure certain variables. This refers to almost all variables, but especially to the measurement of technology, human capital, trade, and environmental quality. Therefore, much more emphasis should be paid on an improvement of empirical proxies for theoretical phenomenon. Related to that, in growth regressions always a high level of aggregation is assumed, both for the dependent and independent variables. More firm-level studies seem to be highly relevant, especially for a better assessment of effects of R&D and human capital (cf. Branstetter, 1996).

Nevertheless, something can be learned from the recent empirical analyses. The growth regressions strongly confirm the relevance of human capital and thus education. Political stability and trade openness also seems to be important, although not all studies support this. Especially, the effects of trade on economic growth differ very much per study. This is partly the result of measurement problems: some proxies for trade suggest a robust positive effect of trade on growth, whereas other proxies for trade seem to imply that trade does not significantly affect economic growth. However, conflicting results concerning the effects of trade on growth also stem from differences in the set of countries taken into account. It may well be the case that a positive relationship between export orientation and economic growth only exists for relatively developed countries (Helleiner, 1986). Related to this, it is interesting to refer to a study by Berthélemy and Varoudakis (1996). They show that a policy of trade openness has favorable effects only in countries with a developed financial system. The reason for this is simple. According to the neoclassical trade theory, trade mainly affects economic growth via a more efficient reallocation of production factors. However, when the financial system is poorly developed this reallocation of production factors is hampered considerably. This once again confirms the importance of financial development for economic growth, as has been indicated in many growth regressions.

The growth regressions also suggest that many variables do not robustly affect economic growth. These include variables, such as alternative measures of external trade and fiscal and monetary policies, which according to theory should be important for economic growth. Does this imply that these variables really do not matter for economic growth? In our opinion, this can not be concluded from the existing empirical studies. All linear regressions, including the most sophisticated, may suffer from—serious— misspecifications. Theoretical analyses often suggest the existence of nonlinear relationships, such as threshold effects and inverted-U curves, between explanatory variables and economic growth. This refers to all variables, but in particular to inflation. These possibilities are almost never taken into account in the growth regressions. Moreover, the causality between variables is often unclear, especially with respect to the relation between trade and financial development on the one hand and economic growth on the other. King and Levine (1994), by referring to recent causality studies, even doubts whether there is a causal link from investment to growth. The causality may well run the other way around.

In our opinion, much deeper work on how variables affect each other is necessary.[113] An important drawback of the reduced-form growth regressions is that the growth-inducing variables under consideration, such as education, technology, financial development and so on are assumed to be exogenous. This is in line with the standard neoclassical growth theory, so that the growth regressions in fact can be characterized as tests for augmented Solow models. However, one of the main messages of the new growth theory is that variables affect each other and hence are endogenous. This is the case for the relationships between the stock of human capital and the diffusion of technology, between technology and trade, and between financial development and the effectiveness of trade. But it also appears to be true for the relationship between well-developed institutions and almost all other standard regressors in the growth regressions. Moreover, economic growth affects education, trade, technology, domestic financial development, foreign capital inflows, institutions, and the environment. In our opinion, this calls for much more emphasis on estimating structural models and less on the current habit of estimating reduced-form regressions.

References

Aghion, P., and P. Howitt. (1992). "A Model of Growth Through Creative Destruction." *Econometrica* 60, 323–351.

Aghion, P., and P. Howitt. (1996). "A Schumpeterian Perspective on Growth and Competition." Paper prepared for the seventh World Congress of the Economic Society, Tokyo, August 1995.

Aghion, P., and P. Howitt. (1998). *Endogenous Growth Theory*. Cambridge, MA: MIT Press.

Alesina, A., and D. Rodrik. (1994). "Distributive Politics and Economic Growth." *Quarterly Journal of Economics* 109, 465–490.

Archibugi, D., and M. Pianta. (1992). "The Technological Specialization of Advanced Countries." Report to the EEC on International Science and Technology Activities.

Arrow, K.J. (1962). "The Economic Implications of Learning by Doing." *Review of Economic Studies* 29, 155–173.

Azariadis, C., and A. Drazen. (1990). "Threshold Externalities in Economic Development." *Quarterly Journal of Economics* 105, 501–526.

Barro, R.J. (1991). "Economic Growth in a Cross Section of Countries." *Quarterly Journal of Economics* 106, 407–443.

Barro, R.J., and X. Sala-i-Martin. (1995). *Economic Growth*. New York: McGraw-Hill.

Baumol, W.J. (1986). "Productivity Growth, Convergence and Welfare: What the Long-Run Data Show." *American Economic Review* 76, 1072–1085.

Benabou, R. (1996). "Inequality and Growth." In B.S. Bernanke and J. Rotemberg, eds., *NBER Macroeconomics Annual* (pp. 11-74). Cambridge, MA: MIT Press.

Bernard, A.B., and C.I. Jones. (1996). "Technology and Convergence." *Economic Journal* 106, 1037–1044.

---

[113] For similar conclusions, see Fagerberg (1994).

Berthélemy, J.C., and A. Varoudakis. (1996). "Financial Development, Policy and Economic Growth." In N. Hermes and R. Lensink, eds., *Financial Development and Economic Growth: Theory and Experiences from Developing Countries* (pp. 66-89). London: Routledge.

Birdsall, N., and C. Rhee. (1993). "Does Research and Development Contribute to Economic Growth in Developing Countries?" Policy Research Working Paper 1221, World Bank, Washington, DC.

Boone, P. (1994). "The Impact of Foreign Aid on Savings and Growth." Unpublished manuscript, London School of Economics.

Boone, P. (1996). "Politics and the Effectiveness of Foreign Aid." *European Economic Review* 40, 289–329.

Boyd, J.H., and E.C. Prescott. (1986). "Financial Intermediary Coalitions." *Journal of Economic Theory* 38, 211–232.

Branstetter, L. (1996). "Are Knowledge Spillovers International or Intranational in Scope? Microeconomic Evidence from the U.S. and Japan." Working Paper 5800, National Bureau of Economic Research, Cambridge, MA.

Brunetti, A., and B. Weder. (1997). "Investment and Institutional Uncertainty: A Comparative Study of Different Uncertainty Measures." IFC, technical Paper 4, World Bank, Washington, DC.

Burnside, C., and D. Dollar. (1996). "Aid, Policies and Growth." Policy Research Working Paper, World Bank, Washington, DC.

Caballero, R.J., and A.B. Jaffe. (1993). "How High Are the Giants Shoulders: An Empirical Assessment of Knowledge Spillovers and Creative Destruction in a Model of Economic Growth." In O.J. Blanchard and S. Fischer, eds., *NBER Macroeconomics Annual* (pp. 15–86). Cambridge, MA: MIT Press.

Chenery, H. (1986). "Growth and Transformation." In H. Chenery, S. Robinson, and M. Syrquin, eds., *Industrialization and Growth.* Washington, DC: World Bank.

Chiu, W.H. (1998). "Income Inequality, Human Capital Accumulation and Economic Performance." *The Economic Journal* 108, 44–59.

Coe, D.T., and E. Helpman. (1993). "International R&D Spillovers." Working Paper 4444, National Bureau of Economic Research, Cambridge, MA.

Crafts, N.F.R. (1995). "Endogenous Growth: Lessons for and from Economic History." Paper prepared for the seventh World Congress of the Economic Society, Tokyo, August.

De Haan, J., and C.L.J. Siermann. (1996). "Political Instability, Freedom, and Economic Growth: Some Further Evidence." *Economic Development and Cultural Change* 44, 339–350.

Deininger, K., and L. Squire. (1995). "Inequality and Growth: Results from a New Data Set." Working Paper, World Bank, Washington, DC.

Denison, E.F. (1967). *Why Growth Rates Differ.* Washington, DC: Brookings.

Diamond, D.W. (1984). "Financial Intermediation and Delegated Borrowing." *Review of Economic Studies* 51, 393–414.

Diamond, D.W., and P.H. Dybvig. (1983). "Bank Runs, Deposit Insurance, and Liquidity." *Journal of Political Economy* 85, 191–206.

Dowrick, S. (1992). "Technological Catch Up and Diverging Incomes: Patterns of Economic Growth 1960-88." *Economic Journal* 102, 600–610.

Durlauf, S.N. (1996). "On the Convergence and Divergence of Growth Analysis: An Introduction." *Economic Journal* 106, 1016–1018.

Fagerberg, J. (1994). "Technology and Growth Rates." *Journal of Economic Literature* 32, 1147–1175.

Fagerberg, J. (1995). "Technology and Competitiveness." *Oxford Review of Economic Policy* 12, 39–51.

Galor, O. (1996). "Convergence? Inference from Theoretical Models." *Economic Journal* 106, 1056–1069.

Galor, O., and D. Tsiddon. (1996). "Income Distribution and Growth: The Kuznets Hypothesis Revisited." *Economica* 63, S103–S117.

Greenwood, J., and B. Jovanovic. (1990). "Financial Development, Growth and the Distribution of Income." *Journal of Political Economy* 98, 1067–1107.

Griliches, Z. (1994). "Productivity, R&D, and the Data Constraint." *American Economic Review* 84, 1–23.

Grossman, G.M., and E. Helpman. (1991). *Innovation and Growth in the Global Economy.* Cambridge, MA: MIT Press.

Guile, B.R., and H. Brooks, eds. (1987). *Technology and Global Industry: Companies and Nations in the World Economy.* Washington, DC: National Academy Press.

Helleiner, G.K. (1986). "Outward Orientation, Import Stability and African Economic Growth: An Empirical Investigation." In S. Lall and F. Stewart, eds., *Theory and Reality in Development* (pp. 139-159). London: Macmillan.

Jaffe, A.B., M. Trajtenberg, and R. Henderson. (1993). "Geographic Localization of Knowledge Spillovers as Evidenced by Patent Citations." *Quarterly Journal of Economics* 108, 577–598.

Jappelli, T., and M. Pagano. (1994). "Savings, Growth and Liquidity Constraints." *Quarterly Journal of Economics* 109, 83–109.

Keller, W. (1997). "Trade and the Transmission of Technology." Working Paper 6113, National Bureau of Economic Research, Cambridge, MA.

King, R.G., and R. Levine. (1993). "Finance and Growth: Schumpeter Might Be Right." *Quarterly Journal of Economics* 108, 717–737.

King, R.G., and R. Levine. (1994). "Capital Fundamentalism, Economic Development and Economic Growth." Policy Research Working Paper 1285, World Bank, Washington, DC.

Krugman, P. (1991). *Geography and Trade.* Cambridge. MA: MIT Press.

Krugman, P. (1993). "International Finance and Economic Development." In A. Giovannini, ed., *Finance and Development: Issues and Experience* (pp. 11-23). Cambridge: Cambridge University Press.

Levine, R., and D. Renelt. (1992). "A Sensitivity Analysis of Cross-Country Growth Regressions." *American Economic Review* 82, 942–963.

Lewis, W.A. (1954). "Economic Development with Unlimited Supplies of Labour." *Manchester School of Economic and Social Studies* 22, 139–191.

Lichtenberg, F.R. (1992). "R&D Investment and International Productivity Differences." Working Paper 4161, National Bureau of Economic Research, Cambridge, MA.

Lin, J.Y., and J.B. Nugent. (1995). "Institutions and Economic Development." In J. Behrman, and T.N. Srinivasan, eds., *Handbook of Development Economics* (pp. 2301-2370). Amsterdam: North-Holland.

Lucas, R.E. Jr. (1988). "On the Mechanics of Development Planning." *Journal of Monetary Economics* 22, 3–42.

Maddison, A. (1987). "Growth and Slowdown in Advanced Capitalist Economies: Techniques of Quantitative Assessment." *Journal of Economic Literature* 25, 649–698.

Maddison, A. (1995). *Monitoring the World Economy, 1820–1992.* Paris: OECD Development Centre.

Mankiw, N.G. (1995). "The Growth of Nations." *Brookings Papers on Economic Activity* 1, 275–326.

Mankiw, N.G., D. Romer, and D.N. Weil. (1992). "A Contribution to the Empirics of Economic Growth." *Quarterly Journal of Economics* 107, 407–437.

Marshall, A. (1920). *Principles of Economics.* London: Macmillan.

McKinnon, R.I. (1973). *Money and Capital in Economic Development.* Washington, DC: Brookings Institution.

Myrdal, G. (1968). *Asian Drama: An Inquiry into the Poverty of Nations.* New York: Twentieth Century Fund.

Nadiri, M.I. (1993). "Innovations and Technological Spillovers." Working Paper 4423, National Bureau of Economic Research, Cambridge, MA.

North, D.C. (1990). *Institutions, Institutional Change and Economic Performance.* Cambridge: Cambridge University Press.

North, D.C., and R.P. Thomas. (1973). *The Rise of the Western World: A New Economic History.* Cambridge: Cambridge University Press.

Nurkse, R. (1953). "Problems of Capital Formation in Underdeveloped Countries." Oxford: Oxford University Press.

Obstfeld, M. (1995). "Effects of Foreign Resource Inflows: A Methodological Overview." Unpublished, University of California, Berkeley.

Obstfeld, M., and K. Rogoff. (1996). *Foundations of International Macroeconomics.* Cambridge, MA: MIT Press.

OECD (1992). *Technology and Economy. The Key Relationships.* Paris: OECD.

Pack, H. (1994). "Endogenous Growth Theory: Intellectual Appeal and Empirical Shortcomings." *Journal of Economic Perspectives* 8, 55–72.

Pagano, M. (1993). "Financial Markets and Growth: An Overview." *European Economic Review* 37, 613–623.

Perotti, R. (1996). "Growth, Income Distribution and Democracy: What the Data Say." *Journal of Economic Growth* 1, 149–187.

Persson, T., and G. Tabellini. (1994). "Is Inequality Harmful for Growth." *American Economic Review* 84, 600–621.

Quah, D. (1996). "Twin Peaks: Growth and Convergence in Models of Distribution Dynamics." *Economic Journal* 106, 1045–1055.

Rebelo, S. (1991). "Growth in Open Economies." Policy Research Working Paper 779, World Bank, Washington, DC.

Renelt, D. (1991). "Economic Growth: A Review of the Theoretical and Empirical Literature." Policy Research Working Paper 678, World Bank, Washington, DC.

Rensman, M. (1996). *Economic Growth and Technical Change in the Long Run.* Research Report 96C10, Graduate School/Research Institute Systems, Organisations and Management, University of Groningen, Groningen.

Rensman, M., and G.H. Kuper. (1998). "Do Technology Spillovers Matter for Growth?" Paper prepared for the Conference on Productivity and Standards of Living, Groningen, September.

Romer, P.M. (1986). "Increasing Returns and Long-Run Growth." *Journal of Political Economy* 94, 1002–1037.

Romer, P.M. (1990). "Endogenous Technological Change." *Journal of Political Economy* 98, S71–S102.

Romer, P.M. (1994). "The Origins of Endogenous Growth." *Journal of Economic Perspectives* 8, 3–22.

Romer, P.M. (1995). "Comments and Discussion." In N.G. Mankiw, ed., *The Growth of Nations* (pp. 313-320). Washington, DC: Bookings Institution.

Rosenstein-Rodan, P.N. (1943). "Problems of Industrialization in Eastern and Southeastern Europe." *Economic Journal* 53, 429–439.

Sachs, J.D., and A.M. Warner. (1997). "Fundamental Sources of Long-Run Growth." *American Economic Review* 87, 184–188.

Sala-i-Martin, X. (1996). "The Classical Approach to Convergence Analysis." *Economic Journal* 106, 1019–1036.

Sala-i-Martin, X. (1997a). "I Just Ran Two Million Regressions." *American Economic Review* 87, 178–183.

Sala-i-Martin, X. (1997b). "I Just Ran Four Million Regressions." Unpublished Paper, Columbia University and Universitat Pompeu Fabra.

Schmookler, J. (1966). *Invention and Economic Growth*. Cambridge, MA: Harvard University Press.

Schultz, T.W. (1961). "Investment in Human Capital." *American Economic Review* 51, 1–17.

Schultz, T.W. (1988). "Education, Investment and Returns." In H. Chenery, and T.N. Srinivasan, eds., *Handbook of Development Economics* (pp. 543–630). Amsterdam: North-Holland.

Schumpeter, J.A. (1934). *The Theory of Economic Development: An Inquiry into Profits, Capital, Credit, Interest, and the business Cycle*. Cambridge, MA: Harvard University Press. Reprinted in 1983.

Shaw, E.S. (1973). *Financial Deepening in Economic Development*. New York: Oxford University Press.

Social and Economic Council (SER). (1995). *Kennis en Economie*. Den Haag: SER.

Solow, R.M. (1956). "A Contribution to the Theory of Economic Growth." *Quarterly Journal of Economics* 70, 65–94.

Swan, T. (1956). "Economic Growth and Capital Accumulation." *Economic Record* 32, 334–361.

Szirmai, A. (1994). *Ontwikkelingslanden: Dynamiek en Stagnatie 1997*. Groningen: Wolters-Noordhoff.

Uzawa, H. (1965). "Optimal Technical Change in an Aggregative Model of Economic Growth." *International Economic Review* 6, 18–31.

Van de Klundert, T.C.M.J. (1996). *Groei en Instituties: Over de Oorzaken van Economische Ontwikkeling*. Tilburg: Tilburg University Press.

Van Wijnbergen, S. (1985). "Aid, Export Promotion and the Real Exchange Rate: An African Dilemma." Center of Economic Policy Research Discussion Paper 90, World Bank, Washington, DC.

White, H., and J. Luttik. (1994). "The Country Wide Effects of Aid." Research Working Paper 1337, World Bank, Washington, DC.

Wolff, E.N., and M.I. Nadiri. (1993). "Spillover Effects, Linkage Structure, and Research and Development." *Structural Change and Economic Dynamics* 4, 315–331.

Young, A. (1993a). "Invention and Bounded Learning by Doing." *Journal of Political Economy* 101, 443–472.

Young, A. (1993b). "Substitution and Complementarity in Endogenous Innovation." *Quarterly Journal of Economics* 108, 775–807.

Epilogue

Jan Pronk
Minister for Development Cooperation

From adjustment to growth

Five years ago in this same building we organised a seminar under the title 'structural adjustment and beyond'. Structural adjustment was the theme of the eighties and the early nineties. What should have come beyond adjustment is economic growth. Indeed economic growth is back on the agenda nowadays. The last two decades growth theory has come up with new insights and a wealth of empirical evidence. New growth theory could have direct implications for policy. Is the long term growth rate determined by investments and technological developments largely outside the control of policy or is it policy-driven? Has recent research led to a counter-revolution in development theory? These are the sort of questions that came to mind when I suggested that the EU-LDC network should initiate a dialogue on growth between academics and policy makers.

Relevance of recent research

Explaining long term growth rates of countries is in my view one of the most important challenges for the economic science. The results of theoretical analysis on this issue in the past have been mixed. Neoclassical growth theory remained unsatisfactory because it explained everything but long-term growth. Since then attention has shifted towards the relation between theory and actual data. Again, the outcome is not completely satisfactory in its diversity. But whatever factor is stressed as the driving force, technology or human capital, or institutional capacity, endogenous growth theory seems to underline the importance of policies for growth. But if policies are so important, what explains policies? And what then is the relevance of recent research for development policies? The answer in the issue paper for this seminar by Lensink and Kuper is pretty clear: not that much. They claim that the main insights were known already for a long time by policy makers.

Certainly contact between growth theory and development policy has been lacking. That does not mean, by the way, that Lensink and Kuper are right. Personally, as a policy maker, I found the convergence between new growth theory and traditional development theory quite helpful.

Growth and development

The concept of economic growth in itself is sometimes overrated as a policy benchmark. Economic growth is a means to enhance people's wellbeing, not an end. Economic growth can be seen as a necessary but not sufficient condition for human progress. Some forms of economic growth may even jeopardize future progress. The conditions under which economic growth can be optimised in terms of human development have not been a major issue at this seminar, though they were touched upon in the fascinating paper by Deepak Lai. But such issues nowadays are the subject of many other seminars on growth and development and I wanted to focus again on the old questions: what determines growth and what should we do to foster growth rather than destroy it?

Differentiation

There now is a wealth of empirical work using cross-section regressions to isolate determining factors of growth, but an integrated approach is still lacking. Time series analyses for individual countries using data over a much longer period of history may help, but will also not suffice. Other research methods will have to be explored, ultimately leading to a more integrated structural model of growth. One wonders if it is possible to use one universal growth model for all types of countries, including the most marginalised countries or countries with completely different cultural systems.

It has always been the strength of development economics to incorporate insights from the other social sciences. Many of the present day discussions on economic growth can indeed trace their roots to older theories of development. In my view the new growth theory, trying to explain long term growth within the model, is a contribution to bridging the gap between growth theory and development theory, though, reading various studies on the new growth theory, I wonder whether current work sufficiently builds on older insights.

Basic determinants of growth

Divergence rather than convergence has been dominant in this century. Poorer countries should in theory tend to grow more rapidly than richer countries, but these potential advantages of backwardness did not materialise for many of these countries. Convergence is clearly conditional. If convergence is conditional, what are the basic conditions that have to be fulfilled?

Barro has summed up many of the recent empirical findings. Data comparability and causality present formidable problems for such cross-section exercises. I sympathise with Pyatt and others who said that we need to add a sense of historical perspective, rather than confining ourselves to data that make the world start in 1960.

From a developmental perspective I would like to see more factors relevant for a developing country to be included in the analysis. For instance the sector structure seems to be missing. Most of the factors that did show a positive relationship with growth were hardly surprising. Their difficult translation into effective policy measures already present a daily challenge to development policy. Other factors, still to be researched, would present us even greater challenges, in particular if one takes the interaction between variables and the various interrelationships into account. It has been said a number of times during these days that many of these policies have to come in a package.

Openness and growth

If we look at Easterly's "Joys of Openness", the recipe for economic growth and development seems remarkably simple, openness is the answer. Open economies tend to converge, closed economies do not. Openness may not be a panacea for poverty alleviation, its contribution to growth seems undisputed. But what kind of openness and what amount of openness?

The question for policy makers is how to achieve this goal of openness, because they realize that it is a bumpy road with many roadblocks and deviations. Those on the way to openness take higher risks in terms of a higher variability of their growth rates, especially developing countries. In my view, the international economic system should help to minimise these. The Asian crisis serves as a reminder that we have not yet succeeded in creating such a growth-preserving international financial system. Asian countries also showed that the sequence and pace are important when liberalising trade and financial flows. The optimum strategy is determined by local factors: the technological, institutional and human capacities available.

Technology and growth

Is the diversity of growth experience somehow related to technology? Technology is the driving force behind the globalisation process. Obviously, technological developments constitute a crucial factor explaining growth. Endogenous growth theory has brought new insights about the role of technology, in particular incentives for technological development as Danny Quah has reminded us.

Intellectual property rights obviously play a major role in this field, either as an incentive or as a barrier. One would expect that technological diffusion would lead to convergence given the relatively easy access to knowledge. Further research to identify the mechanisms that lead to knowledge spillovers would indeed be interesting. Here we have an example of the interrelated character of all these growth-inducing factors. In practice, reform, learning and openness go together. The introduction of foreign know-how is related to the openness of an economy and to trade, direct investments and other capital flows. Human development, including schooling, is needed to adopt knowledge.

Human capital and growth

Human capital should in theory be considered as one of the most important factors determining growth. It is directly related to the capacity for technological development of a society. The empirical evidence has however not always been convincing.

Berthelemy addresses this question in his paper: why do heavy investments in education in some developing countries have apparently only minor effects on their growth results? His explanation that skilled labour is employed in non-productive activities as a result of policy distortions leads us back to the conditions of governance. Policy distortions can create a poverty trap at low levels of human capital. But how to define policy distortions? Investment in education still deserves priority, but should go hand in hand with minimising the opportunities for rent seeking behaviour. This is one of the lessons that is already firmly incorporated in development cooperation practice. At last corruption now seems to feature on the agenda of the international institutions.

Financial system and growth

Asia has reminded us how crucial the financial system is for fast growing economies. Fry has demonstrated the key role of the financial system as an intermediate factor in development, while at the same time underlining the fragile character of the financial system in a globalising world economy. He emphasised the importance of a level playing field. My confidence in the efficiency of financial markets may be somewhat less. Externalities and market failures would seem to justify government intervention in this sector, not only at the national level but also at the international level. Globalisation may be inevitable, but a phasing of financial liberalisation may help supporting stability in my view.

Financial liberalisation in developing countries certainly is a delicate art, and should be accompanied by sound prudential supervision and regulation of the banking system as Levine stressed. This combination is a particularly difficult policy prescription for most developing nations where the financial infrastructure is underdeveloped. Better supervision requires good governance, again both at the national level as well as at the international level.

This brings me to the contribution of external aid to policy reform. If economic policies and institutions are the key to long term growth the effectiveness of aid depends on its contribution to better policies. In a much quoted recent article Dollar and Burnside came to the conclusion that aid did not have a measurable effect on policies. This is quite a challenge. In my view many examples of the key role of foreign assistance in postwar reforms contradict this finding. I do think there is a role for development assistance in the process of improving government performance. I realise that there is a possible negative effect of foreign interference, a lack of local ownership and commitment to reform. Aid can help both good governments and bad governments to survive. I still think, however, despite the findings of Dollar and Burnside, that external assistance, well conditioned, does have to play a role in sustaining good policy making.

Institutions and growth

In the end, the strength of informal and formal institutions determines the policy outcome: the market, the state, the family and civil society.

Going to the heart of the matter Deepak Lal has chosen for an impressive historical and cultural perspective on these issues. Indeed, he sees institutional development as a form of cultural evolution.

What kind of institutions are essential for growth, the institutions of the West, where intensive economic growth started, or is there room for alternative value systems? I sympathise with Lal's plea for cultural diversity, based on what he calls differing cosmological beliefs. However, I have two questions. Firstly, are there within such cultural diversity key universal institutional requirements for growth? Lal himself refers to the market as essential for intensive growth. I agree, but then the second question is to which extent the spread of the market, with the help of capital, technology and communication, will not by itself change the cultural value systems related to the family and the state. I think it will. Globalisation of the market, aimed at for reasons of economic growth, will tend to create a uniform value system, necessary for the market to flourish. A fair degree of individualism seems to be a prerequisite. This may have negative consequences for economic and social relations within the family household, resulting in a burden on the state and continuing growth. Could we envisage another convergence, between the West and the rest, a convergence towards an optimum economic regime, conducive to both growth and stability? And if so, what is the role of the state and the government in such an optimum regime? Certainly not rent-seeking, but perhaps again a mix of leadership ("enterprise association" in Lal's terminology, but is this a purely Western label?) and the facilitation of civilians to pursue their own ends. This after all requires trust and could be seen as precondition for economic growth to be translated in human development.

Index